The Present is a Gift

To My Kaiser Colleagues in Santa Clara!

With best wishes,

Michael
2014

also by Michael F. Hoyt

<u>author</u>:

Brief Therapy and Managed Care: Readings for Contemporary Practice (1995)

Some Stories Are Better than Others: Doing What Works in Brief Therapy and Managed Care (2000)

<u>interviewer</u>:

Interviews with Brief Therapy Experts (2001)

<u>editor</u>:

The First Session In Brief Therapy (1992)
    (with Simon Budman and Steven Friedman)

Constructive Therapies, Volume One (1994)

Constructive Therapies, Volume Two (1996)

The Handbook of Constructive Therapies (1998)

The Present is a Gift

❖

Mo' Better Stories from the World of Brief Therapy

Michael F. Hoyt

iUniverse, Inc.
New York Lincoln Shanghai

The Present is a Gift
Mo' Better Stories from the World of Brief Therapy

All Rights Reserved © 2004 by Michael F. Hoyt

No part of this book may be reproduced or transmitted in any form or by any means, graphic, electronic, or mechanical, including photocopying, recording, taping, or by any information storage retrieval system, without the written permission of the publisher.

iUniverse, Inc.

For information address:
iUniverse, Inc.
2021 Pine Lake Road, Suite 100
Lincoln, NE 68512
www.iuniverse.com

ISBN: 0-595-31105-9

Printed in the United States of America

Live (and work) Aloha

All words have roots, histories, families, genders, off-spring. They reach back through the centuries to the dead tongues of ancient peoples, and they go on accumulating wealth and shedding outworn baggage as they travel from region to region. They bring blessings—like a long-awaited letter from your son or your father; and they bring curses so that even the most soberly abstract term can fix us in spells that last for years, like a psychiatric diagnosis. Because words are so laden with hidden messages, they cannot help but be metaphors, by nature "poetic," opening beyond their commonsense definitions into mystery and myth. In fact, the Italian philosopher Giambattista Vico wrote, "a metaphor is a myth in brief."
—James Hillman, "Language: Speaking Well and Speaking Out"

For my own part I never had the least thought or Inclination of turning Poet till I got heartily In Love, and then Rhyme and Song were, in a manner, the spontaneous language of my heart.
—Robert Burns, *First Commonplace Book*

This was another divinely beautiful day. Each morning the world rediscovers its virginity; it seems to have issued fresh from God's hands at that very instant. It has no memory, after all; that is why its face never develops wrinkles. It neither recalls what it did the day before nor frets about what it will do the day after. It experiences the present moment as an eternity. No other moment exists; before and behind this moment is Nothing.
—Nikos Kazantzakis, *Report to Greco*

My life is not this steeply sloping hour,
in which you see me hurrying.
Much stands behind me; I stand before it like a tree;
I am only one of my many mouths,
and at that, the one that will be still the soonest.
I am the rest between two notes,
which are somehow always in discord because
death's note wants to climb over—
but in the dark interval, reconciled,
they stay there trembling.
  And the song goes on, beautiful.
—Rainer Maria Rilke, "My Life Is Not This Steeply Sloping Hour"

Less energy, more comprehension.
  —Philip Roth, *The Dying Animal*

….and when I love thee not,
Chaos is come again.
  —William Shakespeare, *Othello*

Contents

Preface xi

Chapter 1 Toward a More Effective Brief Therapy 1

Chapter 2 Connection: The Double-Edged Gift of Presence 8

Chapter 3 Some Things I Have Learned from Friends and Clients about Empowerment and Rehabilitation 18

Chapter 4 "The Present Is a Gift": A Clinical Demonstration 30

Chapter 5 Interview I—"Some Stories are Better than Others": A Conversation about Hope, Passion, and the Challenges of Work (with Victor Yalom) 48

Chapter 6 Solution-Focused Couple Therapy 70

Chapter 7 The Squeaky Wheel: Don't Let Managed Care Shortchange Your Clients 126

Chapter 8 Early HMO Chart Note 130

Chapter 9 The Pros and Cons of Postmodernism in Psychotherapy: Stepping Back from the Abyss (with Phillip Ziegler) 132

Chapter 10 Interview II—"Burn In, Not Out!": A Conversation about Truth and Beauty in Brief Therapy (with Tapio Malinen) 182

Chapter 11 Interview III—"Snow and Sand": A Conversation about Culture, Alcohol and Empowerment (with Lotta Lehmusvaara and Tracey Powers-Erkkilo) 207

Chapter 12 Road Trip 216

Chapter 13 How I Embody a Narrative Constructive Approach 220

CHAPTER 14   I've Always Been This Way—Thanks to Them!... 230
References 245
About the Author 289
Credits....................................... 291

Preface

The real voyage of discovery consists not in seeking new landscapes but in having new eyes.

—Marcel Proust

Near the end of the bestselling novel *Life of Pi* (Martel, 2001), investigators are interrogating Pi, a young East Indian man, about the sinking of the Japanese cargo ship he and his family had been travelling on, and the subsequent events of his survival at sea. His story is extraordinary.

> Mr. Okamoto: "But for the purposes of our investigation, we would like to know what really happened."
> "What really happened?"
> "Yes."
> "So you want another story?"
> "Uhh…no. We would like to know what really happened."
> "Doesn't the telling of something always become a story?"
> "Uhh…perhaps in English. In Japanese a story would have an element of *invention* in it. We don't want any invention. We want the 'straight facts', as you say in English."
> "Isn't telling about something—using words, English or Japanese—already something of an invention? Isn't just looking upon this world already something of an invention?"
> "Uhh…"
> "The world isn't just the way it is. It is how we understand it, no? And in understanding something, we bring something to it, no? Doesn't that make life a story?" [p. 302][1]

We humans make sense of our experience, conceiving our subjective realities by assigning meanings to what happens. We weave these meanings into narratives or stories. These stories, in turn, conceive us—that is, they shape our awareness and guide our actions, round and round.

> I have found that the person with a sense of story built in from childhood is in better shape than one who has not had stories, who has not heard them, read

them, acted them, or made them up....Story coming early on puts a person into familiarity with the validity of story. One knows what stories can do, how they can make up worlds and transpose existence into these worlds. One maintains a sense of the imaginal world, its convincingly real existence, that it is peopled, that it can be entered and left, that it is always there with its fields and palaces, its dungeons and long ships waiting. One learns that worlds are made by words and not only by hammers and wires. [Hillman, 1983, p. 46]

"Stories" can be great myths and tales—Adam and Eve, Moses and the Ten Commandments, Mohammad's Ascension, Buddha's Enlightenment, Christ's Passion, Odysseus' journeys, and so on—as well as the more mundane.

A story may be about the past, the present, or the future; it may be about what things should be, what they could be, or why they are. Stories appear in our minds hundreds of times a day—when someone gets up without a word and walks out of the room, when someone doesn't smile or doesn't return a phone call, or when a stranger *does* smile; before you open an important letter, or after you feel an unfamiliar sensation in your chest; when your boss invites you to come to his office, or when your partner talks to you in a certain tone of voice. Stories are the untested, uninvestigated theories that tell us what all these things mean. We don't even realize that they're just theories. [Katie, 2002, pp. 4-5]

Stories are usually told in words—prose, poetry, and song—but they are also experienced somatically and emotionally, and can be expressed in other forms of language, such as art and dance. Stories that evoke affect are recalled.

---

1. In his memoir, *Off to the Side*, Jim Harrison (2002, p. 2) puts it more bluntly: "Of course your own life is your truest story and it blinds you unless it's heavily edited....I'm not sure I'm particularly well equipped to tell the truth. What our parents and teachers taught us as truth usually dealt with moral abstractions or the illusory notion of coming to grips with what they loosely termed as reality. Certain things happened and certain things didn't happen, and then the not very agile leap to certain things are true and others false. The wild humor of ten-year-olds comes from the first reading between the lines of this paralyzing bullshit that is destined to suffocate most of us."

   My 82-year-old friend, the psychologist Murray Korngold (2004, p. 25), also notes the impact of age and perspective: "When I reflect on scenes from my childhood I have the fear that the story I tell is biased from the point of view of my present self. Suppose that the eight-year-old boy I once was could talk with me and tell his story of this octogenarian. I expect that narrative would also be biased. But it would certainly be interesting and as authentic a tale as my description of him would be."

> A story can be defined as a unit of meaning that provides a frame for lived experience. It is through these stories that lived experience is interpreted. We enter into stories, we are entered into stories by others, and we live our lives through these stories.
>
> Stories enable persons to link aspects of their experience through the dimension of time. There does not appear to be any other mechanism for the structuring of experience that so captures the sense of lived time....It is through stories that we obtain a sense of our lives changing. It is through stories that we are able to gain a sense of the unfolding of the events of our lives through recent history, and it appears that this sense is vital to the perception of a "future" that is in any way different from a "present." Stories construct beginnings and endings; they impose beginnings and endings on the flow of experience. [M. White, in Epston & White, 1992, pp. 80-81]

Stories can be liberating and/or ensnarling.

> Our many life stories are both our creations and our creators. They are the principal way that each of us participates with other in the making and remaking of ourselves as social beings. When the relationships we count on to sustain and invigorate us are in trouble, however, we often feel ourselves to be less agents in creating our stories than actors playing roles shaped, if not scripted, by others, in dramas that consign us to unsatisfying repetitions or direct us toward some painful end. [Roth & Chasin, 1994, p. 187]

Stories create a subjective world that defines our identities (Parry, 1997; Lodge, 2002). There is a *there* there, however, a reality beyond our personal constructions.

> Go to the pine if you want to learn about the pine, or to the bamboo if you want to learn about the bamboo. And in doing so, you must leave your subjective preoccupation with yourself. Otherwise you impose yourself on the object and do not learn. [Matsuo Basho, quoted in Shawson, 1999, p. 40)

When the stories that people tell themselves do not provide them with the experience of happiness and satisfaction, they may come to therapy. This is what I mean by the term *constructive therapies* (Hoyt, 1994a, 1996a, 1998): the building of solutions, based on the recognition that we are constructing, not simply uncovering, our psychological realities. Drawing on the theories of constructivism and social constructionism, the term deliberately connotes activity that is positive, productive, and creative (Hoyt, 2000a, p. 139).

> A constructivist therapist assumes that there are any number of viable ways the client's view of reality could change that would dispel the presenting problem, and in a spirit of collaboration, the therapist and client consider and try out such possibilities. The differences among constructivist therapies are differences in how they select an alternative, symptom-free view of reality for the client to experimentally inhabit, and in how they invite and assist the client to do so....In the constructivist view, then, a client's presenting symptoms are the unacceptable costs or consequences of the client's current way of construing reality. Because it is the client who set up that construction of reality in the first place, it is the client who can change it, if skillfully guided to do so, in order to eliminate those unwanted consequences. Competently executed, this approach tends to result in particularly durable therapeutic change and can occur rapidly. [Ecker & Hulley, 1996, pp. 6-9]

Messer and Warren (1995, p. 170) name some of the related paradigms:

> *Perspectivism* as a philosophy of science emphasizes the observer's point of view within a particular set of contexts. *Constructivism* implies that what is known about the object of study is inevitably a function of preexisting models, theories, and assumptions. The notion of *"narrativity"* suggests that acts of perception and of knowing are prestructured and actively mediated by intrinsic requirements of coherence and human sensibility. *Participant-observation* as a method likewise stresses the involvement of the subject in the object of study.

It is important to recognize that there are many powerful forces—biological, familial, social, political, cultural, historical—that impact individuals' subjectivities. Inner and outer, the subjective and the objective, "interpenetrate" (Cade, 1986). "Any act of epistemology affects how you act as well as perceive—the two are linked as a recursive process" (Keeney, 1983, p. 98).

> We assume that the universe is really existing and that man [sic] is gradually coming to understand it. By taking this position we attempt to make clear from the onset that it is a real world we shall be talking about, not a world composed solely of the flitting shadows of people's thoughts. But we should like, furthermore, to make clear our conviction that people's thoughts also really exist, though the correspondence between what people really think exists and what really does exist is a continually changing one....Any living creature, together with his perceptions, is a part of the real world; he is not merely a near-sighted bystander to the goings-on of the real world. [Kelly, 1955, pp. 6-8]

Although we make sense of the world through language, it is also important to keep in mind that changes in story are the vehicle, not the destination. We are most interested in *effects*. As my colleague Michael White has written:

> Thus, the stories that we enter into with our experience have real effects on our lives. The expression of our experience through these stories shapes or makes-up our lives and our relationships; our lives are shaped or constituted through the very process of the interpretation of experience within the contexts of the stories that we enter into and that we are entered into by others.
>
> This is not to propose that life is synonymous with text. It is not enough for a person to tell a new story about oneself, or to assert claims about oneself. Instead, the position carried by these assertions about the world of experience and narrative is that life is the performing of texts. And it is the performance of these texts that is transformative of person's lives. [in Epston & White, 1992, p. 81]

There is no time but the present. As St. Augustine noted in his *Confessions* (quoted in Boscolo & Bertrando, 1993, p. 34):

> What is by now evident and clear is that neither future nor past exists, and it is inexact language to speak of three times—past, present, and future. Perhaps it would be exact to say: there are three times, a present of things past, a present of things present, a present of things to come. In the soul there are these three aspects of time, and I do not see them anywhere else. The present considering the past is the memory, the present considering the future is expectation.

Change (or stasis) always happens NOW (Borges, 1964; Goulding & Goulding, 1979; Hoyt, 1995; Stern, 2004; Tolle, 1999). Sometimes seeing one's constructions and changing one's storying is not too difficult. Othertimes, however, the challenge can be daunting, especially if much is at stake or circumstances are adverse. Even then—especially then—it is good to remember that we still have choice, that the present is a gift.

> To be hopeful in bad times is not just foolishly romantic. It is based on the fact that human history is a history not only of cruelty, but also of compassion, sacrifice, courage, kindness.
>
> What we choose to emphasize in this complex history will determine our lives. If we see only the worst, it destroys our capacity to do something. If we remember those times and places—and there are so many—where people have behaved magnificently, this gives us the energy to act, and at least the possibility of sending this spinning top of a world in a different direction.

And if we do act, in however small a way, we don't have to wait for some grand utopian future. The future is an infinite succession of presents, and to live *now* as we think human beings should live, in defiance of all that is bad around us, is itself a marvelous victory. [Zinn, 2002, p. 208][2]

THE BOOK IN HAND

This volume represents my continuing exploration of how the concepts of narrative constructionism can help to make therapy more effective and efficient (i.e., "brief").[3] Appreciating that "the present is a gift" and that change occurs in the moment, I continue to draw heavily from the strengths-based worlds of solution-focused therapy, narrative therapy, and redecision therapy, with their respective concepts of "making a difference" (de Shazer, 1991), "reauthoring" (White & Epston, 1990; White, 1995), and "redeciding" (Goulding & Goulding, 1979), as well as from ideas about "utilization" associated with the work of Milton Erickson and others.

Since the publication and warm reception of *Some Stories Are Better than Others* in 2000 and *Interviews with Brief Therapy Experts* in 2001, my professional life has continued to be busy. In addition to moving my fulltime practice as a clinical psychologist to a Kaiser Permanente Health Plan facility (San Rafael, California) much closer to home, it has been my good fortune to have been invited to present speeches and teach workshops in a number of places, both in the United States and abroad. Some of the chapters contained herein are based on those lectures, as well as on several published interviews. Some have appeared, in modified forms,

---

2. Colleagues John Sharry, Brendan Madden and Melissa Darmody (2001, pp. 106-107) remind us that this is true also in our work as therapists: "It is one thing to be respectful, optimistic, curious and flexible in a well-resourced agency with clients who are largely at the customer level of motivation. It is quite another thing to maintain a respectful constructive stance in a context where clients are largely at a visitor or complainant level of motivation, in a very under-resourced agency where you feel undervalued and unsupported; or worse still where there are high levels of conflict (either within the agency or outside). In these instances it is easy to become 'burnt out' or pessimistic....For example, therapists become visitors when they feel detached or disinterested in their work or clients; and they become complainants when they feel pessimistic about change and hopeless about being effective. If this happens therapists do not have the optimism and energy to take on difficult cases. It is therefore crucial for therapists to take steps to monitor and maintain their own mental health and resourcefulness, to ensure that they stay as customers to their work."

as journal articles and book chapters, and are brought together here for the first time. All provenances are listed in the Credits that conclude this volume.

Chapter 1, "Toward a More Effective Brief Therapy," records the keynote address I was honored to give at the opening of the Second Pan-Pacific Brief Psychotherapy Conference, held in Osaka, Japan, only a few weeks after the terrible events of September 11, 2001. Before turning to the specific characteristics and various theories of brief treatment, I began the speech by noting that many of the basic principles—such as building alliances, communicating clearly, and showing respect for the others' abilities and values—are ideas that can go far beyond our offices and clinics. Recent world events have done nothing to diminish the urgency of this message.

Chapter 2, "Connection: The Double-Edged Gift of Presence," addresses various implications of the conventional term *countertransference* and proffers the alternative idea of *client-inspired therapist contributions*, with various clinical examples to illustrate.

Chapter 3, "Some Things I Have Learned from Friends and Clients about Empowerment and Rehabilitation," was originally presented at the Finnish Rehabilitation Foundation conference held in Helsinki in March 2001. Using numerous case examples as well as excerpts from poetry, ways are illustrated for developing and maintaining our human connection within the therapeutic alliance, for establishing and renegotiating treatment goals and responsibilities, for valuing strengths and opportunities instead of problems, and for appreciating the overarching importance of language in the construction of worldviews and stories that inspire, facilitate, and empower rehabilitation and therapy.

Chapter 4, "'The Present is a Gift': A Clinical Demonstration," from which this omnibus collection takes its name, is the edited transcript (with commentaries) of a session demonstrating "Integrated Brief Therapy" conducted at the "Brief Therapy: Lasting Impressions" conference held in New York City during August 1998 under the sponsorship of the Milton H. Erickson Foundation.

---

3. "In addition to meaning 'efficient' and 'to the point,' *brief therapy* is also used sometimes to refer particularly to time-sensitive intervention based on certain (social constructionist) theoretical principles, not on the length of treatment. Directly or indirectly, these approaches—which are sometimes loosely associated with the work of the famous psychiatrist-hypnotherapist Milton Erickson (with Gregory Bateson and the word *epistemology* waiting in the wings)—involve a wide variety of creative methods that operate at the level of cybernetics and hermeneutics, strategies and 'language games,' all more-or-less intended to influence how clients interact and construe ('story') their experience" (Hoyt, 2001, p. xiv).

Chapter 5, "Some Stories Are Better than Others: A Conversation about Hope, Passion, and the Challenges of Work," is the first of three interviews contained in the present book. Victor Yalom, the President of PsychotherapistResources.com, explores with me ways to be innovative and remain excited in the difficult face of practicing therapy today.

Chapter 6, "Solution-Focused Couple Therapy," is an extensive review of the principles and practices of solution-focused therapy, with special application to work with couples. Excerpts from interviews with Steve de Shazer, an elaborate literature review, myriads of typical solution-focused questions, connections between solution-focused therapy and other methods, and a case history are featured.

Chapter 7, "The Squeaky Wheel: Don't Let Managed Care Shortchange Your Clients," is a practical, nuts-and-bolts discussion of ways to increase the likelihood of getting managed-care companies to make appropriate authorizations for couple therapy.

Chapter 8, "Early HMO Chart Note," is a pithy satire about the tendency to pathologize and the (mis)use of the *DSM*. Imagine what would happen if Jesus of Nazareth were to appear at your local mental-health crisis clinic!

Chapter 9, "The Pros and Cons of Postmodernism in Psychotherapy: Stepping Back from the Abyss," was written with my friend Phillip Ziegler. We trace the history of postmodernism and appreciate its emphasis on the importance of language and the influence of power and perspective on social discourse, but draw the line at the invitation to step into a potentially destructive netherland of unreality, anti-science, and alienation. Rather, we put forward the related but alternative theory of social constructionism with its connotations of multiple perspectives, interpersonal coordination, relational responsibility, and therapeutic collaboration.

Chapter 10, "'Burn In, Not Out!': A Conversation about Truth and Beauty in Brief Therapy," is the second of three interviews. Tapio Malinen, a Finnish school psychologist, therapist, and journal editor, and I met in Helsinki, Finland, in March 2001. The edited transcript of our discussion highlights ideas about solution-focused therapy, social constructionism, the meaning(s) of truth and beauty, and the mindful and evocative uses of language.

Chapter 11, "'Sand and Snow': A Conversation about Culture, Alcohol, and Empowerment," is the third interview in the book. While in Helsinki in March 2001, I also met with Tracey Powers-Erkkilo and Lotta Lehmusvaara, two staff members at the A-Clinic there. We talked about ways to intervene respectfully and effectively with problem drinkers, and also discussed the role of culture and some ideas about the building blocks of children's self-esteem.

Chapter 12, "Road Trip," recounts an adventure I had with my father. We often get unstuck from life's calamities by letting go, changing attitudes, thinking outside the box, shifting perspectives and accessing our overlooked personal resources. Sometimes that's not enough, however, as I learned once in the middle of the night.

Chapter 13, "How I Embody a Narrative Constructive Approach," was originally presented as part of a symposium entitled *How Do Eminent Psychotherapists Personally Embody Their Own Theories?* held in August 2001 at the annual convention of the American Psychological Association. I provide a candid view, emphasizing the importance of language, compassion, politics, poetics, pragmatics, and mystery in my construction of constructivism.

Chapter 14, "I've Always Been This Way—Thanks to Them!" was originally presented at another APA symposium, this one entitled *Honoring Our Teachers: Eminent Psychotherapists Describe Who Influenced Them, and How*, held in August 2002. In this extended version, I discuss some of my influences—including family, professional teachers, patients, good luck, Mother Nature, and art and literature. I also emphasize both the value of being open to input from others and the importance of listening to oneself.

Each chapter has been written to stand on its own, although the whole is intended to be greater than the sum of its parts. Throughout, my emphasis is on the elevation of the client's and clinician's creativity and humanity within the therapeutic relationship; on the importance of focusing on strengths and competencies, more on what is possible than what is not; and on the skillful use of language in the construction of preferred realities. As readers will see, at places I provide numerous quotations from the professional psychotherapy literature so that some of the many contributors that have added to my understanding can be heard directly. I have also attempted to describe instances of my own way of relating to clients, which sometimes involves the sharing of a personal anecdote or a joke or a line from a song or a poem. Although often intuitive and plucked from the resonating ground of what sometimes is called "countertransference," these are usually carefully selected to heighten clients' awareness and to put them in touch with a less familiar part of themselves that may be useful in their continued "re-storying."

How we look influences what we see, and what we see influences what we do. We all conceive the world through our "lenses" (Hoffman, 1990).

> So it matters a great deal how a psychiatrist is taught to look at mental illness, because the "how" cannot be clearly separated from the "what" of the disease. To understand psychiatric ways of seeing, we have to proceed knowing that what counts as "fact" is a tinted window onto a world you cannot step outside to see. [Luhrmann, 2000, p. 10]

The psychotherapy case history itself is an interesting form. To what extent (or in what ways) are case histories true? In his brilliant book *Healing Fiction*, James Hillman (1983, p. 3) quotes Freud: "I am a scientist by necessity, and not by vocation. I am really by nature an artist. My books, in fact, more resemble works of imagination than treatises on pathology." Appreciating the central role of stories in therapy (and life), Hillman notes that case histories are *fiction* is three senses of the word: (1) as representing factual history of events as they unfolded, (2) as invented accounts of another's (the patient's) interior experiences, and (3) as the presentation of literal statements transposed to where they cannot be controverted or verified. A case history is an intrapsychic and interpersonal process as a particular moment in time. It might capture much of the spirit, but much gets colored by memory. Even a videotape of the actual events would only reveal certain aspects.

I also agree with Hillman (1996, pp. 6-7) when he indicts much of what mental-health professionals have proffered as "conventional wisdom":

> Because the "traumatic" view of early years so controls psychological theory of personality and its development, the focus of our rememberings and the language of our personal storytelling have already been infiltrated by the toxins of these theories. Our lives may be determined less by our childhood than by the way we have earned to imagine our childhoods....[W]e must set aside the psychological frames that are usually used, and mostly used up. They do not reveal enough. They trim a life to fit the frame: developmental growth, step by step, from infancy, through troubled youth, to midlife crisis and aging, to death. Plodding your way through an already planned map, you are on an itinerary that tells you where you have been before you get there, or like an averaged statistic foretold by an actuary in an insurance company.

Truly "good stories" are well told (McKee, 1997), and more. As I have written in *Some Stories Are Better than Others* (Hoyt, 2000a, pp. 19-22):

What makes some stories better than others? Ultimately, of course, the answer must come from each individual freely, lest we impose our own values or beliefs. In general terms, stories involve a plot in which characters have experiences and employ imagination to resolve problems over time....From this perspective, therapy can be understood as the purposeful development of a more functional story; "better" stories are those that bring more of what is desired and less of what is not desired....

Aesthetics, effects and ethics are all important. We like stories that are well told; that are vivid and eloquent; that involve the generation and resolution of some tension; that see the protagonist[s] emerge successfully, perhaps even triumphantly. A "good" story does more than merely relate "facts"; a "good story" invigorates.

I hope that you and your clients, dear reader, may find ways of putting stories together that gets them more of what they want.

Michael F. Hoyt, Ph.D.
Mill Valley, California
New Year's Day 2004

Acknowledgments

While I cannot do justice to my many gratitudes, I would be particularly remiss if I did not thank for their ideas, comments, opportunities, and inspiration: Insoo Berg, Nick Cummings, Steve de Shazer, Albert Ellis, Milton Erickson, John Frykman, Bob Goulding, Mary Goulding, Alan Gurman, Jay Haley, Sandra Hoben, Tobey Hiller, Tatsumi Kojima, Murray Korngold, Lotta Lehmusvaara, Alvin Mahrer, Tapio Malinen, Donald Meichenbaum, Scott Miller, Karin Olssen, Bill O'Hanlon, Jeffry Ordover, Tracey Powers-Erkkilo, Harvey Ratner, Ritva Saarelainen, Carl Whitaker, Michael White, Victor Yalom, Jeffrey Zeig, and Phillip Ziegler. Thanks also to the anonymous patients and clients that allowed use of their stories; to the various authors, editors, and publishers that permitted use of materials; to Alex Hoyt and Sean Dwyer for computer assistance; and to Kaiser Permanente Health Plan and to the Mill Valley Public Library for their continuing support.

To my wife Jennifer and my son Alex: As always, I love you more than words can say.

1

Toward a More Effective Brief Therapy

It is a great honor to be here. I remember with pleasure our meeting at the First International Conference six years ago in Fukuoka. The challenge before us now, the reason for this conference, is to continue to describe and exchange therapeutic models and methods that efficiently achieve good results. Keeping with the theme, "Toward a More Effective Therapy," I have prepared some remarks that I hope you will not find too boring.

We are all here to learn together; we are all part of the heart and soul and brain of this wonderful international meeting. I think it is especially fitting—given the terrible recent events that have been occurring in the world—that we are joining together to discuss ways of helping and healing. This is a good time for learning and friendships to be international. Brief therapy is not the answer to all the world's problems, of course, but some of the principles we will be studying here—such as building alliances, communicating clearly, showing respect for the others' abilities and values—are ideas that can go far beyond our offices and clinics. I hope so.

What is *brief therapy*? A simple definition might say *"Time-sensitive treatment to relieve psychological distress and promote growth."* But what does this mean: *"Time-sensitive treatment"*? Originally, "brief" simply meant "short" or "not long," and was often used to contrast with traditionally "long-term" (usually psychoanalytic) therapy. While "brief" is sometimes used to mean treatments generally going from 1-20 sessions, the basic idea of "brief therapy" is more an attitude or orientation than a specific number of sessions: *"to the point—not one more than necessary."* Following these length-of-treatment notions, there can be many different schools of brief therapy—brief cognitive-behavioral, brief family systems, brief solution-focused, brief redecision, brief narrative constructive, even brief psychodynamic. All have the commonality of being focused on resolving a presenting problem as quickly as possible.

The term *brief therapy* has also come to mean a set of therapeutic principles and practices that are often loosely associated with the work of the famous Dr. Milton Erickson. As some of you may know, Erickson-Sensei (who died in 1980) was a brilliant psychiatrist and hypnotherapist who was known for his creative use of multi-level communication and therapeutic directives. Underlying his often highly innovative techniques was the basic principle of *utilization*—the idea being to find ways to use (or utilize) whatever the client brings to therapy.

Ericksonian influences and themes can be seen in many diverse schools. While they have important differences in how they conceptualize problems and think about power and the roles of the therapist/client, and in their subsequent techniques, they all endeavor to recognize and therapeutically use whatever capacities and competencies the client (and the therapist) may bring to the session, with an emphasis on strengths, abilities, and resources rather than on pathology, defects, or weaknesses.

Regardless of the specific theoretical approach or technical method, the goal of brief psychotherapy is to help the patient resolve a problem, to get "unstuck" and to move on. Techniques are specific, integrated, and as eclectic as needed. Treatment is focused, the therapist appropriately active, and the patient responsible for making changes. Each session is valuable, and therapy ends as soon as possible. Good outcome, not good process, is most valued. More is not better; *better* is better. The patient carries on, and can return to treatment as needed (Hoyt, 1995a).

Looking across different efficient and effective brief therapies, we can identify a set of six common characteristics. In their own ways and to varying degrees, they all emphasize certain features:

1. *the development of a rapid and positive alliance.* The alliance is the soil in which all else may take root. Brief therapists—knowing that imposition generates opposition, that insistence produces resistance—attend carefully to forming and maintaining a good working relationship, gauging and attempting to match methods with client motivation and readiness.

2. *a focus on specific, achievable, measurable goals.* What are the client's preferences? Their intentions? What would tell them that our work is done—and done well? Negotiating (and at times, re-negotiating) treatment goals involves the client from the beginning: It excites expectations, calls upon the client's skills, highlights personal autonomy, and sets a template for the con-

tinuing client-therapist alliance. Identifying and respecting the client's goals communicates respect for the client.

3. *the clear definition of client and therapist responsibilities*, often with tasks or assignments to be carried out between sessions. Brief therapists know that much of therapy happens *between* sessions, and that the possible enduring value of therapy cannot be assessed at the end of the last session but only after some time has passed during which the client has opportunities to apply what has occurred in the meeting(s) with the therapist.

4. *an emphasis on strengths and competencies*, with an expectation of change and the cultivation of motivation. We often use the language of supposition, talking about "*When* things are better…" and "*After* the miracle…"

5. *the introduction of novelty, assisting the client toward new perceptions and behaviors.* As Jay Haley-Sensei (1976, p. 49) has written about his problem-solving therapy approach, "The main goal of therapy is to get people to behave differently and so to have different subjective experiences." In addition to suggesting directives and 'homework' tasks, we endeavor to help clients change their 'viewing and doing' with education, skill instruction, metaphoric communication, reframing, and an emphasis on their possibly overlooked abilities and choices.

6. *a here-and-now (and next) focus on the present and future more than on the past.* As part of time sensitivity, there is recognition that there is really no time but the present, as well as the concept of *intermittency*, the idea that clients can return to treatment as needed in the future.

What makes therapy work? This is a big question, and I am looking forward to hearing the valuable ideas that each speaker at this conference will contribute to answering the question of how to make therapy more effective and efficient. No one method works all the time. To my mind, therapy is a craft, one that can be sometimes practiced artfully and studied scientifically. Recent research evidence suggests that what is most predictive of a good outcome is a good therapist-client alliance and the utilization of the client's abilities and resources. So-called "therapist factors" and "placebo effects" by themselves do not contribute much to the eventual outcome of a case. Specific techniques and nonspecific factors (like hope) are valuable to the extent that they encourage clients to participate actively and to use their own sometimes overlooked resources.

My own perspective is limited, of course, by many factors. Still, it seems to me that therapy works better when we form a good alliance, when we negotiate a clear goal or therapeutic contract with the client, when we actively involve the client in the work and help them to experience something new and desirable in the session, when we discuss how they will apply the lessons of therapy outside the consulting room, when we make plans for possible relapse and unforeseen events, and when we discuss follow-up. From my experience, there is often a structure to sessions and to treatments—and we do well to pay attention to the different tasks that need to be accomplished at the beginning, in the middle, and near the end of meetings. I will attempt to discuss this further at the workshop I will be presenting as well as in my book, *Some Stories Are Better than Others* (Hoyt, 2000a).

Many different theories and models have been offered about what is the most important key in therapy to help unlock clients from their distress, what needs to happen to assist them in leaving the past behind them. Each has an idea about what is the fulcrum on which treatment turns. Some will suggest it is using language to create a sense of reality that highlights solutions and competencies; others may say that what is most important is making the unconscious conscious or bringing forward and releasing painful feelings; others will suggest that it is giving directives and teaching skills to alter maladaptive relationship patterns; yet others may suggest emphasizing people's choice and personal power to help them reauthor their stories and narratives.

Long ago but not far away, at Osaka Castle, legend has it that three lords revealed their very different characters when asked what they would do with a bird that did not sing. Every model or theory opens doors and closes doors. What do we gain and what do we lose by thinking in a certain way? As you listen to descriptions of different therapies over the next few days, I would invite you to consider three questions:

1. Is it *effective*—does it work?

2. Is it *aesthetic*—is it attractive and interesting?

3. Is it *ethical*—is it respectful, does it enlarge the person?

We are all in the business of trying to influence people, but does the particular approach endeavor to help the client feel more of his or her own power or does the approach leave the client feeling that it was the Professional Expert who solved the problem?

How we look influences what we see, and what we see influences what we do, 'round and round. The doors of therapeutic perception and possibility have been opened wide by the recognition that we are actively constructing our mental realities rather than simply uncovering or coping with an objective "truth." We build our worldview through the stories we tell ourselves and each other. Some stories are better than others, some ways of thinking and looking and acting are more enlivening and encouraging and help people get more of what they want, than others. I hear a haiku muse whisper (from Hoyt, 2000a, p. 167):

> Solution focus
> Find exception and increase
> Otherwise stay same
>
> More of same, no change
> More of difference, not same
> When will you notice?

What makes us most human is not our opposable thumbs nor our use of tools but, rather, our capacity to conceive a future, recall a past, construct meanings, and make choices. How we choose to conceive and pattern the present, the past and the future profoundly influences our course. To use a modern image from computers, one of the keys to happiness, for ourselves and our clients, is knowing where to double-click!

Therapy happens in relationship, through language. Again, I hear a haiku (from Hoyt, 2000a, p. 47):

> Focusing language
> On solutions, not problems
> Miracles happen.

One effective way to guide clients toward new perceptions is to ask good questions. We can arouse people's imagination and curiosity and invite them to refocus their attention toward where they want to go. Notice, for example, the excitement generated when Insoo Kim Berg-Sensei asks the solution-focused Miracle Question, *"Suppose one night a miracle happens—how will you notice?"*; or when Mary Goulding-Sensei asks the redecision therapy question, *"What are you willing to change today?"*; or when David Nylund-Sensei asks the narrative therapy question, *"When are you able to control the problem rather than it controlling you?"* Therapy becomes more effective and efficient when it is done collaboratively, not forcefully. During these days together, let's see what good questions we can hear, and ask.

As with our clients, in the true spirit of cultural diversity, we have before us a wonderful opportunity to learn *from* each other as well as *about* each other. It is especially interesting to be here in an international setting, since it helps us to notice things that we normally take for granted. Who gets to say what is *normal* and what is *valid* and what is *healthy*, and what is not? So much is simply (and not so simply) culturally determined. For all of us, our vision is both empowered and delimited by the lenses through which we view the world. These 'lenses' are shaped by our personal histories, by our family histories, by our social class and education and language and cultural histories. Indeed, therapy can be thought of as helping people to look through new lenses, helping them to open their eyes, helping them to see things in ways they haven't noticed or appreciated before.

I love the idea that I may be able to get a glimpse of the world through Malaysian eyes or Korean eyes or Chinese eyes or Filipino eyes or Japanese eyes. In preparing these remarks, I have to confess that I searched through the literature for the right quotation to illustrate the value of cross-cultural awareness. There were many interesting comments, but none seemed just right. Finally, in frustration I put aside my psychology books and picked up something much more enjoyable—a book entitled *"Baseball is Just Baseball"—The Understated Ichiro*! And there I read the words of the great Seattle Mariner, Ichiro Suzuki, from an interview done a few months ago:

> There are a lot of things to worry about, unexpected things, because the mentality and the manners are different. Even if there are things that become somewhat stressful, I think they're interesting. Isn't it because of those things that I am able to be struck by the significance of being alive? [from an April 2001 interview, in Shields, 2001, p. 17][1]

Let us celebrate our diversity. Some cultures may put more emphasis on the value of having and expressing feelings than others. Different cultures may have a different sense of time and how quickly it is appropriate or allowable for change to occur—even the very idea of what may be "brief" may vary from one place to another. It is important to recognize that we may not all mean exactly the same thing when we say *emotion* or *self* or *family* or *therapist-client relationship*. An approach or technique that may work in one situation may not be appropriate in another—the idea of helping clients to better use their own competencies is a good one, but how to do that in a culture that sees the doctor or therapist as a Special Authority may be very different that doing that in a culture where roles are more egalitarian. In California, where I live, patients sometimes ask if they may call me by my first name, and sometimes even call me by my first name without asking; I'm not sure how often that would happen in Tokyo or Seoul or Beijing or Hong Kong.

So, as we move toward a more effective therapy, I hope that you will be curious and receptive, but also generative. There are useful general principles to be learned for building a respectful alliance, co-creating achievable treatment goals, and evoking client skills and capacities, but I would suggest that you consider asking, *"How can I apply some of what I am hearing and seeing and imagining in my own situation, with my own patients, in my own style?"*

In closing, I would like to thank you for your patience and interest, and again express my appreciation to our hosts and colleagues for this time together.

Domo arigato!

---

1. Writing a century ago, Lafcadio Hearn (1898/1984, p. 228) counseled "Even with the kindest of intentions it is impossible to estimate correctly at sight anything of the extraordinary in Japanese custom, because the extraordinary nearly always relates to feelings, beliefs, or thoughts about which a stranger cannot know anything." Readers of *Shogun* (Clavell, 1975) and watchers of the subsequent T.V. mini-series may recall, for example, that the 1860s English sailors echewed bathing, fearing that they would wash off what they imagined to be their protective coating, whilst the Japanese took daily soaks and were appalled at the English lack of hygiene.

   As a number of Western writers (e.g., Feiler, 1991; Horn, 1996; Iyer, 1992; Mura, 1991) have illustrated, culture clashes are instructive as well as sometimes amusing, helping us to see ourselves and our taken-for-granted assumptions. After I taught a workshop in Tokyo in 2003 for the Japan Clinical Counseling Association, the executive committee and I had a wonderful dinner together. I had been in Japan twice before and several of my hosts had been to the U.S. As the evening progressed, we talked about various topics, including what had seemed "strange" in visiting the other's country. I had noticed that in Japan, at the entrances to temples, dragons produce water for purification; whereas in the West, dragons are depicted as fierce fire-breathers. "That's sooo American!" one of my colleagues smiled. "Well, what seemed strange when you visited the U.S?" I asked. They mentioned guns and litter, and then someone offered "the food plates are too big" and someone else chimed in "and the desserts are too sweet." As a course of delicious grilled *unagi* (eel) was served, one woman (who had gotten a graduate degree at a school in West Virginia) added, "And they eat squirrels!"—which is kind of weird.

2

Connection: The Double-Edged Gift of Presence

My heart rouses
       thinking to bring you news
              of something
that concerns you
       and concerns many men.
—William Carlos Williams (from "Asphodel, That Greeny Flower," 1969a, p. 150)

One must be receptive, receptive to the image at the moment it appears.... The poetic image is a sudden salience on the surface of the psyche, the lesser psychological causes of which have not been sufficiently investigated.
—Gaston Bachelard (1964, p. xv)

Many psychotherapists have been so conditioned by the term *countertransference* that they have become almost phobic, hoping not to have it, or hoping if they do, that at least it won't show. The term is often used to connote a distortion, an error, the "acting out of unresolved pathology," therapeutic blunders, and the like (Robertiello & Schoenewolf, 1987). Therapists are right to avoid reactions that would interfere with their clients, of course, but processes of responding to the client that sometimes are termed *countertransference* also inform the connections we call *presence, attunement, empathy, rapport, resonance, inspiration, caring, compassion,* and the like. As such, it can be useful, desirable, enlivening, inevitable, and sometimes necessary. Like Janus, the Roman diety, *countertransference* is two-sided; like the Chinese ideogram for "crisis," opportunity and danger may both be present.

Some questioning of the term *countertransference* may help us to better understand what's under where we're standing. I'm not saying that *countertransference* is good or bad, but rather, that different constructions of the term carry different implications, with different consequences. How we look influences what we see, and what we see helps determine what we do (Hoyt, 2000a). Both the phenomena we call *countertransference* and our understanding of that phenomena are interpersonal creations. As Kenneth Gergen (1985, p. 267), one of the significant voices in the social constructionist movement in (post)modern psychology, has put it:

> The terms in which the world is understood are social artifacts, products of historically situated interchanges among people. From the constructionist position the process of understanding is not automatically driven by the forces of nature, but is the result of an active, cooperative enterprise of persons, in relationship.

We all have *theory countertransference* (Hubble & O'Hanlon, 1992), our theories shaping and coloring our lenses, opening our eyes *and* delimiting our vision, affecting how and what we see and telling us how and what to think about what we think we see.

In the *brief therapy* and *constructive therapy* literature that I am particularly familiar with—especially the worlds of solution-focused therapy, narrative therapy, strategic-interactional therapy, Ericksonian therapy, and the like—the term *countertransference* isn't much used. Rather, recognizing that "some stories are better than others" (Hoyt, 2000a), brief therapists tend to think more in terms of how to frame and constructively utilize whatever emerges in their work with clients. *Client-inspired therapist contributions* can be very useful, although there needs to be keen recognition of the power gradient and the importance of honoring clients' goals and not imposing our values while maintaining a collaborative client-therapist relationship.

Of course, even if one eschews the term *countertransference*, we are still susceptible to various pulls and pressures in brief or time-sensitive treatment, from both without and within. Indeed, operating under a requirement to almost immediately "make something happen" may create special "countertransference" potentials for brief therapists. In addition to various "therapist resistances to brief therapy" (Hoyt, 1995a), there may be the temptation to quickly impose a particular theoretical framework, resentment at a client's balking response, and the development of a kind of *institutional countertransference* (the therapist begins to relate in an officious, impersonal manner).

I recall the opening words of William Carlos Williams (1969b, p. 132) from his poem, "The Descent":

> The descent beckons
>   as the ascent beckoned.
>   Memory is a kind
> of accomplishment,
>   a sort of renewal
>   even
> an initiation, since the spaces it opens are new places
>   inhabited by hordes
>   heretofore unrealized,
> of new kinds—
>   since their movements
>   are toward new objectives
> (Even though formerly they were abandoned).

Initially, the term *countertransference* was used by Freud very specifically to signify the therapist's reaction (or *counter*) to the patient's transference, as when a therapist becomes exceptionally active in response to the patient's neediness, or guilty in response to the patient's complaining, or sexually aroused in response to the client's flirting, and so forth. In this sense, the therapist's reactions can serve as information or clues about the way the client transacts.

This conception distinguishes *countertransference* from the therapist's *own transferences* toward the client/patient, as when a therapist's overactivity or guilt or anger or sexual excitment originate in the therapist's own psychology, not in the interaction that the patient initiates. (As an audience member noted in the discussion section of the symposium where this paper was first presented, the term *countertransference* can also be applied to how the *patient* responds to the transference of the therapist.) Imposition tends to generate opposition, and some of what gets called patient *resistance* may actually be an attempt to avoid being psychologically 'colonized' (having a meaning framework forced upon one). The distinctions can be subtle and complicated; let it suffice here to say that invitation, not imposition, is the key.

If a client genuinely announces some bad news and you feel sad, it's different than if their "m.o." (*modus operandi*) is to announce bad news to get your sympathy (what T.A. therapists would call a 'racket'), or if you always dig for bad news (who's 'issue' is that?). This became clear to me in a seminar with Erik Erikson some twenty years ago. We were discussing whether a particular response was *transference* or *countertransference*. Erik shrugged and said, "Have you thought that maybe it's *reality?*"

The concept of *countertransference* is situated in the belief that *we* are "treating" *them*, that we can objectively determine which components belong to whom, who is the source and who is the reactor. In my experience, however, practice is much more reflexive and seldom that clear-cut: like the famous Escher print, countertransference is an interpersonal process, one hand drawing the other (Matthews, 1985). Long ago it was Carl Jung (1929/1966, p. 72) who commented: "[T]he doctor is as much 'in the analysis' as the patient. He *[sic]* is equally a part of the psychic process of treatment and therefore equally exposed to the transforming influences." (Carl Whitaker, 1989, pp. 164-165, referred to this process as *co-transference*.) As William Butler Yeats (1928/1989, p. 217) wrote:

> O chestnut-tree, great-rooted blossomer
> Are you the leaf, the blossom or the bole?
> O body swayed to music, O brightening glance,
> How can we know the dancer from the dance?

I am not suggesting that everything be blurred or that 'anything goes.' There is a useful middle ground. What therapist worth her salt or his salt has not sometimes had their "heart aroused" and been inspired to share an emotionally personal experience or to quote a famous Zen story or Bible passage, or maybe simply laugh or even cry with a patient? Too much worry about "countertransference" can inhibit our humanity and therapeutic creativity and block the magic that dwells in every moment.

In *Brief Therapy and Managed Care* (Hoyt, 1995a, pp. 320-323), I recounted an episode during the course of a therapy with an older man in which his interest and my interest in baseball served as a point of connection, not just in the content of our stories and metaphors but also in terms of a felt sense of shared kinship. We sparked one another's imagination, which helped us co-construct a solution to the predicament that had brought him to therapy. In another instance, a woman whose husband had recently died nervously asked me if it was "crazy" that she wanted to take his ashes in the trunk of her car to a rock concert to hear his favorite group. They had both been deep into music. From somewhere deep inside myself—from my family connection to rock music, a his-story rooted in my late brother being a business manager in the music entertainment world—I suddenly heard the lines from an old Dobie Gray album:

> *Give me the beat boys and free my soul,*
> *I want to get lost in your rock and roll*
> *And drift away.*
> —from "Drift Away" (M. Williams, 1973)

Somehow forgetting my self-consciousness, I looked at her and sang the words. She paused, then asked me how I knew *that* song. Before I could answer, she sang the verse, and the next, then laughed: "That settles it—I know it's not really John, but Friday night I'm taking him to the concert anyway." The words and music we shared acknowledged her reality and opened space for her mourning process to continue.

In his book *The Poetics of Space*, the French phenomenologist Gaston Bachelard (1964; also see Hirsch, 1999; Hirshfield, 1997) discusses *reverberation*, the idea that a poem becomes alive because the writer provides a stimulus that sets off something kindred in the reader's mind. Bachelard writes (in English translation):

> [W]hen I shall have occasion to mention the relation of a new poetic image to an archtype lying dormant in the depths of the unconscious, I shall have to make it understood that this relation is not, properly speaking, a causal one. The poetic image is not subject to an inner thrust. It is not an echo of the past. On the contrary: through the brilliance of an image, the distant past resounds with echoes, and it is hard to know at what depth these echoes will reverberate and die away. Because of its novelty and its action, the poetic image has an entity and a dynamism of its own; it is referable to a direct *ontology* ....
>
> The poet does not confer the past of his image upon me, and yet his image immediately takes root in me. (1964, pp. xvi-xvii)

A few pages later, he continues:

> This is where the phenomenological doublet of resonances and repercussions must be sensitized. The resonances are dispersed on the different planes of our life in the world, while the repercussions invite us to give greater depth to our own existence. In the resonance, we hear the poem, in the reverberations we speak it, it is our own. The reverberations bring about a change of being. It is as though the poet's being were our being....Through this reverberation, by going *immediately* beyond all psychology or psychoanalysis, we feel a poetic power rising naively within us. After the original reverberation, we are able to experience resonances, sentimental repercussions, reminders of our past. But the image has touched the depths before it stirs the surface. (1964, pp. xxii-xxiii)[1]

This sympathetic vibration sometimes happens between therapist and client—a vibration that can be touching and inspiring as well as informational. Rather than thinking of *countertransference* as the enactment of an anachronistic distortion, there are times it might better be understood—and perhaps even appreciated—as a well-directed sensitive emotional reaction (Erving Polster, in Kernberg et al., 2000).

If one story amplifies another in a not-so-useful direction, however, sometimes we have a not-so-therapeutic problem. In one situation, a very anxious woman kept asking me the same goddamn questions over and over. I knew that she was neurotic, that she was a constant worrier and suffering (but did not have OCD); I also knew that she reminded me of my mother. I answered patiently, I answered impatiently. I asked her to identify times she had resisted the urge to worry; she ignored my answers and my efforts to redirect her. I asked her to reflect on why she kept asking despite having heard my answers. I shared with her my frustration and asked her to consider what impact her repeated questioning had on me (and others). She smiled, then resumed her litany of questions. Finally, after the umpteenth time, I gently snapped—I stood up, announced that I would no longer be her therapist, and asked her to follow me to the front desk where she could sign up to see someone else if she so desired (see Kottler & Carlson, 2003, pp. 157-164).

Such a confrontation can be therapeutic and even necessary. Sometimes "being real and losing your temper" (Whitaker, 1989, pp. 210-211) is what is needed; not just a contrived "use of self" technique, but a real I-and-thou (not a role-and-thou) expression. Consider the well-known scene in the movie *Good*

---

1. Some things to ponder, from Muriel Rukeyser's *The Life of Poetry* (1949/1996): "Helmholtz says, in his basic study of tone, that water in motion has an effect similar to that of music; the motion of waves, rhythmic and varied in detail, produces the feelings of repose or weariness—and he adds, reminds us of order and power and the fine links of life. Meter, in poetry, is allied to these effects and the long search for their causes. We begin to believe that there are resonances according to which the body responds, in its rhythms, to external motion and rhythm....In this recognition, both empathy and memory present new possibilities. We know that memory has a great deal to do with the power of poetry. We know that verse has a certain value as a mnemonic device. This value depends partly on the rhythm itself; partly on the meter, the segmenting of rhythm into measurable parts; and partly on the sounds, not even of the words this time, but of the syllables" [pp. 115-116]; and "The search of man is a long process toward this reality, the reality of the relationships. One meaning of that search is love; one meaning is progress; one is science; and one is poetry. For there is no human level on which the search does not exist" [p. 165].

Will Hunting wherein the therapist (played by Robin Williams) angrily grabs his client. The story was fiction and seizing a patient by the throat is problematical—right on the hairy edge, if not over it—but until then everything was impactless game-playing, not real.

In his classic paper, "Hate in the Countertransference," Donald Winnicott (1949) tells of an instance wherein anger toward the client was genuine and anything else would have been phony and failed to register. (I thought of calling the present paper "Hoyt in the Countertransference" but thought the allusion might be a bit obscure and also didn't want to conflate my family name with enmity.) In the case I've just been describing, however, while my frustration and anger may have dented her attention, I don't think it did so for very long. My 'buttons got pushed,' I lost it, and lost the patient, too.

Our countertransference potential exists long before the transference (James Hillman, in Goulding & Hillman, 1995). Lately I've been in the process of moving to a new location in a different city. I've been saying goodbye to many clients and colleagues. One elderly woman, who is very dear to me, failed to keep the appointment at which I had been planning to tell her of my impending departure. I had just recently made the decision, and she didn't know yet that I was leaving. When she failed the appointment, I had the fantasy that she had died—and I felt relieved. When she called a few days later to apologize and reschedule, I felt chagrined by my morbid fantasy. I also felt better informed and prepared to deal with my grief—and hers—about our impending loss.

In another recent situation, a colleague and I came to the difficult juncture in an ongoing co-therapy case of needing to tell a client-couple that I would soon be leaving the clinic. The question arose of how to continue—should my colleague see the couple by herself? Should she just see one member, the woman, who was the one who initiated the conjoint therapy and who also wanted one-on-one therapy? Should the couple therapy end, or should the couple be referred? The patients were clinically very challenging, both together and individually, and the issues became quite intense and complicated. My colleague and I felt rushed and pressured, and were not at all satisfied with the way we concluded what was supposed to be our last conjoint session. It took two brief conversations and then a long walk-and-talk before we felt sorted out—we then called the couple and arranged a second and much more mutually satisfying session to terminate our co-therapy arrangement and to make plans for what the clients and we hope will be in their best interests. The details and outcome of our deliberations are not the point here, however. Rather, it was important for us to step back and examine why our process had gotten so disjointed and dissatisfying—my guilt at leaving my colleague in mid-stream and my relief at escaping such a difficult case, her feelings of being overwhelmed by their intense demands and being considered 'second choice' by the couple, the possible reverberating parallels between our processes and those of the client-couple. We can use such imbroglios for in-sight and advancement (see Taffel, 1993), and it was good to have a skilled and thoughtful colleague with whom to process the process.

Beyond the obvious ethical and clinical guidelines, such as don't sleep with your patients, I learned from my training with Carl Whitaker that there may be times when it is useful to surrender the safety of the shore and go with the flow as a coparticipant or co-author. (As symposium co-panelist Florence Kaslow reminded us during the discussion that followed our formal paper presentations, Whitaker often recommended that clinicians have a co-therapist to help them maintain perspective and separation from a family's maladaptive patterns.) At the risk of distracting from our discussion about countertransference, I want to say that I agree with Arnold Lazarus (1997, pp. 20-24; also see Bograd, 1992) that we have become overly cautious (read: rigid) in our concern regarding boundaries. Sexual relations and exploitative or abusive conduct are off-limits, of course, but there are many times when therapeutic goals can be advanced without much risk of harm if reasonable clinical judgment is exercised.

Let me conclude with an extended case description for your consideration. Bill and Maria were a Portuguese-American, working-class, Catholic couple in their late 50s who I had known on and off for several years. Bill was a good guy, a truck driver, outgoing and a bit gruff in his way; Maria, who sold cosmetics at a local department store, was somewhat of a compulsive caregiver, very accomodating, always thinking of others. Early on, she even recognized a cologne I was wearing, Lagerfeld, and brought me an expensive bottle as a gift.

The tragic death of a child, who had died around age 20 under ambiguous circumstances—a gun had discharged while he was alone with it—brought them to therapy. Over time they consulted me regarding a variety of problems, some having to do with their grief, some with their marriage, some with raising their other children and dealing with other family relationships. The death of their oldest son was sometimes in the foreground, while at other times it receded, although often still casting a long shadow.

After many meetings, in one session Bill and Maria described to me an uncanny experience. They had finally gone for a little vacation, to Las Vegas, the first time they had been away together since their son's death. It had been a good experience, but what had really gripped them was something that happened on their last night there. They were in a lounge and they both saw at another table a young man who they described as looking startling like their son. They knew it wasn't him, but the resemblance was amazing. He was at a table with some friends, laughing. Bill and Maria were mesmerized—they couldn't stop looking at him, and eventually even called the waiter and sent an anonymous bottle of champagne to the table to keep the young party there so that they could watch longer. From their poignant description in my office, the experience was magical and wonderfully bittersweet.

A year or more later in the course of our meetings, Bill and Maria were in the midst of a very rough patch. They had recently gone through another anniversary of their son's death; other stressors were also active, including some conflicts with a daughter as well as problems at Bill's job. They had not been getting along, and their marriage appeared to be in trouble. In the session, they bickered and argued; but near the end of the hour Bill mentioned that they were going out to dinner the next night, to the local Black Angus Restaurant, for their wedding anniversary.

After they left my office, I had an urge. It just occurred to me. I thought for a few minutes, then saw my next patient, then got ready to leave. I picked up my phone, called Information and got the address of the Black Angus. I drove over and spoke to the *mai'tre d'*. I explained that I had some friends who were coming to dinner the next night and that I wanted to leave a present for them. I paid for a bottle of champagne and wrote out a brief note to accompany it: "Happy Anniversary! Love, Dr. Lagerfeld."

On the way home I knew I had just done something unusual. I rushed into the house and spoke with my wife. I explained to her what I had done: the couple, the kid in Las Vegas, the champagne, Dr. Lagerfeld and the perfume. "Should I call the restaurant? Should I cancel the order? What will the couple think? Will it make it so they can't express anger toward me? Am I invading their privacy? What will this do to the therapy?" I was very nervous. My wife looked at me and then said, "Honey, that's probably the nicest thing you've ever done!"

I did not call the restaurant.

A week went by. The next Thursday Bill and Maria arrived for their appointment. We sat down in my office. I looked at them, first Maria, then Bill. Suddenly, Bill smiled. "Doc, I got to tell ya', I don't usually let myself get too emotional, but what you did last week made me wanna cry. Nobody's ever done anything like that for us. It was wonderful. At first, I thought it must be a mistake when the waiter came to the table with a bottle of champagne. Maria and I really enjoyed it, and I sat there and every time I looked at that champagne bottle and at Maria I thought about how much we've been through and how much I love Maria. I don't know what else to say. Just, I really want to thank you."

This did not resolve all their problems, of course, but the work went on. I think my gesture—and the abiding feeling it signified—may have helped weather the storm. Was it countertransference? Transference? Reality? Love? Maybe it was just me—and them.

3

Some Things I Have Learned from Friends and Clients about Empowerment and Rehabilitation

He sang day after day, he sang night after night.
The sun stopped to hear, the lovely moon to look;
The waves stood still in the sea, the billows at
    the head of the bay.
The streams stopped flowing, the rapids of
    Finnmark stopped foaming,
The rapids of the Vuoksi stopped flowing, the
    river Jourtan came to a stop.
    —(from *The Kalevala*, Elias Lonnrot, 1849/1963, poem 17, p. 111)[1]

There are two kinds of music, good and bad. Any music that makes you tap your foot is good music.

    —Louis Armstrong (quoted in Ken Burns, *Jazz*, PBS television, January 9, 2001)

---

1. *The Kalevala*, the national epic poem of Finland (comparable to *The Odyssey* or *The Iliad*), was compiled by Elias Lonnrot, who travelled through Finland recording mythic folk poetry beginning in the 1820s.

Empowerment and Rehabilitation 19

When Karin Olssen first asked me to speak at the Finnish Rehabilitation Foundation conference while I was in Helsinki, I was honored, of course, but I was also a bit apprehensive. "What do I know about rehabilitation?" I thought. "It's not my area of speciality. I'm not a rehabilitation psychologist, and (knock on wood) thus far I've never personally had to go through any extensive rehabilitation. While I admire the work and the people who do it—I don't know much about spinal-cord injuries, strokes, multiple sclerosis, burns, blindness and deafness,amputations, dementia, and so on.[2] Furthermore, I live near San Francisco, California, and my knowledge of Finnish culture and society is very limited: take away the words *Suomi, sauna, Sibelius, Marimekko, Nurmi, Nokia,* and maybe a few others, and I'm speechless." So I wrote her back an e-mail, saying essentially, "Thanks—but why me?"

While I was waiting to hear back from Karin, my best friend Jeff Ordover came with his girlfriend to San Francisco for a visit. Jeff, who is a psychiatrist, has

---

2. In their editors' introduction to the new 700-page *Handbook of Rehabilitation Psychology*, Frank and Elliott (2000, pp. 3-6) write:

   "Rehabilitation psychology is concerned with the treatment and science of disabling and chronic health conditions....Rehabilitation psychology directly affects outcomes that are beyond the circumscribed definitions of traditional mental health practice (e.g., individual therapy for emotional adjustment). Rehabilitation psychologists are involved in resolving issues with physical health and health-related quality of life and are well acquainted with biopsychosocial mechanisms associated with disease, injury, disability, and well-being in a fashion other psychological disciplines could emulate....Rehabilitation psychology taxes the entire wealth of clinical skills applicable to professional psychology from individual psychotherapy to neuropsychological assessment to group therapy to consultation."

   As I was preparing this chapter, I came across the remarks of Phillip Zimbardo (2002, p. 5, emphasis in original), then president of the American Psychological Association, about his recognition of his own disability: "It might be that I was a tree unaware of the forest around me, or rather that I was in denial of being part of that forest....Disability is not only about being blind or deaf or paralyzed, it is also about transient handicaps, about many impediments to optimal functioning, about the social dynamics and lifecourse development of disabled people interacting with their behavioral settings....The most basic lesson I have learned is that the line between abled and dis-abled is a *permeable* one that we will all move across throughout our lives for varying durations and with varying degrees of limitations. As we move into and out of disability, we do not make that voyage alone, but bring along a community of others who are affected by their connections to those who are disabled. Their supportive, understanding response to disability helps increase awareness of the disability experience while also fostering the will to be resilient."

a special interest in rehabilitation—both professional and personal. He is a Western doctor, but has also studied various Eastern philosophies. Amongst his specialties, he works with people who have had strokes, as well as some who have had chronic and severe psychiatric illnesses. Fifteen years ago he became paraplegic when he was run over by a big truck while riding his bicycle. (When this first happened and I went to see him at the rehabilitation center, I remember telling him I was feeling guilty about being so physically able amongst so many people with disabilities. He told me, "Don't be guilty—just be grateful!") One night over dinner I asked Jeff what he thought might be an important message to carry regarding psychology and rehabilitation. He thought for awhile, then called my attention to the *distinction between pain and suffering*, pain being what the body does, suffering being what the mind does with the pain. He also spoke about the importance of *transformation*, and encouraged me to look at the fine book entitled *Still Here: Embracing Aging, Changing, and Dying* by the psychologist and meditation teacher, Ram Dass (2000), about his post-stroke awareness. I read:

> I realized that what I was accustomed to calling 'reality' was, more accurately, my subjective perception of things, and what's more, that *I was capable of changing that perception*. I realized that the suffering I experienced as a result of perceived reality was, to a large degree, self induced, and could be shifted by watching my thoughts, and moving from my Ego to a Witness perspective....Please understand that I am not for a moment denying the very real difficulties and pain of aging....nor am I making light of the physical troubles that come our way as the body loses its youth. But there is a fundamental difference between pain and suffering....a difference that involves our minds, and how we react to experience....We can see reality from different angles, so we can choose how we wish to respond to events. We tend to forget the flexibility of our own minds....And yet we have the power....if we take the time to know the mind and how it determines the quality of life. [Ram Dass, 2000, pp. 32-33, emphasis in original]

In the same book (p. 79) I also read a lovely passage quoted from the 19th century American poet Henry Wadsworth Longfellow[3]:

> Age is opportunity no less
> Than youth itself, though in another dress,
> And as the evening twilight fades away
> The sky is filled with stars invisible by day.[4]

---

3. From the poem, "Morituri Salutamus" (Longfellow, 1875/1943, p. 434).

My dictionary tells me that *habilitate* means to "to clothe or dress," or more generally, "to fit out or equip for working." *Re-habilitate*, then, does not necessarily mean "to restore to a former capacity." Everything cannot be "fixed" or put back as it was. We need to go forward. *Transformation*. Patients (and those who care about them) may need to grieve and accept that some capacities are truly lost—no easy task—but there comes a time when the shift may be helped by recognizing other satisfying ways of being that may become available. *"The sky is filled with stars invisible by day."* 5

I suddenly remembered one of my patients, a woman named Karen, who had taught me some things about making one's reality in the face of difficult circumstances.

> Karen had been a very attractive young woman, a fashion model. She had developed a severe case of multiple sclerosis. Over time, she had become bedbound, incontinent, and barely able to speak. I would visit her at home, where she lived with daily assistance and her collection of cats. We talked some about 'depression' and 'adjustment,' but also about art and fashion and ideas from movies and books. One day she told me, in halting speech, "You know, this isn't all bad." I asked what she meant. "Well, when you drive 65 miles per hour down the superhighway, you miss a lot of scenery." "Huh?" "Having to lay here has forced me to learn to pay attention to lots of little details I never

---

4. This also led me to recall some lines from Basho (1644-1694), the great Japanese haiku master:
   During the daytime
   A firefly is
   Just an insect.

5. *Transformation* may require *surrender*. In his fine book *Flowers of Wiricuta: A Gringo's Journey to Shamanic Power*, Tom Pinkson (1995) connects true personal power ultimately to having right relationship with the Great Spirit. He writes (p. 78): "Surrender....is not the same as quitting. The latter is usually accompanied by feelings of anger, despair, frustration, depression, and lowered self-esteem; after all, you weren't good enough to win. Surrender, on the other hand, is a conscious choice. You voluntarily choose to take yourself and your burden—or whatever you are working on—to that which is higher than you, that which is bigger than you, the Great Mystery. You then surrender it into the infinite 'hands' of the Sacred Mystery to work for the greatest good with divine intelligence, divine order, and divine timing....Sometimes our physical life, not just our emotional and psychological state, can be at stake when we are called to release what no longer serves us." For another useful perspective on letting go and dealing with inevitable change, see Spencer Johnson's (1998) bestselling parable, *Who Moved My Cheese?*

noticed before. If you have some patience, you can learn a lot more about cats, and about your world, a lot more." And you can.[6]

Even when things declined further, when she approached the endstage of her illness, she sent me a holiday card with the following inscription (she had an attendant write it): "Memory is what God gave us that we might have roses in December."

While I was musing this over, Karin Olssen e-mailed back. She was encouraging and helpful: "We know you are not a rehabilitation specialist. Perhaps you could think of the term *rehabilitation* more broadly, and speak about patient empowerment and the integration of resources."

I read her message on my office computer, then saw my next patient.

> Luke, a man in his early 70s, contacted our Psychiatry Department looking for some help. A semi-retired businessman, he was used to being successful and very much on the go. About six months prior, his wife had a serious stroke. She was making progress in her rehabilitation and recovery, slow but steady, and Luke was in the process of learning how to cope with his wife's changed capacities and the impact on their life together. We were working to

---

6. In *The Call of Stories*, Robert Coles (1989, p. 39) recounts the words of a young man whose polio, while not a good thing, had been a gateway to wisdom: "I've seen a lot, lying here. I think I know more about people, including me, myself—all because I got sick and can't walk."

    In *Quantum Change: When Epiphanies and Sudden Insights Transform Ordinary Lives* (Miller & C'de Baca, 2001, p. 122) I read the report of a man who broke his neck on a trampoline: "The slowing down of my lifestyle allowed me to see a lot more of the beauty in the world, just to take the time to see and to analyze it. To see people and not judge them on a quick first impression, not judge them for what they do right then, but to see them more compassionately in a longer-term picture. It makes for a whole lot nicer world." He also offered an observation (pp. 122-123) that has affected my golf game (see Hoyt, 1996f/2000): "After the accident, I lived with my parents, and my bedroom looked out onto a golf course. One of the first poems I wrote after the accident was of watching the golfers as they played, walking on the golf course, walking up the fairway and taking a wood out and hitting it and getting mad and stomping off and running off. If they'd just stop to see and just take it easy, take a deep breath, just relax and enjoy the *game* of golf! Sure they're out there doing a sport, trying to be competitive and doing the best they can, but it also can be so relaxing, if they'd take the time, just seeing all the green and the beautiful forest all around them. I know I did the same thing, and I probably missed out on a lot of beauty. I missed out on just seeing a lot of things that I probably could have seen, had I taken the time and slowed down in the things that I was doing."

help him develop strategies and social supports to cope with his role overload and sense of loss of self in his new caregiver role (see Shewchuk & Elliott, 2000). In one session, he was telling me about his wife's slowly recovering her ability to ambulate without a walker, and, while proud of her accomplishments, he also worried about his frustration and impatience at the new pace they have together. He got up and moved slowly around my office, demonstrating how he would hold his wife's arm and walk with her. "I'm proud of her and happy for her making progress," he said, "but I'm so used to doing things quickly, and I don't want her to feel discouraged by my impatience. I need some help, Doc—how can I think about this differently?" As I watched him accompanying his (imaginary) wife around my office, an image become clear: "Luke, it looks like you're walking your bride down the aisle at your wedding. How about if you think you're slowly walking together to the altar?" We were both moved by this image—which he has referred to several times in the subsequent months—and he told me (not knowing about Karin Olssen's invitation!) "You ought to remind other people to use what they already know to help themselves."

So, here I am.

How we look influences what we see, and what we see influences what we do. *Some stories are better than others*—some ways of looking and thinking are more enlivening and invigorating than others. Can we help clients reframe their experience to look at themselves in ways that work with their goals for rehabilitation? What clues lie in their presentation and history about talents, interests, motivations, passions? How can we encourage their active participation?

It is important that we pay great attention to what our patients tell us about what may be helpful for them. As Shakespeare (*All's Well that Ends Well*, Act I, Scene 1, line 216) wrote, "Our remedies oft in ourselves do lie." How can we help them ignite their initiative, help them get motivated to use their resources, help them to become the heroes in their stories? (W.R. Miller & Rollnick, 1991; Duncan & S.D. Miller, 2000) What moves them?

> In an initial interview a Jewish woman told me about her efforts at psychiatric rehabilitation. As a child, she (and her sister) had developed anorexia. She had been through addictions to bulimia, alcohol and cocaine, multiple dissatisying relationships, and other 'life in the fast lane' problems. She was now in a 12-step program with a sponsor. She was 'clean and sober' but was struggling and feeling discouraged. "Oh, did I tell you that my parents were Holocaust survivors?" she added. "Maybe I'm just permanently screwed up." I interrupted her. "It's difficult and painful, I'm sure, but with your history, it's in your genes to succeed." She paused. "What do you mean?" I thought, then told her: "If your parents could survive Auschwitz and the Nazis, you can survive

depression and learn to be healthy." She looked at me and nodded in agreement.[7]

In the true spirit of cultural diversity, we need to learn *from* our clients, not just *about* them. What do the stories that Finnish people (like all cultures) tell about themselves that may be helpful (see Erickson & Simon, 1996; Saarelainen, 1999)? What stories are there of courage, of challenge and endurance and resurrection that can inspire and guide our work together? If "The sun is king and the queen is silence" (Sodergren, 1993, p. 57), how will this effect patients expressing their needs? How can the virtues of hard work, stoicism, and self-reliance be harnessed and used therapeutically?[8]

We know that we're helpers—or at least think we are—but sometimes our clients may not realize this, or may not be ready for the help we're eager and educated to give (Hoyt, 2000; Ram Dass & Gorman, 1993). It's good to remember that it's not *our* therapy or *our* rehabilitation—it's the *patient's*. Imposition tends to generate opposition, so we need first to form a good working alliance, the soil in which all else may take root.

> A physical therapist colleague asked for consultation regarding a difficult case. She was working with a young woman who had a complicated neurological condition, a strange dystonia that over many years had twisted her limbs and torso. As a teenager, the patient had also suffered some physical abuse, it was reported, including some at the hands of health-care workers when she had been in a hospital. Even though the current P.T. was quite kind and gentle, the patient was having great difficulty allowing herself to relax and be touched. Their work had reached an impasse.
>
> We met in the treatment room. The patient was on the table, next to Nina, her P.T. Her power-driven wheelchair was nearby, with her assistant dog tethered to it. She acknowledged the history that the P.T. had relayed and

---

7. At the Museum of African-American History in Baltimore, as you leave the exhibit of a horrific slave ship, you are confronted with a life-size photograph of several Africans in chains looking out at you with the caption beneath saying: "Remember: You are the dream they kept alive." A similar idea is echoed in the movie *Amistad* when the protagonist calls upon his ancestors and says "they must come, for at this moment I am the whole reason they have existed at all." (see Hoyt, 2000a, p. 72)
8. At the Helsinki conference where this paper was first presented, one audience member shared cultural metaphors drawn from the Finnish war experience that she had used with patients, another commented on the abilities required to survive the long winters, and a third told a joke that illustrated the Finnish mentality that appreciates independence rather than following orders that don't make sense.

said that she wanted help, but that she sometimes couldn't help getting tense and reflexively pushing Nina away. As we talked, I was extra careful not to be presumptuous or intrusive. I did not touch her wheelchair. I explained that I had a dog named "Snowball" at home, asked her dog's name, and asked respectfully if I might pet her dog. She agreed.

I was aware of how closely she watched me as I crouched and made friends with her dog. As I gently scratched—ears, neck, behind, wagging tail—I also became aware of a memory of taking Snowball to visit my mother when Mom was living in a care institution near the end of her life. I told the story, in detail, of how the old people loved the dog, how we would move through the solarium where they would sit and delight in petting the friendly big white dog. The people and the dog both enjoyed it, a lot. One woman was a bit frightened, however, and held back. She watched for awhile, I remembered, then commented to the lady sitting next to her: "Look—he likes to be petted." And the second lady turned to her and said, in a way I'll never forget, "*Nu?* We ALL like to be petted!"

Things relaxed in the room. This did not solve everything, of course, but as trust was rehabilitated, the alliance was strengthened and the work was able to continue.

Is the person we're meeting with relating as a *customer*, a *complainant*, or a *visitor?* (de Shazer, 1988). In what stage of readiness are they approaching and participating in rehabilitation: *precontemplation, contemplation, planning, action, maintenance* (Hoyt & Miller, 2000; Prochaska, 1999; also see Hanna, 2002)? What are their preferences? Their intentions? What would tell them that our work is done—and done well? Negotiating (and, at times, renegotiating) achievable goals is empowering. It recognizes and appreciates the person's authority.

I was very nervous as I tried to talk my way through the neuro-psychological test results with an elderly patient and her family. Her memory deficits and cognitive impairments were bad and getting worse, but I was choking on the words *dementia* and *Alzheimer's*. Seeing my discomfort, the lady kindly helped me. "It's OK, doctor. I think I understand what you're saying. It's clear that the past is going and is almost gone, and it sounds like the future isn't going to get any better. We'll all just have to learn how to live in the present!"

Looking beyond the injuries and illnesses, past the bandages and braces, and talking about common human interests, theirs and ours—news and current events, children and pets, work, favorite sports teams, even gossip and telling jokes—can help remind the patient (and the therapist) that there is more to life than meets the eye, that *"The sky is filled with stars invisible by day."*

Persons with difficult situations often become experts about their situation and ways to better manage it. Necessity may be the mother of invention—and intervention. Their "special knowledges" can be used to assist others facing similar circumstances—a process that can facilitate empowerment and the restoration of morale as clients learn that they are not alone and that they can give, as well as get, help. Group therapists know that it can be very helpful to organize opportunities for the sharing of information and support. (One creative use of "communities of concern" is described by Madigan & Epston, 1995.) Professionals may have their place, but persons who have dealt with a particular problem in their own life have unique qualifications.

> In one extraordinary situation, a woman received help from her dead husband! The story is too sweet not to tell. I met Mary in the medical hospital a few months after Hank had died. They had been very close, and she was having a terrible time letting go. To make matters worse, she had become dehydrated, developed kidney problems, and needed hospitalization.
>
> After her medical crisis had passed, we met in my office. Following a session in which she had struggled with grieving his loss and with what she would now do with her life, she went home. It was the anniversary of their first date. On her doorstep she found a dozen red roses with a card written in her (deceased) husband's handwriting. She opened it and read:
>
> *'These are the last flowers you will receive from me. Thank you for the best 9 years of my life. Please don't grieve too much longer—go forward. I love you.'*
> —Hank
>
> (He had called a florist and made the arrangements, unbeknowst to Mary, a couple of weeks before he died.)

Sometimes, when we're faced with a terrible situation, it is especially difficult to remember the "I and Thou," that we are not just "on a case" but that we are with another human being. I was inspired when I heard on a film interview the answer Mother Teresa gave when asked how she could do such things as comfort lepers and touch the so-called 'Untouchables.' She said: "I remember that I am washing the wounds of Christ." (One need not be Christian, of course; in India people press their hands together and say *Namaste*, 'I salute the Divine in you.')

Mother Teresa: For all kinds of diseases there are medicines and cures. But for being unwanted, except there are will-

	ing hands to serve and there's a loving heart to love, I don't think this terrible disease can ever be cured.
Interviewer:	And that is the disease you're looking after?
Mother Teresa:	This is what we're aiming at, to bring to the people the willing hands to serve and the hearts to go on loving them, and to look at them as Christ.

(from Malcolm Muggeridge, *Something Beautiful for God*, 1971, pp. 78-79)

While more mundane, it can help—both client and clinician—to separate the person from the problem. Labeling can be powerful and pernicious, sometimes producing a self-*un*fulfilling prophecy (Goffman, 1963; Wright, 1991; Hoyt, 1995a). The person is not the disability, and may need (sometimes frequently) to be reminded of this. They can 'own' the disability, rather than it completely 'owning' them. This can be done in various ways.

> I referred a patient with cerebral palsy to one of my mentors, Robert Goulding, M.D., for help with her "self-esteem problems." She went to a week-long workshop. Later she told me of their first encounter, which she said had changed her life. She had started to 'present' herself to Bob, describing her cerebral palsy. "I can see that you've got a few scrambled brain cells," she said he said as he looked into her eyes, "but I'm much more interested in finding out who *you* are." Figure and ground, flipped forever!

> Consulting in the hospital with a medical-surgical patient who had undergone a total hip replacement, I asked if I could get some advice. "I've never had this kind of surgery—I know each person is an individual, but is there any information or any helpful tips you can give me that I can pass on to other people who have the same kind of procedure? What would be good for them to know?" As the patient described various practical ways to manage pain, cope with boredom, and how to get up and around to use the toilet, the patient became The Expert, their knowledge transcending their individual experience and now benefitting others.

> There's a lovely film called *Milton H. Erickson, M.D.: Explorer in Hypnosis and Therapy* (Haley & Richeport, 1993), about the life and work of the famous psychiatrist-hypnotherapist who overcame polio and considered his 'disabilities' to have made him a better doctor because in many ways they increased his awareness and his empathy. In one poignant scene, Erickson meets at a training seminar with a young woman whose back was broken in a car accident. He asks her "What can I do for you?" With pleading eyes she whispers, "I'd like to walk again." Sitting in his wheelchair next to her wheelchair, Erickson pauses then replies, "And if not that, then what?" (This is negotiating a realistic treat-

ment goal, since he could not repair her spinal column.) They focus on ways of redirecting her attention to reduce pain and to increase the use of the muscles she is able to use. Later, in a follow-up film clip, we see her telling the well-known family therapist John Frykman about her progress. She now has three children and a full life (Frykman, 2001).

Narrative psychotherapists, following the work of Michael White and David Epston (1990) and others, often use two related techniques called *externalization* and *relative influence questioning*. The person is not the problem; the problem is the problem. By encouraging the patient to form a relationship *to* the problem (such as a disability), their identity is separated and strengthened. "What name do you call your disability? How does it influence you? And how do you influence it? When is it able to take you over and control you? And when are you able to control it, or work around it? How do you do that?" And so on.

To conclude: We need lots of *specific technical knowledge and training*. We also need to focus on developing and maintaining our *therapeutic alliance* and to remember *our humanity and our clients' humanity*. We need to *clarify goals, motivations and responsibilities*, and to recognize that these emerge and change as therapy and rehabilitation progress. We need to *use our imaginations and appreciate and evoke resources*—those of the client, the family, the social systems, and our own. We also need our own supports and self-care to *avoid burnout* (see Elliott et al., 1996).

We need to *watch our language*. Do we use "solution talk" or "problem talk" (Furman & Ahola, 1992; see Chapter 6)?

To me the language of psychotherapy, psychiatry, psychology and rehabilitation is almost a total wasteland. For me these are names for collections of dead words, dead gestures. They are masses of words which only seldom, and with a great difficulty, can be made to caress or to have music. They have some powers left, a power to scare perhaps. There could be a glimpse of divinity: the promise of telling about the deepest secrets of the soul, about mysteries of creativity, etc. [Riikonen & Smith, 1997, pp. 66-67]

Empowerment involves self-definition. *"Nothing about us without us."* Shouldn't the people who are the true experts on disability, the so-called 'disabled,' be the ones who decide—or are at least seriously consulted—about what terms are helpful and preferred? Is it more empowering and respectful to speak of *persons with disabilities* or *disabled persons*? *survivors* or *victims*? *challenges* or *impairments*?[9] While appreciating and respecting that the people we serve are experiencing pain and very real limitations and restrictions that they did not choose (see Olkin, 1999), does our language focus on *opportunities and what may be* or on *frustrations and what cannot be?* on *not yet* or on *never?* on *the stars* or on *the darkness?*

> There is much that remains to be said about the language of this work, about how it evokes the images of people's lives that it does....These images reach back into the history of people's lived experience, privileging certain memories, and facilitate the interpretation of many previously neglected aspects of experience. So the language of the work, of the very questions that we ask, is evocative of images which trigger the reliving of experience, and this contributes very significantly to the generation of alternative story lines. [Michael White, in Hoyt & Combs, 1996/2001, p. 81]

So much happens through language, how we say what we say, our choice of words, the way we connect and stimulate and inspire hope and understanding and effort and acceptance.

If you will permit me, please let me leave you with these words:

> Steadfast old Vainamoinen uttered these words:
>
> *"Now I have already got a hundred charms, thousands of magic formulas;*
> *I got the charms from a hiding place, magic words from a cranny."*
> *Then he went to his boat, rich in charms to his workshop.*
> *He got the boat ready, the side planks fastened,*
> *The stern finished, the bow structure mounted.*
> *The boat was produced without using a tool,*
>   *the ship without removing a chip.*
>
> —[Lonnrot, *The Kalevala*, 1849/1963, poem 17, p. 112]

---

9. While the term *handicapped* is still problematical, in Rhoda Olkin's (1999, p. 38) excellent book, *What Psychotherapists Should Know about Disability*, I was enlightened to read: "Although it is often reported that 'handicapped' comes from 'cap in hand' (i.e., beggar), this is not the origin of the word. Rather it comes from the older usage of the sports term meaning an advantage or disadvantage imposed on a contestant to equalize chances of winning (the forfeits were held in a cap)."

4

"The Present Is a Gift": A Clinical Demonstration

The case presented here was a one-session clinical demonstration interview conducted at the "Brief Therapy: Lasting Impressions" conference held in New York City during August 1998 under the sponsorship of the Milton H. Erickson Foundation.[1] I was asked to demonstrate how I might begin an "Integrated Brief Therapy" interview, which endeavors to increase effectiveness and efficiency by drawing from different schools and methods to enhance clients' sense of choice and the fuller utilization of their competencies and resources.

The client, "John" (a pseudonym), was a mental-health professional attending the conference. The work was relatively straightforward, nothing fancy. I like this session because it appeared to be helpful to the client, although without follow-up we don't know what lasting impact it may have had (see Barber, 1990).

The session started quickly and rather intensely:

HOYT: I appreciate your volunteering to join with me in this, John. What's up?

JOHN: I have a baby daughter—she's 11 months old. And my mom died, died last year. *[chokes up]* And she never saw the baby, but before she died she told me that she always felt she worked too hard and didn't spend enough time with the kids. Well, having 7 kids she had to work hard—a good Catholic family. And I really want to spend more time with my daughter and I'm a hard worker, too, so I'm kind of struggling with being with my daughter and not working too hard. I'm just

---

1. A videotape of the complete session is available from the Milton H. Erickson Foundation. For more information, visit www.erickson-foundation.org.

	worried I'll work too hard and not spend enough time with her.
HOYT:	How can I be helpful to you? What would you like to change?
JOHN:	I guess I just kind of need to slow down and just, just enjoy her. I'm feeling some pressure: she's facing major surgery and...
HOYT:	...your daughter is?
JOHN:	...Yes. It's 9-hour surgery....

Some additional discussion about the impending surgery (which was to deal with fused skull plates, reshaping an eye socket, and other problems) helped to establish some initial alliance and comprehension of the presenting situation. I then endeavored to clarify the client's goal in seeking the consultation. Note the future focus and positive assumptions, as well as the use of the narrative therapy techniques of externalization *and* relative influence questioning *(White & Epston, 1990).*

HOYT:	After the surgery, when things are better and she's recuperating, it sounds like you want to learn to slow down.
JOHN:	Yeah, well, I want to do it now. That's one reason I've been doing things with her, but also you know, with my wife, too, because that gets neglected for Grace [the daughter] and I just want to not always feel like I have to work.
HOYT:	What do you call this pressure, this sort of not being able to relax? Does it have a name?
JOHN:	Hmmm. "What do I call it?" *[musing to himself]* "Anxious," I guess. "Does it have a name?" Yeah: "Anxious."
HOYT:	From what you're telling me, it sounds like sometimes you're able to control It, and sometimes It controls you.
JOHN:	Yeah.

HOYT: What's the difference? When are you able to manage Anxiety and when does Anxiety seem to get the best of you?

JOHN: Ah, if I don't think about work and just enjoy what's happening and that work will take care of itself, it's not going to go away, I don't always have to be on top of things, always kind of rushing, and so what if things are done a day later, this whole notion that it has to be done today.

HOYT: So that's how you manage Anxiety. How does it sometimes trick you and take over?

JOHN: Hmm, "trick me and take over." *[long pause]* Sometimes, like I don't know what to do, I guess is the only thought that comes to my mind. I get restless. I don't like waiting. I wouldn't do well in New York—you have to wait a lot.

HOYT: Right.

JOHN: I don't like to wait.

HOYT: Uh huh. So when you have to wait, that's when Anxiety can work on you?

JOHN: Yeah, because I could be doing something, you know, I could be off getting things done. Which is sometimes a good thing.

HOYT: So during this time while you're having to wait for a couple of weeks, what do you need to do so Anxiety doesn't take you over while you're waiting?

JOHN: Ah, stay out of the future.

HOYT: Stay out of the future and keep staying in the moment, huh?

JOHN: Yeah, not think about the surgery and stuff. I mean it's all been taken care, there's nothing else we can do but be there Wednesday morning. Um, and just don't think about that.

While I would usually, in solution-focused fashion (de Shazer, 1985, 1988; see Chapter 6), have inquired after details of times when John had "stayed in the moment," the connection between his obsessive worrying and his deceased parents seemed almost palpable. I inquired:

HOYT: How did you learn to worry so much about the future?

JOHN: Probably from my mom.

HOYT: Your mom?

JOHN: Yeah.

HOYT: Tell me more, how did she teach you that?

JOHN: Um, well, she worried, you know, about how to take care of a large family and just worried about taking care of us, and sometimes my dad drank too much. I think she probably worried about that, and I think sometimes he wasn't real faithful, you know [....]

HOYT: So she had some real things to worry about.

JOHN: Oh, I worried, too.

HOYT: Do you find yourself now sometimes worrying about things you don't need to worry about?

JOHN: Yeah, yeah. I do well in my practice and I don't need to worry about that. I'm successful and it doesn't seem to kind of penetrate, you know, that I'm doing very well, very nice lifestyle, we can do lots of things my parents couldn't really afford to do. There doesn't ever seem to be enough.

HOYT: So what do you say to yourself in your head, how do you keep yourself scared about "never enough"?

Identifying the client's negative self-talk can be a gateway for his changing his "viewing and doing" (O'Hanlon & Wilk, 1987).

JOHN: "How do I keep myself scared?"

HOYT: That's my way of putting it; you may have a different way of thinking about it.

JOHN: Right, right. I guess I don't like being scared, but I get scared. *[sighs]* I guess "I'm not good enough" is what comes to mind. But I am, I mean, I'm successful.

HOYT: As you think back, can you think of a time when you got that message, "you're not good enough, you haven't done enough"?

We might attempt to change this "story" or "self-conceptulization" via several channels: rational-emotive disputation (Ellis, 1994); consideration of times ("exceptions") when he resisted the message (de Shazer, 1985, 1988) and alternatives he might tell himself; a redecision-therapy guided role-playing of an internalized "critical parent" and his "free child" response (Goulding & Goulding, 1979; also see White, 1989; Hoyt, 2003); and so forth.

JOHN: My dad was pretty critical and stuff. I'd help him fix things but he'd always criticize my mistakes. *[pause]* You know, I'd be a hard worker. I work hard. *[cries]* I guess a lot to please my dad.

HOYT: Sounds like no matter what you did, it wasn't going to be enough for him, huh?

JOHN: Well, he wasn't always critical, I mean he bought me things. He bought me a beautiful bike, I kind of smashed it after a week—I ran into a fire hydrant. So he's done some nice things for me, too. But I kind of like my mom more than my dad. I think my dad knew that. Maybe that's what some of that was all about. I liked them both; I loved them both.

There are several threads we could take up. The client reinforces the story of his not being good enough, referencing a time he wrecked a new bicycle. He also raises the question of his different feelings toward each parent, and their possible reactions. Given the one-session nature of our consultation, I chose to focus on his initial complaint. It might have been better to present the time constraints and ask him which of the various issues he wanted to focus upon.

HOYT:	Sure. You said when we sat down you didn't want to be so pressured and so critical.
JOHN:	Uh huh.
HOYT:	What will it take, do you think, for you to finally say, "I love my parents but I'm not going to march to my father's demands"?
JOHN:	I want to do that. Some of the stuff was between my mom and dad. You know, I somehow got in the crossfire of some of their stuff, it had nothing to do with me.
HOYT:	True.
JOHN:	Yeah. I could just be me and they can whatever, I don't have to fix that.
HOYT:	When you say that now, does it sink it, do you feel that all the way through?
JOHN:	*[sighs]* I kind of feel less nervous. I'm a parent now and, you know, while Carla [his wife] and I have our disagreements, it has nothing to do with Grace—she's not responsible for that. I mean I want my baby to like me a whole bunch and she's really close to her mom and that's really great and I enjoy seeing those two play together and she loves me, too, and I guess that what's triggering all this is that, you know, I'm a parent now so I can understand. Plus I can see from the other side.
HOYT:	Yeah.
JOHN:	And I understand more about that. I like being a parent.
HOYT:	Good.
JOHN:	You know. I started a little bit late, but that's all right.
HOYT:	Me, too. I have a small son.

JOHN: Oh, do you?

I'm not sure why I made this self-revelation just then, but it seems to be a "joining" and "supportive" attempt in response to his feeling a bit older and being worried about his child.

HOYT: Oh yeah. Is this helpful, what we're talking about?

JOHN: Well yeah, I never thought about my dad really in some ways probably being jealous because I was closer to my mom. I was. Not that it was a bad thing. He was working, he worked a lot, my dad, and he was gone a lot, he worked really hard. And so I was with my mom more.

HOYT: Is your dad living now?

JOHN: No, both my parents are deceased, dad died a long time ago. I'm going to live longer than him, I hope. He died when he was 70.

HOYT: Uh huh. Is there something you wish you had said to him?

JOHN: I wish I told him I loved him. I tried. Before he died, I tried to as much as I can express the love—it's not easy for me. I guess I was afraid of how he would respond.

HOYT: What did you think he would do?

JOHN: I was hoping he'd say he loved me, too. I think he would say that. I wasn't the best of kids. *[laughs]* I certainly gave them gray hairs over the years. But it helps me being a parent and knowing that in terms of my own daughter—she can't date until she's 30, that's the rule! *[laughs jokingly]* I laugh about that. I think he would have.

HOYT: Even if he wouldn't of, can you still feel good about yourself?

Asked in a somewhat rhetorical manner. It might have been more efficacious to ask, "What do *you have to tell yourself so that you can still feel good about yourself?"*

JOHN:	Well, if he couldn't, he would just have difficulties saying that. That'd be his difficulty. I think he did, but I just think he may have had trouble saying that. I don't know. I wish he had saw my daughter, too. *[looks down, sadly]*
HOYT:	Sure. What are you thinking of?
JOHN:	Oh, that my dad died in August, around this time, and my mom died in July, so the anniversary and the sadness with that and that they won't see my little daughter and—she's really beautiful.
HOYT:	Yeah, that's hard.
JOHN:	Yeah.
HOYT:	We had the same situation in our family. My wife's mother passed away just before our child was born. It was just a couple weeks, and she was ill with cancer and I remember we were talking with her, and feeling sad, of course, and she said 'It just can't be helped,' and that's true, and it was sad.

Therapist's self-disclosure signals acceptance and appreciation and thus promotes increased openness and vulnerability (see Tomm, 1991; Tomm, Hoyt & Madigan, 1998).

JOHN:	Well, my mom was laughing about me going to be a father, she thought that was quite funny. *[chokes up]*
HOYT:	What are you holding back?
JOHN:	Just some sadness. I did tell my mom I loved her and I hugged her before she died, so I feel good about that. Of course I miss her.
HOYT:	Especially this month and surgery coming and…
JOHN:	Yeah. One of my sisters died and she was six months old and I remember that. It was tough for my mother. I was talking with my mother and she [the baby sister] had hydroencephalitis, water on the brain. So I thought about that. My mom knew there was something wrong

with the baby and they didn't want to believe it, and then finally they realized there was something wrong, so she died when she was six months. I remember that was really tough on my mom—I know she felt bad about that. You know, she was telling people there's something wrong, and they didn't have shunts back then and it was all experimental and stuff, so she didn't survive the surgery. So my mom would have been real supportive.

HOYT: Does that come up now in terms of your own daughter's surgery?

JOHN: Well, as I think about it, it does now. I didn't really think about that until just now. You know, it was tough on my mom.

HOYT: Of course. How do you remind yourself that your sister's not your daughter, that what happened with your sister doesn't mean anything in terms of the outcome for your daughter?

Therapist offers rationality to help the client control his emotional spill-over.

JOHN: Oh, it doesn't. I mean, it's a totally different thing. The prognosis for my sister was really low, it was experimental.

HOYT: Sure.

JOHN: With my daughter, the technique, the procedure, they do the surgery like every other week. It's very common. Well, it's not an uncommon problem to have. I'd never heard of it before, but one out of 200 babies have this problem, and the doctor has never lost anybody.

HOYT: Good.

JOHN: Better not lose this one either—he'll be in deep trouble. He's real perfectionistic—I guess you want that for a plastic surgeon, though.

"The Present Is a Gift": A Clinical Demonstration 39

HOYT: Yep. When we first sat down you mentioned being critical and pressured.

JOHN: Yeah. Well, it's okay to be sad.

HOYT: Yeah.

JOHN: You know, and have those feelings. They're just feelings, nothing wrong with them. I guess sometimes I work to avoid those feelings. Yeah, sometime they're not very pleasant.

HOYT: I'm impressed by how much you've got going on right now. As a father, thinking about if my child was facing surgery in two weeks...my voice even trembles saying it now.

JOHN: Umm.

HOYT: I'd be nervous, worried, scared, trying to keep my mind in the present but it'd be very hard not to also be thinking ahead and "how many more days and what's going to happen" and...

JOHN: *[nods]*...I guess I really want to enjoy Grace and have her have a nice experience in New York, and she's having a great time. So am I. It was my idea to come here just before the surgery, and ah, so the biggest worry now is if the airline goes on strike *[referring to the morning newspaper headlines]*, we may be here longer, which wouldn't be so bad, so I'm not really going into the future at this point. I mean, I know that it's going to be uncomfortable and I can't change that. It's going to be...

HOYT: ...cross it when you get to it, huh?

JOHN: Yeah, really. Not much more I can do about that. I'm not feeling guilty about it. We thought this through and it's for her benefit to have this surgery. And she won't remember it at all, she won't remember New York either, for that matter. You know, so I just want to

	get that behind us—I kind of want to skip September and enjoy Halloween or something with her.
HOYT:	So, when it's Halloween or down the road…

Joins with patient to imagine a better future.

JOHN:	…yeah…
HOYT:	…and you're enjoying her, what are some of the things you're looking forward to doing with her?
JOHN:	Well, go out for Halloween, get her dressed up. She won a prize last year [….] We went to a benefit for some people, there was a fire, their house burned down so we went to a benefit. We dressed her up as a pumpkin and she won a prize—she got two free ice cream cones which she gave to her cousins. So we'll take her out for Halloween and…
HOYT:	Do you know yet what she's going to be this year?
JOHN:	No, I haven't even thought about that yet. Her charming self, that's for sure. Then we want to go to Scotland next year, that's our plans, and want to do a lot more vacations with her in the summer, find a conference some place in either California or Colorado, take her there and just spend some real vacation times with her. And just show her things that either my wife or I've seen already and just enjoy vacations with her—that way I can spend more time with her on vacation. I'll take more vacations. I don't need to work all the time now. I don't want to wait until my retirement like my dad did. I can do it sooner.
HOYT:	How are we going to help you remember this?
JOHN:	Remember?
HOYT:	"Smell the roses, be in the moment, take a vacation."
JOHN:	*[long pause]* I guess I'm planning to do those things. I'm really realizing I've got to spend more time with my daughter and to enjoy it. The best way to do it is

	through vacations and stuff…and not work so much on weekends.
HOYT:	So, in a few months from now when it's Saturday or Sunday and you're tempted to get on the computer or do whatever you do *[John laughs in apparent self-recognition]*, how are you going to say, "Wait a minute, I'm supposed to take it easy here"?
JOHN:	Well, part of it, I'll remember what my mom said that she had some regrets about not spending enough time with us, and I do tell myself that. And, I guess, just sit back and have my feelings I may have about things. I guess I'm still grieving my mother's death and stuff. I do talk to my daughter about my mom and, ah, the world's not going to fall apart if I'm not in there on the computer.
HOYT:	Do you think your mom would be glad to see you taking more time?

Evoking internalized other to reinforce client's desired change.

JOHN:	Oh yeah, she would be. I think she'd be pretty pleased about how I'm being a father and a parent. I think she'd be real happy.
HOYT:	And in a few months when you're tempted by Anxiety to get on the computer…
JOHN:	Oh, not me! *[laughs]*
HOYT:	She'd approve of you taking it easy, huh?
JOHN:	Oh yeah, she'd be okay with that.
HOYT:	It might even be a way of kind of honoring her memory.
JOHN:	Yeah. *[nods thoughtfully]* I wish she [daughter] knew my mom and my dad, too. But in a way she does, through me. I mean, I'm like my mom and dad, in different ways, so in that way she'll kind of know them and I just have to tell her the stories about them, you know.

HOYT: Yeah, I've come to think that if we don't want to completely lose somebody, we have to take the qualities in them that we love and manifest them, carry it on. Otherwise they get lost, the parts that should be carried forward.

JOHN: Yeah. Yeah.

HOYT: I think your daughter is very lucky to have such a good dad.

JOHN: Thanks.

HOYT: Yeah.

JOHN: Yeah, we're pleased.

Client's desired changes are again future-paced and also explicitly linked to his social system.

HOYT: When you begin to make some of these changes now and into the next months, who else is going to help you with that? Your wife?

JOHN: Yeah, yeah. We both are making a more strong commitment to slow down. That's certainly possible because my income flow is increasing and by not even doing more work, which is even nicer. So that's really happening—I do some contractual work and I'm getting a substantial increase in income by doing the same amount of work, so I can work on just Fridays and not Saturdays and do fine.

HOYT: Is there anything you should ask your wife or anybody to help you stay on track with this?

"Thickens the path" with interpersonal links.

JOHN: Well, we just need to plan our weekends and our time together, because if I don't plan it, it tends not to happen. So, we just need to plan things together.

HOYT: I've found with my life, it helps me with my appointment book if I block out the times—like "nature abhors

	a vacuum" and if I don't schedule time not to do things there's always something interesting to do. I don't know if you're similar, but in some ways it sounds like you need to…
JOHN:	…I do that at work. Yeah, my wife and I just need to plan our leisure time more.
HOYT:	The world has got all these demands that kind of impinge, so I wonder how you're going to deal with the outside world's demands on your time while you're telling yourself "I want to slow down, be with my daughter more."
JOHN:	Financially we're doing fine. I don't have to accomplish everything so quickly, I have these goals, I'll have my daughter's education paid for in the next couple of years.
HOYT:	Wow.
JOHN:	I don't want to work my whole life, so I'd like to at least semi-retire in my early 60s.
HOYT:	It sounds like in some ways you want to take a very different path than what your folks did.
JOHN:	I'm able to.
HOYT:	You are able to.
JOHN:	Yeah, but I don't know if they were able to—with seven children, you're kind of stuck working, you know. I value some parts of my father, though, in terms of being a real hard worker and real persistent and my mom, too. So I have this work ethic. It's okay, but also I can enjoy the fruits of my labor, too. So, it would be fun to have more time off with my daughter, take her to things and do things. You know, my dad used to watch me play football and I used to enjoy him being there and so I'm sure my daughter would want me to be there when she's doing various activities. I'd like to be there. Not a super parent, but just to enjoy her.

HOYT: In a couple of minutes we'll stop, but I wanted to ask you before we stop—what's been helpful in our talking? What's something you'll carry with you?

In the termination phase of the session (see Hoyt & Miller, 2000), therapist encourages "lexical encoding" (putting it into words) to help client conceptualize and store ideas or lessons in a retrievable way.

JOHN: *[pauses]* I guess not being in a hurry to get anyplace. Kind of just sharing with you what I was feeling and just being me and just talking about it and having my feelings, whatever those were. They've kind of subsided and it's nice being able to talk about my mom or my dad without crying. It doesn't mean I don't love them. It's okay to be sad. Now I'm able to breath. I'm enjoying that, not really feeling anxious.

HOYT: Good.

JOHN: For a compulsive, you know, that's kind of a trick. I'm not as compulsive as my sister, though. And just realizing that I am making plans to spend more time with my daughter, I'm actually doing that, and it's starting to happen and it's real joyful. That it's really going to happen, I'm going to have a real good life, for her and my wife and myself, and just really enjoy that. It's like we're enjoying New York.

HOYT: The other day, I was obsessing and a friend of mine said something…

Normalizing.

JOHN: …You obsess?

HOYT: Of course! *[laughter]* And when she said it, it was just 'Wow!' She said—let's see if I can get the words *[pauses]*: "Yesterday is history and tomorrow's a mystery, today is a gift, and that's why they call it the present."

JOHN: *[laughs]* That's great!

HOYT:	Yeah, even though it's sort of corny, probably five or six times in the last week when I've started to obsess, I'll say: 'the present, a gift—be here now.'

A catchy refrain, like a well-targeted joke or song lyric or memorable image, can be a useful mnemonic or 'anchor' to help recall a learning when the pressure's on (see Beaulieu, 2004).

JOHN:	Yeah, I can do that at times. It's been very valuable to do that. I just need to acknowledge my feelings and I don't need to be in a hurry. I don't have to worry so much about other people. Just take care of me—it's an occupational hazard being a caretaker, you know, taking care of others. Take care of me, I think that's what I need to do. If I take care of me, I'll be taking care of my daughter. She needs me to do that.
HOYT:	Yeah. You need to do unto yourself as well as you do unto others.

John then mentioned that he and his wife had taken the time to enjoy a night out together. This provided a reinforcement opportunity.

JOHN:	That's true. We went out last night and saw the play "Rent." It was really fantastic. It was all about love. I don't know if you've seen the play or not. I didn't understand all the words of the play—I was just getting into the feelings and raw emotions and I didn't have to figure things out. It's just a real emotive experience, you know.
HOYT:	How did you do that? That's fantastic!
JOHN:	All of a sudden in this play I began to see the beautiful lust, and see the attraction and struggles with the attraction.
HOYT:	Yeah.
JOHN:	And they're all struggling towards attachment and the difficulties with that and I didn't, I couldn't understand the words too well, but I didn't need to.

HOYT:	You got the message.
JOHN:	Well, yeah, the message was really be into the emotions and the feelings they were having and their struggles. It was a very beautiful night—expensive but very beautiful—but that's all right.
HOYT:	You're worth it.

We then concluded:

HOYT:	I'll be thinking about Wednesday next, wishing you well.
JOHN:	Oh, thank you, I appreciate that. I could use the warm thoughts. I'll think about you at that time.
HOYT:	Yeah, prayers are with you.
JOHN:	Thanks.
HOYT:	Would this be a good place for us to stop?
JOHN:	Yeah. Certainly.
HOYT:	Thank you.
JOHN:	Thank you.

<u>*Therapist's Comment*</u>. *My personal involvement and "use of self" is fairly typical. I could certainly relate to both the client's concerns as a father and his tendencies toward worry and overwork. People attending the interview commented on the sense of presence and intimacy, which may not be well conveyed in the written form of a truncated transcription.[2] I had no further*

---

2. In his review of the videotape, John Gladfelter (2001) graciously commented: "The client clearly wants an opportunity to talk about a current life crisis and is responsive to a thoughtful invitation to discuss his distress. A lot of good psychotherapy can be done in one session by a wise interviewer who has both the experience and orientation that allows the client to move at his own pace. This client is experiencing a lot of scare and a lot of sadness and the therapist gently invites him to go as far as he wants to go. Hoyt's warmth, caring and contact with the man makes this interview easy to watch. The dialogue has the character of a discussion between two friends rather than a therapist and client, and yet is clearly an intelligent strategy for enabling the client to explore his choices, comtemplate the status of his life and review the nature of his feelings."

contact with John. If we met for (an)other session(s), I expect I would ask about his daughter, of course, and also follow up (and attempt to amplify) practical, behavioral details of how he was taking time to "smell the roses." I find that many times we mental-health professionals know about our "issues" and what we need to do—a superficial level of "insight" (see Kaslow, 1984)—but may not actually follow through to make the changes we desire. I was impressed by all that John had going on, and I hope things work out well for him and his family.

5

Interview I—"Some Stories are Better than Others": A Conversation about Hope, Passion, and the Challenges of Work (with Victor Yalom)

The following interview was conducted on May 27, 2000, while I was attending the Evolution of Psychotherapy conference being held in Anaheim, California. Victor Yalom is a psychologist and business consultant in San Francisco. He teaches at the California School of Professional Psychology, and is President of PsychotherapistResources.com.

YALOM: I'm really pleased you agreed to join me today for this conversation. I'm going to try to pick your brain in the short time we have, to really find out about you as a therapist and as an innovative thinker in this field.

HOYT: I appreciate the opportunity to meet with you. I wanted to start by asking you a question, if I could: What was your particular interest in inviting me to participate in this exciting series?

YALOM: My vision for this interview series[1] for psychotherapist.net is to present therapists that are doing really innovative yet practical work, despite the pressures that

---

1. The list of interviewees includes James Bugental, Albert Ellis, John Gottman, Otto Kernberg, Donald Meichenbaum, Frank Pittman, Thomas Szasz, Irwin Yalom, and others.

	we are all facing on various fronts. I'm most interested in those who are finding a way to be excited about what they're doing. I've had a sense from your work that you fit in that camp.
HOYT:	Thank you. I'm delighted to be included. I'm very excited to participate.
YALOM:	So, you've written a new book.

Narrative Constructivism: Is It All in the Mind?

HOYT:	Yes. It's called *Some Stories Are Better than Others* (Hoyt, 2000a). It was just published two weeks ago by Brunner-Mazel Publishers.
YALOM:	How did you come up with that name? Obviously, it has a lot of meaning for you.
HOYT:	It does have a lot of meaning. I've become in the last several years more and more interested in what is sometimes called narrrative constructivism, in how people put their stories together. Rather than having the idea that we discover our reality, or that it's an objective thing that we find, we are oftentimes creating it. How we look at things affects what we'll see; and what we see affects what we'll do. I think that as people live their lives, they may generally be doing fine, but when they get stuck it's often because they're telling themselves a story or constructing a worldview or a narrative that isn't satisfying to them—it isn't self-fulfilling in a good way, but instead it's frustrating. And people will come to therapy looking, in essence, for a new story, a new way of understanding, a new perception—which can lead to new behaviors and new outcomes. So *some stories are better than others,* because some stories give people more of what they want in life, whereas other stories will be more self-limiting. My recent influences include the work of Don Meichenbaum, Michael White, and Steve de Shazer, and other constructivist thinkers going back centuries.

YALOM: Just this morning, I was reading a book by Zerka Moreno about her late husband, Jacob Moreno. That's what he said about psychodrama—that it's used as a way for people to construct their life. Existentialists thought the same thing: we're here, we have to create our meaning, we create our lives with the resources we have. In that way, you're following yet another tradition.

HOYT: It's a long tradition. As I begin to say a few names of the people who've influenced me recently, I begin to think of all the people I haven't mentioned, including Irvin Yalom [who is Victor's father], George Kelly, and a whole host of people. I think it's important to realize, though, that this idea of narrative or story is not the entirety of people's existence. Some people have misunderstood constructivism as meaning "it's just in your mind" or "that's your opinion." It's very important to recognize the realities that people are living in. To use the title of one of Michael White's books, *Narrative Means to Therapeutic Ends* (White & Epston, 1990): the narrative is a means, it's a vehicle.

YALOM: There is a quotation in your book; something to the effect that social constructionism does not mean that external reality is irrelevant.

HOYT: Yes. As obvious as that is to say, there's been a lot of misunderstanding, I think, and it's become a kind of tiresome argument. We're not saying that there's nothing outside. We're saying the knower has to know the reality, and that knowing involves construal, construction, meaning-making, and so on. It gets filtered, mediated through our consciousness, and that we can affect consciousness. The situation that people are in can be very significant. Existence determines consciousness as well as consciousness determines existence. Salvador Minuchin has spoken a lot about this. Take the example of people in terrible situations of oppression and poverty—a radical constructivist might say it's all in the way they're looking at it—but that would be an absurd position to take, not really appreciating the horribleness of their situation. So, obviously, we have to take into account social and economic issues, not just internal, intrapsychic processes.

YALOM: What you are saying, and relating it to the current reality of the therapy world, and what's driving the idea of this website, is exactly this. Many therapists feel very oppressed, very disillusioned by the phrase "realities of practicing therapy today"—managed care, a glut of therapists in many urban areas, lower fees. And the story that some therapists tell about themselves is that "we're in the wrong profession at the wrong time, and there's not much opportunity."

HOYT: I've seen and experienced some of that personally as well. There's a lot of demoralization. I think at the extreme psychotherapists are somewhat of an endangered species [see Simon, 2001]. On the one hand, there are the pressures of managed care: Get it done real quick, keep it on the surface and get it done quick. Then there are the pressures of biological psychiatry: Use medication and you don't have to talk too much about it. It's a very hard time. It's an interesting coincidence that we're meeting here at the Evolution of Psychotherapy Conference. "Evolution" requires pressures in the environment, and some kind of genetic variability, and then some new things can emerge. You don't want to become extinct; you want new things to emerge.

I wrote a different book, in 1995, called *Brief Therapy and Managed Care*. At that time, I expressed the view that there are ways of working with managed care. And I still think there are ways of working with some managed care, but more and more I've heard too many horror stories that have impressed me with how much difficulty managed care—especially in the for-profit sector—has been thus far in the world of psychotherapy. Managed care has not produced the promise we were hoping for, of being more efficient and distributing services to more people. It seems mostly that it's been cost containment, which has meant cutting people off, rather than finding new ways to help people.

The Archaeology of Hope

YALOM: How does your recent book shift your focus?

HOYT: Well, the reason I called my new book *Some Stories Are Better than Others* is because I think we're going to need to have a real shift in the field, in many directions, including looking more for clients' strengths and resources, not just focusing on their problems, pathologies, and pain. The "archaeology of hope" (to borrow the subtitle of the 1997 book *Narrative Therapy in Practice*, edited by Gerald Monk et al.) involves looking for competencies, strengths, overlooked possibilities, latent joy, and other little nuggets that we can pluck and bring forward. So when I say *Some Stories Are Better than Others*, I think it's going to be incumbent upon therapists more and more to see the whole person, not just the problems. I think it's going to be much better if we're competency-oriented, more collaborative, somewhat more future-oriented.

YALOM: I think, going back to Freud, the model is "what's unconscious is usually bad." A seething pit of conflict and aggression. While those things certainly exist, my experience has been that some of the most powerful changing moments in therapy are when people discover the positive things about themselves that they didn't know, that may have been repressed, or forgotten, or dismissed. Often therapists are looking for problems, they're looking for pain and conflict, rather than helping the client develop the capacity to sit with positive feelings which is no easy feat either. If a client comes in

	with something happy or joyful, the therapist may redirect them into the pain, rather than helping them sit with and explore and really experience something positive, at a deeper level…They're almost running from the joy. Yet, staying with the positive can lead to profound awareness shifts and life changes.
HOYT:	As one of my colleagues quipped, most people in this field have been trained as "mental illness professionals," not mental health professionals. We spend so much time pursing illness and pain. Somebody will say, "I had a couple of good days, but then some bad things happened" and the response is "Well, tell me about the bad things." If someone mentions pain, or sorrow, or looks sad or angry, we feel that's where the meat is. We're supposed to go for that. It would be interesting to me, not just to take a history of the present problem, but to take a history of the person recovering. "What in your past, what little clues or keys might help you deal with this better?"
YALOM:	Or simply, "How have you overcome difficult circumstances in the past?"
HOYT:	"How have you dealt with difficult circumstances? How have other people? Role models? Parents? People in your ethnic history? Are there examples you can draw upon? Ancestors you can call upon? Can you project yourself into a time in the future when things will be better? Imagine that time, and how are you going to get to that time? Thinking of times when things are better, a time that inspired you, can that give you some energy, some courage to go toward that?"

Some Stories Are Better than Others

YALOM: Can you think of your work with a client where you helped them get to a better story?

HOYT: I'm thinking of a woman—I'm thinking of how to respect her privacy and confidence, how to say this. OK, a woman I've known for some time who developed a terrible case of multiple sclerosis. Over a number of years she became very incapacitated, to the point where she's barely able to speak, incontinent, bedbound. At one time she had been a fashion model—quite a lovely young woman.

YALOM: Pretty heartbreaking.

HOYT: Very heartbreaking, but that's not the whole story. There is a lot of sorrow there, and we cried together over that. But if we see her as only an "MS victim," then she's really stuck. Then she's been terribly delimited. I began visiting her in her home when she couldn't come to the office. She had cats all over her house. So we started talking about the cats—they're sitting in my lap—and I found out that even though she's very limited, she's doing animal rescue. She's a phone counselor and helps place animals. I also discovered that she has a whole world of artistic and aesthetic interests. So we were able, over time, without denying the medical reality, to at least enlarge the picture. That she's not just somebody with MS, but that she's an animal lover/activist, she's an art appreciator.

She sent me a Christmas card last year—her condition has even worsened—in which she said *[voice breaks]*...if I could think of the exact words it would be better...I'm so choked up thinking about it that I'm blocking on it. Heck, it will come back to me.

YALOM: What's the feeling of being choked up?

Interview I: "Some Stories Are Better than Others"

HOYT: The feeling is that of being deeply moved. I love heroism, and heroine-ism. People triumphing over adversity. People who somehow, despite the odds, find a way to be happy. I met a kid recently down the street, a little boy who had some serious medical problems and he was in a wheelchair. In one way, you could look at him and see all the physical problems he had. And this little boy was laughing, and he had a balloon, playing. He was, at that moment, in a certain way healthier than I was. I was fussing and worrying about something, and he was experiencing the joy in life. I'm very interested in finding ways to bring out that joy for people.

And sometimes it's very hard. And it's getting harder for therapists. Most of us, I think, went into this crazy business—this wonderful, strange business—for very good reasons. We want to make the world a better place, we care about people. And oftentimes we get suspected: "You're doing this out of some neurotic need," "Aren't you co-dependent?" or "You're on a power trip" or something like that. The term "countertransference" has gotten to a point now where therapists are sometimes concerned about themselves too much [see Chapter 2, this volume]. I think it's very important for us to keep remembering the positive reasons we're in this field. Otherwise, I think it's a sure burnout.

YALOM: I think one way of doing that is to really be able to celebrate the triumphs with our clients. Were you able to emotionally share that joy with the woman you just so movingly described?

HOYT: Yes, and we both experienced it as a natural, genuine human encounter, not as a technique. It's very important for us to anchor, reinforce, praise, acknowledge, celebrate—whatever terminology you like—our clients' successes and forward movements. In this case, our relationship has become very important to both of us. She had sent me a note and I wrote back thanking her for the session. I told her that there had been a couple of times that I had been very worried about something, and I thought of her example and it gave me courage. She inspired me: if she could find a way to live her life meaningfully and have joy in it, given the challenges she has, then that inspires me to do the same in my life. And for me not to tell her that would have felt inauthentic and incomplete.

YALOM: That's wonderful! I think one way to avoid burnout is to give yourself permission as a therapist to really be human. So much of the training in our profession runs counter to this and teaches us to hold back so much of ourselves.

HOYT: It's a fine line. I don't want her to feel that she has to take care of me, or "I can't tell him I'm having a problem because he'll be disappointed," so I think we have to be judicious.

YALOM: Yes, we don't want to self-disclose simply because it feels good. You always ask yourself, "Is it for the benefit of the client?" In this case it seems like a no-brainer that sharing your joy about her triumphs is a good thing to do.

HOYT: Yes. I can see ways it would not be if it became her obligation; if she needed to prop me up somehow. But most of the time I think we're much too invisible; if we're a blank screen, then we're not real. A colleague of mine, David Nylund, and I have developed an interesting exercise. It's in my new book [see Hoyt & Nylund, 2000]. We interview therapists, but we interview them as if they were one of their patients. So, you would interview me as though I had been this patient. And you would ask, "What was it like working with Michael Hoyt? What was helpful and what wasn't helpful? What did he do that was really good for you? Did you ever let him know that you appreciated him?" There's a whole series of questions which are useful in evoking the internalized clients that we all carry around. We've used this in a lot of workshops, and people often say it's a breath of fresh air, or "It's like getting a different take on myself." Particularly when we make it very real, if we start to ask a lot of specific questions. We all internalize our parents, our clients, our friends—all sorts of people. And I think they're a source of revitalization. You can be reinvigorated if you can find a way to access what inspires you. And this particular lady really inspires me...

Hey, now I remember what the card said: "Memory is what God gave us that we might have roses in December."

YALOM: My...how very sweet.

HOYT: Yeah!

Goals and the Discovery Process

YALOM: I want to go back to some of the other things in your work, in the brief/strategic/solution-focused types of therapy. One of the concerns I have involves the emphasis on goal-setting. How the hell can you set a goal with a client in the first session, when it is often the case that clients don't really know what they're there for? Their presenting problem is often so vastly different than what you're working on four sessions later.

HOYT: I think that most clients do know what they're there for, at least initially. And so I might say, "What's your goal at this time?" or "As we start today, what do you think would be useful? What would you like this to be like? How will you know this has been useful?" And then, now and then in the course of therapy—whether it's one-session therapy or 10 sessions or 100 sessions—I'll ask "How's this going for you? Where are you at now? How have we done in terms of the initial things we were talking about? What should be our focus now?"

YALOM: "How are we working together?"

HOYT: Yes. And "What's next? Do you feel this has been adequate and sufficient? Do you think there are other things?" I think there's a danger that we can act as though we know more about the client, or what's best for the client, in ways that actually disempower the person. Jay Haley (1969) wrote a great paper years ago called "The Art of Psychoanalysis." You can keep saying to the patient, "You think that's the problem, but there's a deeper level." Oral interpretations trump. You can always go "deeper." You can say it was pre-Oedipal: "You'll have to have years to absorb me, because we can't even talk about it." Doing that can undermine the patient's sense that they really have autonomy, that they really know what's best for them. I think sometimes people come in and their goal is not the goal I would pick; it seems to me too superficial, or it's just skimming the surface. And I'll ask them: "Does that work for you?" And if they say it really does, I'll say "Fine." I might say—if I think they're taking a solution that's not really in their best interest—"I was thinking of some other things that might be of some interest to you. Does that sound like something you might want to look at?" I might try to open some space. If the person says, "Nah, I don't think so" or "Maybe someday," I'll say, "I just want to let you know it would be available. I'm not necessarily saying it's good for you, or even true for you, but it might be something to consider." I don't want to give people the message, "You think you've dealt with this, but you really haven't," where you keep undermining their sense of self-control and autonomy.

Oftentimes I think we've had the idea that we somehow have superior knowledge. And even if in some ways we know a lot, I think by following the client closely, rather than leading the client, in the long run the person will become more empowered and more of a person. You become a "person" by making "personal" decisions.

YALOM: I agree with a lot of what you say. We can't know more about our clients, regarding the content of their lives, or in terms of what their actual goals should be. What we bring to the table is that we're process experts. We can see ways that they're holding themselves back, how they're defending themselves. And we have real skills to help deepen their awareness, to deepen their inward searching abilities.

From another angle, one limitation of the question, "What are your goals?" is that it's a cognitively-framed question, and you're going to get a cognitive response. A few sessions later the goals and the awareness can get larger if they've explored new territory and are starting to think and feel differently about themselves or their body.

HOYT: Yes. We are using certain metaphors: "superficial versus deep," "cognitive versus in your heart." And they can be useful metaphors, sometimes. So my deconstructive mind says, "What do we gain and what do we lose?" I'm familiar with the "deep" concept, and I sometimes think that way. I might, even in brief therapy, say: "Does that solution fit all the way through? I know it sounds good in the 'top of your head,' but how does it set in your gut?" or "Does it fit all the way in your life?" or "Is there any part of you that doesn't feel right with that yet?" We have all sorts of language—we say "the old tapes are playing," "what part of you," there's an "unconscious," and all these different metaphors. They all can be useful. I think it's helpful to try and stay as much as I can in the client's frame, in the client's phenomenology. I am not an expert at everything, by any means, but I am something of an expert at asking questions. We want to help create a discovery process, and we can ask questions that will open vistas, that will get people to look at things differently, without necessarily directing them.[2] Not "You should do this and this and that." For example, you might say to a depressed patient, "What you call depression, what else might you call it? Some people would call that sadness. Or some people would call that oppression rather than depression. Is something putting you down or holding you back?"

Managed Care...Or is it 'Mangled Care'?

YALOM: Let's switch to some practical issues. You've worked at Kaiser, a large HMO that gets a lot of bad rap from psychotherapists, as any HMO or managed-care company does. How have you dealt with that? Obviously you care passionately about the field, and it's clear from this conversation that you do deep, meaningful work. And yet I've heard so often that at Kaiser you have to average 5-6 sessions or less per client. Also, you might see them for the first session, and then your schedule is so booked you can't schedule a follow-up session for three weeks. How do you work within such a system?

HOYT: I'm not here as a Kaiser spokesperson, but let me respond to several things you said. It's true I've worked at Kaiser for 20 years, and I'm certainly aware of people's comments, that it's "get them in and get them out." I think the pressures of managed care are affecting everyone, unless you have private-pay clients and their income is such that they don't have to worry about the economics of it and can come as often as they want. There is a major distinction between the for-profit HMOs, who generate most of the complaints, and the not-for-profit HMOs, of which Kaiser is one. No system can be everything for everyone, but it's the for-profits that rake a large profit off the top rather than

---

2. For further discussions of discovery versus direction, see *Interviews with Brief Therapy Experts* (Hoyt, 2001a).

putting it back into services. Many years ago I coined the phrase "mangled, not managed care" to describe what some companies often wind up providing. According to all the polls—*Time* and *Newsweek* and *U.S. News and World Report* and various newspapers—Kaiser has actually gotten excellent ratings within the HMOworld.

There's also a conflating or confusion between the idea of length of treatment and depth of treatment and quality of treatment. There are some patients that I have seen once or twice or three times and it was "deep" or "heart" work or whatever one would call it. And other patients I've seen for long periods, it never really had much "soul" or "passion" in it, but the patients found it very helpful. So I don't think that length or "depth" of treatment is always the indicator of what is better.

What I try to do is a number of things. I'm fascinated with people, and I'm almost an anthropologist at times. I'm curious how people got to be who they are, what makes them tick, what their hopes are.

YALOM: How does that work in your brief therapy?

HOYT: For me, the hallmarks of brief therapy are the development of a collaborative alliance and an emphasis on clients' strengths and competencies in the service of an efficient attainment of co-created goals. In brief therapy, people can get unstuck, or get back on track, get their process going, but I usually don't get to hear the whole story. I might get to hear one or two chapters or an interesting pivot or turn and then they carry on and do their work without me. I think it's one of the differences between more traditional longer-term versus briefer treatment. At the risk of oversimplifying it, with the former, the therapist goes well down the road with the patient, around lots of turns, with this shared idea that "eventually we're going to terminate." Whereas the brief therapist, as soon as things really start moving, they're saying "We're only going to meet a couple more times, let's talk about relapse prevention."

YALOM: So you can do some very useful things within the constraints of the system. And certainly it is better than no progress at all. But in terms of what feeds the soul of the therapist, and prevents us from getting burnout, that may be harder. We have a lot of difficulties in our professional life. We're dealing with lots of people with pain. We're not making as much money as a lot of other equally intelligent professionals. So we want the emotional gratification/satisfaction that the work brings.

HOYT: Freud said somewhere that the therapist should have the most satisfying personal life that he or she can have, so they won't look to their patients to make their life meaningful, to give them satisfaction. And I think some therapists have a strong need—I don't quite call it "addiction" or "codependency"—but there's some emotional reliance on the experience of getting close and being trusted. It's beautiful when it's happening. But sometimes I would ask, "What and whose needs are really getting served? Is it my need to be a long-term therapist for the gratifications—maybe not financial ones…

YALOM: …or maybe financial.

HOYT: Yes, maybe financial. I think there are some monetary incentives as well.

YALOM: Of course it cuts both ways. Clearly, as a private practitioner, there are financial incentives to keep patients long term. There's no way around that. And, conversely, in managed care, where someone has a pre-paid health plan, or a capitated contract, it's to the institution's economic advantage to keep the treatment shorter. So the economic incentives are there; we live in a free market economy; we know the impact of prices and money. And I think private practitioners need to be aware of the point you just raised, just as managed care needs to be aware of the converse dilemma.

How do managed-care therapists and companies deal with this? Weren't you in the management end at one point? How do you deal with that? To know that you're doing the right thing, and not being coerced by economic pressures from up above?

HOYT: As well as being a full-time clinician, I was the director of adult services at a large Kaiser facility for many years. I stopped being the director a few years ago because I had some other interests I wanted to pursue. I think it's a complicated question. I address it at length in two chapters on likely future trends and attendant ethical dilemmas in my book, *Some Stories Are Better than Others*.[3] There are lots of thorny issues, and 40 or 50 pages of discussion. I think we have to find ways to continue to function as professionals, with the intertwined implications of competency, autonomy, responsibility and ethicality.

YALOM: We certainly have to try to.

HOYT: As much as we can. And there *is* the fact that "he or she who pays the piper calls the tune," to some extent. Although it's true that we are economic animals, that we're trying to make a living, we have to safeguard what we think is best for clients, whether we're working in fee-for-service, managed care, or in whatever arena. This long pre-dated managed care. Imagine if a patient came into a private practitioner's office with a long list of issues and problems that obviously required long-term intensive treatment. And imagine he or she says "But I don't really have any money—I can only pay you

---

3. Also see Hoyt (1995a), especially Chapter 2 ("Twenty-Five Questioins to Ask Before Joining a Managed-Care Organization"), Chapter 3 ("Psychotherapy in a Staff-Model HMO: Providing and Assuring Quality Care in the Future"), and Chapter 4 ("Promoting HMO Values and a Culture of Quality: Doing the Right Thing in a Staff-Model HMO Mental Health Department").

$100 total." Many well-intentioned practitioners would say something to the effect of, "Well, I can only see you two or three or four times." They might do sliding scale, and maybe pro bono for awhile. But sooner or later they would also say, "If you can't pay, I'm not going to be able to give you professional services on an ongoing basis." So sometimes I've wound up in a situation discussing with patients—whether it's in an HMO or in a private setting—"How do you propose to pay for this? This is a professional service. For consideration of a certain amount of money you'll get a certain amount of service." It becomes a very complicated thing, because you don't want to just cut people off—but you also need to make a living.

Hoyt Under Pressure

YALOM: Let me put the pressure on you a little bit more.

HOYT: Good!

YALOM: I know that at HMOs like Kaiser, and others, in their benefits they give up to 20 sessions per year, and then if you read the fine print, it says "As needed for medical necessity." Where do you draw the line? Five sessions versus 17 sessions? And what's "medical necessity"? It's not really a medical treatment to begin with.

HOYT: I have a big objection to the term "medical necessity." I much prefer to call it "clinical necessity." And they have defined clinical or medical necessity in terms of four criteria, in general: One is a legitimate *DSM-IV* Axis I diagnosis. A second is "likely to show significant improvement," meaning "it's necessary because it will really help." A third is "necessary to avoid a worsening," meaning that if we don't do it, the patient is going to wind up worse. And the fourth, which has a lot of slimy politics around it, is that some companies are using the *DSM-IV*, Axis V, the Global Assessment of Function-

	ing, just setting a number: they have to be below a 55, or below a 50, or below a 60.
YALOM:	Whatever that means!
HOYT:	Whatever that means. It's semi-operationalized. But, how low do they have to go? How sick do you have to be? It's counterproductive and, in my mind, stupid, to say that you have to really fall apart and then we can start therapy.
YALOM:	There's an incentive for therapists to make the person look worse! An incentive to game the system.
HOYT:	Right. What happened a long time ago is that we, as a field, made an alliance with the medical model. And insurance has been treated as an entitlement: "I'm entitled to my 20 sessions," or "I'm entitled to as much as I want." Whereas it has been written, in contracts, that only if it's a diagnosable "illness" and a "necessity" will treatment be covered.
YALOM:	By doing that we signed a pact with the devil, if you want to call it that. But whoever bought into that is saying, "I'm going to agree that this is the illness model, the medical model." I agree with you: If we're going to go for that, we play by those terms.
HOYT:	And then we're into the language of *DSM* pathology, the language of the medical model. Then we're into "Axis I," "presenting complaint," and "symptom resolution."
YALOM:	And all that jazz.
HOYT:	I do think it can be useful, to a point, at times. It depends what we're doing therapy for. When people are having panic attacks, and it's turned into panic disorder, it's a fairly circumscribed thing. Sometimes diagnosis is not a bad thing. Other times, people want to come to therapy for a kind of growth therapy, or personal enhancement. I've been in therapy for those reasons, more than once. I wasn't there to treat *DSM IV*, I was

	there to grow Michael Hoyt. It's a question about whether insurance should pay for it. Insurance is for one thing, but this was a different process. HMOs and other managed-care companies are needing to specify what will and will not be covered, and for how long [see Hoyt, 1995a, 2000b; Hoyt & Friedman, 2000].
YALOM:	But that's such a hazy line. When you talk about the woman with MS, you talk about despair and hope and inspiration. Where is the line between treating illness and symptoms, and growth?
HOYT:	Yes, and one of the ways that treatment was justified to the insurance company was that there is some well-known research, with many replications, that good psychotherapy services reduce unnecessary medical utilization [see Cummings & Follette, 1967; Mumford et al., 1984; Cummings, Cummings, & Johnson, 1997]. That's one of the ways to sell it to the HMOs, showing them the bottom line. And so, if she could have some visits with the psychotherapist, it was likely that there weren't going to be so many visits to the internist and the emergency room. We may have to be "bilingual," so to speak. I could articulate "symptoms," "enhancing coping" and "reduced medical utilization" when I had to, but when I was with her, I wasn't doing medicine, I was doing humanity.

Words of Wisdom

YALOM:	Before we stop, any words of wisdom or advice or inspiration to the hordes of therapists, many of whom are feeling disillusioned with the field? What do you say to them?
HOYT:	I *hope* these are words of wisdom; they've been wise for me, and they may fit for somebody else. I think it's good to get more training and read books and go to workshops. I think that's helpful, but what we really

need to do is remember why we came into the field, and honor it. We need to come from our heart. We need to come from our soul. We need to follow our passion, as Joseph Campbell used to say. Sometimes there is a lot of pressure and unpleasantness. That's true. But don't let the bastards get you down. Don't let them define your reality completely. Work hard and keep hope alive—right livelihood is worth it.

I think another word of wisdom is that it's important to be multitheoretical, to have different lenses you can look through. The other word is "eclectic," but I don't like that word because it sounds like "chaotic" and "electric" in the same breath, like when you throw techniques at someone and don't know why. But I think it's important to be "multitheoretical."

We're in this wonderful, strange business: we go into small rooms with unhappy people and we try to talk them out of it, so to speak. We're here at the Evolution of Psychotherapy conference. The first speaker was brilliant and right on. And the second speaker was brilliant and right on, and completely contradicted the first. And the third said something really brilliant and right on and had a very different perspective—and each of them and their proponents have helped thousands of clients. Not everything is equal, but there are different ways to go, and nothing works all the time.

I think when you're stuck—and we all get stuck every day, we don't quite know what to do or the therapy isn't going anywhere—the first thing I would do is consult my client: "How is this working for you? What am I missing? I don't think we're looking at this the right way. What are your thoughts and ideas?"

YALOM: Instead of peer consultation?

HOYT: Yes. I would start with asking the client, rather than assuming the resistance is in the client. The first place resistance exists is in the therapist. *We* have a resistance—we are looking at things a certain way that doesn't let thing go forward. I would start with the resistance being in me, then I would look at the resistance in the interpersonal field, that is, something not working between us right. And finally, and only finally, I might ask, "Is the resistance in my client?" Too often, when it's not going where we want it to go, we say "Oh, they're Axis II," or "There's secondary gain," or "They don't really want to change," or "They really like suffering," or "They're too attached to their negative affect because of their early experiences with abuse." We've come up with something to explain it, as though the other person is the problem rather than the difficulty is in our understanding them better.

YALOM: "If it doesn't work, it's their fault."

HOYT: Right.

YALOM: "And if it works, it's our doing."

HOYT: Yes. There's an old saying: "When you point a finger at someone, there are three of them pointing back at you." So I would take this and say, "What's going on with me? What am I missing?" Even if it turns out that it's not something you're doing, being humble and genuinely willing to look at yourself may help open the space for the client to look at himself or herself. So, that's one thing I would do.

I would also suggest talking to people who have a different theoretical orientation than oneself. If you're psychodynamic, go talk to a cognitive behaviorist. If you're a cognitive behaviorist, go talk to a Jungian. If you're Jungian, go talk to someone who does biological psychiatry, and so forth. Because the way you're looking at it, your lenses, your frame, your conception, may not allow you to see the client and to see solutions in a way that's going to be helpful for this person. We often want to go talk with someone we really trust, someone we went to school with, because we had the same professors and the same books are on our shelves. Some-

	times it's like talking to a mirror. You almost know what they're going to say; they're going to confirm your pre-existing beliefs, because they have the same frame. It's OK to do that, because sometimes you get ideas. But if you're not getting the ideas that are going to move the therapy forward, it's time to talk to someone from a different orientation. How you look influences what you see, and what you see influences what you do. And if you're not seeing something helpful, get some new glasses. Some stories *are* better than others.
YALOM:	Thanks. You've helped expand my perspective and greatly enriched my understanding of what your work is all about.
HOYT:	I really appreciate your interest, trying to follow some passion and bring some energy and life into the field by interviewing different people about what turns them on. I would encourage readers to look at this whole set of interviews, not just the ones with people they may already be acquainted with. All the people who are going to be interviewed have something important to say, if you can hear it. Maybe this is another "word of wisdom": It's important to stay curious. I used to think that if something didn't turn me on, it meant that it wasn't good. I have now discovered that if it doesn't turn me on, and (especially) if it turns lots of other people on, maybe it's something I'm not hearing.
YALOM:	Again, the three fingers are pointing backwards.
HOYT:	Thank you for the opportunity.
YALOM:	Thank you so much.

6

Solution-Focused Couple Therapy

When you play songs, you can bring back people's memories of when they fell in love. That's where the power is.
 —Johnny Mercer (songwriter of "Moon River" and other ballads, quoted in John Berendt, *Midnight In the Garden of Good and Evil*, 1994, p. 90)

Suppose that one night, while you were asleep, there was a miracle and this problem was solved. How would you know? What would be different?
 —Steve de Shazer (*Clues: Investigating Solutions in Brief Therapy*, 1988, p. 10)

Solution-focused therapy is an intervention approach developed by Steve de Shazer (1982, 1985, 1988, 1991a, 1994a) and Insoo Kim Berg (1994a; Berg & Dolan, 2000; Berg & Kelly, 2000; Berg & Miller, 1992; Berg & Reuss, 1997; DeJong & Berg, 1997; Miller & Berg, 1995), with additional valuable explications from a number of contributors (e.g., Bonjean, 1997, 2003; Dolan, 1991; George, Iveson & Ratner, 1999; Lethem, 1994; G. Miller, 1997; S. Miller, Hubble & Duncan, 1996; O'Connell & Palmer, 2003; O'Hanlon & Weiner-Davis, 1989; Tohn & Oshlag, 1995; Walter & Peller, 1992, 2000; Weiner-Davis, 1992). While there is a theory-based, teachable model with specific techniques—the topic of this chapter—it is important to recognize that the essence of solution-focused therapy is an overarching worldview, a way of thinking and being, not a set of clinical operations (see Lipchik, 1994). As the name implies, the focus is on *solutions*, on *what works for clients*. It is a "post-structural revision" (de Shazer & Berg, 1992; also see de Shazer, 1993a)—a non-normative, constructivist view that emphasizes the use of language in the social construction of reality (see Hoyt, 1994a, 1996a, 1998, 2000a; McNamee & Gergen, 1992; G.

Miller, 1997). It appreciates the power of the subjective and operates with the assumption that clients have the competency and creativity, sometimes with skillful facilitation, to shift perspectives in ways that will open new options for experience and interaction. Solution-focused therapy respects clients' own resources and is directed toward *building solutions* rather than increasing insight into putative maladaptive psychological mechanisms. It is optimistic, collaborative, future-oriented, versatile, user-friendly, and often effective.

BACKGROUND OF THE APPROACH

Solution-focused therapy was developed in the late 1970s and '80s by Steve de Shazer and his colleagues at the Brief Family Therapy Center (BFTC) in Milwaukee, Wisconsin.[1] de Shazer had been influenced by the work of the pioneering Mental Research Institute (MRI) group in Palo Alto, California (Watzlawick et al., 1974; Fisch et al., 1982; Shoham & Rohrbaugh, 2002), which in turn was influenced by the work of the renowned psychiatrist/hypnotherapist Milton Erickson—especially Erickson's ideas about strategic intervention and the fuller utilization of clients' submerged competencies.[2] As indicated by the title of their keynote book, *Change: Principles of Problem Formation and Problem Resolution* (Watzlawick, et al., 1974), the MRI group had focused on how clients' create and resolve problems, including how efforts to solve a problem sometimes actually perpetuate the problem. de Shazer and his Milwaukee-based group took a somewhat different view, instead focusing on those times ("exceptions") when the presenting problem was not present, as expressed in the title of their signal counterpaper, "Brief Therapy: Focused Solution Development" (de Shazer, et al.,

---

1. While the pressures of managed care for greater efficiency and cost containment have contributed to the increased popularity of solution-focused and other time-sensitive approaches, de Shazer (quoted in Short, 1997, p. 18, emphasis in original) has made his position clear: "We are *not* a response to managed care. We've been doing brief therapy for 30 years. We developed this a long time before managed care was even somebody's bad idea."
2. Erickson wrote: "Patients have problems because their conscious programming has too severely limited their capacities. The solution is to help them break through the limitations of their conscious attitudes to free their unconscious potential for problem solving" (Erickson, Rossi & Rossi, 1976, p. 18); and "The fullest possible utilization of the functional capacities and abilities and the experiential and acquisitional learnings of the patient….should take precedence over the teaching of new ways in living which are developed from the therapist's possibly incomplete understanding of what may be right and serviceable to the individual concerned" (Erickson, 1980, p. 540).

1986). DeJong and Berg (1998, p. 13) describe a watershed moment in their book, *Interviewing for Solutions:*

> De Shazer first hit upon the idea that there is not a necessary connection between problem and solution in 1982, when working with a particular family (Hopwood & de Shazer, 1994). As usual, de Shazer and his colleagues asked, "What brings you in?" In response, family members kept interrupting one another until, by the end of the session, they had listed 27 different problems. Since none of the 27 were clearly defined, de Shazer and his colleagues were unable to design an intervention. Still, wishing to encourage the family members to focus on something different from their problems, de Shazer and his colleagues told them to pay careful attention to "what is happening in your lives that you want to continue to have happen." When the family returned, two weeks later, they said that things were going very well and they felt their problems were solved. According to the assumptions of the problem-solving approach, the family should not have improved so dramatically, because the practitioner had not yet been able to isolate and assess the patterns and nature of the problems. Their experience with such cases led de Shazer and his colleagues towards a solution focus in place of a problem focus. They and many others….have been continuing to work out the implications of this shift ever since.

The two approaches, BFTC and MRI, are complementary (Weakland & Fisch, 1992), both eschewing obfuscating theory in favor of "minimalistic," pragmatic, outcome-oriented approaches. As Shoham, Rohrbaugh and Patterson (1995, p. 143) explain in their review in the second edition of the *Clinical Handbook of Couple Therapy*:

> The hallmark of these models is conceptual and technical parsimony. The aim of therapy is simply to resolve the presenting complaint as quickly and efficiently as possible so that clients can get on with life: Goals such as promoting personal growth, working through underlying emotional issues, or teaching couples better problem-solving and communication skills are not emphasized. Both therapies offer minimal theory, focusing narrowly on the presenting complaint and relevant solutions, and both are nonnormative in that neither attempts to specify what constitutes a normal or dysfunctional marriage. Both pay close attention not only to what clients *do* but also to how they *view* the problem, themselves, and each other; in fact, both therapies assume that the "reality" of problems and change is constructed more than discovered. Both therapies also attach considerable importance to clients' "customership" for change and to the possibility that therapy itself may play a role in maintaining (rather than resolving) problems. Finally, in contrast to most other treatments for couples, therapists following the MRI and Milwaukee models often see the

partners individually, even when the focus of intervention is a complaint about the marriage itself.

The most fundamental difference between problem-and solution-focused therapy concerns the emphasis each gives to the concept of "solution": While the MRI approach aims to interdict existing solutions that maintain the problem and to promote "less of the same," the Milwaukee model seeks to identify exceptions to the problem and develop new solutions that work.

NON-NORMATIVE (IDIOMORPHIC) ASSESSMENT

Solution-focused therapists meet clients where they are (oftentimes beginning a session by asking "What brings you in?" or "What are you hoping to accomplish coming here?") and avoid preconceived notions of what may be healthy/unhealthy or functional/dysfunctional for a particular couple, individual, or family. Although general guidelines can be described, every case is considered to be unique. The therapist attempts to "keep it simple" by "taking the patient seriously" (de Shazer and Weakland, in Hoyt, 1994b), accepting the clients' version of what is—and isn't—a problem. Primacy is given to clients' experiences, goals, ideas, values, motivations, and worldviews, which are respectfully accepted as valid and real. While some discussion of the past allows clients a sense of being heard and acknowledged, and provides an opportunity for exploring clients' ideas about what would be helpful (their theories of change) and a reconnaissance of past successes and exceptions to the problem, the thrust of the solution-focused session is present-to-future oriented.

The therapist needs to have skills to join and work with persons of varying diversities to help them develop solutions that fit *their* frames of reference. The solution-focused approach is client-centered and transcultural in that it truly respects the "local knowledge" (individual, familial, social) of those who seek therapy; "cultural diversity" is honored in that the emphasis is genuinely on learning *from* clients, not just *about* them. The approach tends to be apolitical, however, and sociocultural topics such as ethnicity, class, race, and gender roles are not usually discussed explicitly unless clients make them the focus of conversation.

Initially, the solution-focused approach emerged in an inductive manner, from studying what clients and therapists did that preceded clients declaring problems "solved." It was noticed that problems were described as "solved" (or "resolved," "dissolved," or simply "no longer problems") when clients began to engage in new and different perceptions and behaviors vis-a-vis the presenting difficulty (Hoyt & Berg, 1998). This recognition led to de Shazer's "basic rules" of solution-focused therapy:

> *If it ain't broke, don't fix it.
> *Once you know what works, do more of it.
> *If it doesn't work, don't do it again; do something different. [quoted in Hoyt, 1996b, p. 314]

As previously noted, at times *solutions* may not even seem to have a direct connection to *problems*—development of a solution often involves a reformulation or different construction such that the former position loses its relevance or simply "dissolves." The client-couple has "moved on" and what was once a problem is "no longer an issue."

GOAL-SETTING

It's the *clients'* therapy (and life). The solution-focused therapist is on the lookout for the *clients'* notions of what would constitute a viable solution or success. As de Shazer (1991a, p. 112) has written:

> Early in their conversations, therapists and clients address the question, "How do we know when to stop meeting like this?" Both clinical experience and research indicate that workable goals tend to have the following general characteristics. They are:
>
> 1. small rather than large;
> 2. salient to clients;
> 3. described in specific, concrete behavioral terms;
> 4. achievable within the practical contexts of clients' lives;
> 5. perceived by the clients as involving their "hard work";
> 6. described as the "start of something" and not as the "end of something";
> 7. treated as involving new behavior(s) rather than the absence or cessation of existing behavior(s).
>
> Thus goals are depictions of what will be *present*, what will be happening in the clients' lives when the complaint is absent, when the pain that brought

them to therapy is absent and they therefore no longer depict life in problematic terms.

de Shazer (1991a, p. 113) goes on to suggest using his well-known future-oriented "Miracle Question" to elicit goals within an interpersonal framework:

> Suppose that one night there is a miracle and while you are sleeping the problem that brought you into therapy is solved: How would you know? What would be different? [de Shazer, 1988, p. 5]
> What will you notice the next morning that will tell you that there has been a miracle? What will your spouse notice?[3]

How (and where) we look helps determine what we see (Hoyt, 2000a). In *Words Were Originally Magic*, de Shazer (1994a, p. 10) elaborates the relevance of this for therapists working with couples:

> What we talk about and how we talk about it makes a difference (to the client). Thus reframing a "marital problem" into an "individual problem" or an "individual problem" into a "marital problem" makes a difference both in how we talk about things and where we look for solutions.[4]

---

3. In their book *The Miracle Method*, Scott Miller and Insoo Berg (1995, p. 37) recount the origins of the "Miracle Question," which has come to be a signature characteristic of solution-focused therapy:
   "A woman called us [in 1984] for an appointment demanding that she be seen that day because it was an emergency. She began sobbing as she told the receptionist how her husband's drinking was out of control and that he had even been violent toward her. As [the client] entered the therapist's office and began to sit down, she said, 'My problem is so serious that it would take a *miracle* to solve it!'....The therapist simply followed the client's lead, and said, 'Well...suppose one happened?' Immediately, the client began to describe what she wanted to be different about the situation that was troubling her. As she described what she wanted in more detail, a smile began to creep into her face and the tone of her voice became more hopeful....As she stood to leave the office, she told the therapist that she was feeling 'much better.'[....]The following week she returned and reported that she had turned that feeling into some small but significant changes in her life and her marriage."

"*Goaling*" is an on-going, dynamic process, open to re-negotiation, often more a process of identifying and moving toward possibilities rather than locking in fixed behavioral targets (Walter & Peller, 2000). Partners also may have different ideas, of course, about what constitutes the problem and what would constitute the solution; this provides the opportunity for a *both/and* (not *either/or*) negotiation:

HOYT: What about the situation of the so-called "multiproblem family"? [....]

DE SHAZER: [....] We think about them as "multi*goal* families." [....] First of all, if you ask the miracle question early enough in the session, you oftentimes avoid that difficulty—having all these multiple goals. Sometimes.

HOYT: Who do you ask the miracle question of?

DE SHAZER: Everybody.

HOYT: And if everyone gives a different answer?

DE SHAZER: That's reasonable.

HOYT: Then you have competing goals.

DE SHAZER: That's normal and reasonable. Then you say "Okay, 10 stands for this package—everything you've been talking about, those kinds of things. Whatever it will take for you guys to each individually and collectively to recognize that a miracle has happened, that's 10. Where are we today?" We get different estimates where each of them are. Then we sort of work on getting everybody's number on the scale and ignore, if you will, the fact that their version of 10 is probably different, because it's always going to be different with more than one person. And even with one person, he's going to have more than one goal, and they may conflict with each other anyway. [....] Our studies indicate that most people —most families stop

---

4. As Donald Schon (1982, p. 40, emphasis in original) notes in his book *The Reflective Practitioner: How Professionals Think in Action*: "[A]lthough problem setting is a necessary condition for technical problem solving, it is not itself a technical problem. When we set the problem, we select what we will treat as the 'things' of the situation, we set the boundaries of our attention to it, and we impose upon it a coherence which allows us to say what is wrong and in what directions the situation needs to be changed. Problem setting is a process in which, interactively, we *name* the things to which we will attend and *frame* the context in which we will attend to them."

> with 7 being good enough, and that 6 months later they will have frequently moved up to 8, but that is almost the outer limit. Very few people make 10. Those that do make 10 usually end up going into the teens as well—"overachievers." [in Hoyt, 1996b, pp. 70-71]

Eve Lipchik, a former member of the BFTC group, reminds us of the importance, when working with couples and families, of forming and maintaining a relationship with all the attending members:

> When there are two or more people in the room presenting themselves with a problem, I think of myself as having to establish a relationship with each one....Usually they have different views or are in conflict with each other. I often experience myself pulled by clients to accept one view over another. I try to stay connected in a positive way with each person in the room by reminding myself to be curious about how they see things differently and that I must communicate acceptance and understanding to everyone. A technique that helps me stay centered is not to listen to one person talk too long without asking the other for their view of what they heard. Frequent switching and checking between clients is a way of communicating that I am equally interested in what all of them have to say. I have been told by clients after treatment that what they think helped them the most was that I never took sides. They said that while they disagreed bitterly with each other, they trusted their relationship with me, and my acceptance of all views motivated them to give consideration to the perspectives of other family members. [Lipchik, 1997, p. 163; also see H. Anderson's (1997, pp. 95-96) discussion about *multipartiality*; as well as Ziegler and Hiller's (2001, pp. 39-53) discussion about *active neutrality*.]

Friedman and Lipchik (1999, p. 325) elaborate and note the utility of using a solution-focused approach:

> Differing perceptions between partners requires great sensitivity in acknowledging often strongly held yet divergent points of view while maintaining a working alliance with each member of the couple. In addition, faced with sometimes volatile and emotionally charged communications and affects, the couple therapist must manage high levels of reactivity in ways that offer the couple a path out of its members' problem-saturated reality. To meet these challenges, the time-effective, solution-focused therapist acts as a facilitator of the therapeutic conversation in ways that open space for the couple to move toward a preferred future. Working from a perspective of competencies and strengths, we take a nonpathologizing approach that respects the clients' goals

and utilizes the clients' own resources and "expert knowledges" in reaching these goals (Friedman, 1997; Lipchik, 1993).

THE STRUCTURE OF THE (COUPLE) THERAPY PROCESS

While therapy with a couple may present some particular challenges—such as each member vying for the therapist's attention and trying to get the therapist on his or her side, their presenting differing and sometimes seemingly contradictory histories and goals—the basic structure and therapeutic processes of solution-focused intervention are much the same whoever attends the session:

> Is marital therapy somehow different from family therapy? If so, what is the difference? And if there is a difference, does this difference make a difference?
> Since our practice and the practice of the Brief Family Therapy Center (BFTC) involve seeing individuals (people who live alone, half a marital pair, or one member of a larger family group), couples (married and unmarried, heterosexual and homosexual pairs), and family groups (two or more people, representing at least two generations or parents without the troublesome child), we found that the distinction between marital therapy and family therapy does not apply. A problem is a problem; the number of people (and their relationship to one another) whom the therapist sees to help solve the problem does not seem a useful distinction. This, of course, presupposes a strong belief in the systemic concept of wholism: If you change one element in a system, or the relationship between that element and another element, the system as a whole will be affected....
> The only criterion that seems to make a potential difference is that in "marital therapy" the relationship treated is that between two people of the same generation, whereas in family therapy the relationship of concern is often or usually between people of different generations. But does this affect the nature of the problems encountered or the nature of the solutions or the patterns of intervention-response?
> A quick check of case records accumulated over the years at BFTC and some research we have been doing indicated that the nature of problems, the nature of solutions, and the patterns of intervention-response do not differ along the lines implied by this distinction. In fact, the process of therapy seems relatively constant across situations. The kinds of intervention messages used appear over and over, and the patterns of response appear over and over. *Marital therapy, individual therapy,* and *family therapy* do not seem to be separate classes of brief therapy. [de Shazer & Berg, 1985, pp. 97-98]

On initial phone contact, the caller may be invited to bring to the session whoever is involved. "A part is not apart" (de Shazer & Berg, 1985; also see Weiner-Davis, 1995, 1998, 2000), however, and it is recognized that working with only one of the partners present can still have powerful effects upon all concerned. Indeed, as de Shazer has suggested:

> As I see it, the idea of bringing more people in is based on the idea that you're stuck because you don't have enough information. That's the premise behind it. My idea, following [linguistic philosopher Ludwig] Wittgenstein, is "The problem is you have too *much* information already, but you just don't know how to organize it." Or, furthermore, from Wittgenstein again, "You're in this situation and you've got what you got and that's all there is. There ain't no more." All you got is a problem of organization. So get people out and talk to just one person at a time, and maybe you can simplify it enough to do something. I haven't invited—I can't remember when last I said, "Bring your husband," or something like that. I can't remember that happening. [in Hoyt, 1996b, pp. 69-70]

Usually there is one therapist, who sits across from the clients. In some clinics and training situations, a team may observe (with the clients' informed consent) and consult from behind a one-way mirror, but in common practice most solution-focused therapists work successfully without this "stimulating but not necessary" (de Shazer, 1985, p. 18) arrangement.[5]

Solution-focused therapy is typically time-unlimited (no pre-set session maximum) and session appointments are made one at a time—the implication being that one may be enough. A course of therapy generally lasts 1-10 sessions, sometimes longer, and clients can return on an intermittent or as-needed basis (Hoyt, 1995b, 2000a). Sessions may be scheduled as frequently or infrequently as clients and therapists desire and find convenient and useful—often one to a few weeks apart. A couple wanting another appointment in one week might be complimented for "wanting to get right to it" while a couple wanting to wait a month might be complimented for "wanting time to see some progress" before returning.

In 1991, de Shazer (1991a, pp. 57-58) reported the average number of sessions per case as 4.7; in 1996, he indicated (in Hoyt, 1996b, p. 61) that the average had dropped to 3. Using an approach based on the BFTC model, single-session therapies were demonstrated to be successful in a wide variety of cases (see Talmon, 1990; Rosenbaum, Hoyt & Talmon, 1990; Hoyt, 1994c). Other research results are reviewed in McKeel (1996), De Jong and Hopwood (1996), and Macdonald (2003).

---

5. For some group therapy applications, see Coe and Zimpfer (1996), Hoskisson, 2003, Metcalf (1998), Nelson and Kelly (2001), Sharry (2003), and Shorr (1997).

THE ROLE OF THE THERAPIST

The solution-focused therapist serves essentially as a consultant, interviewing purposefully (Lipchik & de Shazer, 1986; Lipchik, 1987; Weakland, 1993; Weiner-Davis, 1993) to "influence the clients' view of the problem in a manner that leads to solution" (Berg & Miller, 1992, p. 70). The therapist endeavors to help the couple build a solution by asking questions (discussed at length below) and carefully punctuating responses to highlight a positive reality facilitative of clients' goals. Clients usually respond directly to the therapist, as well as talking with one another.

The interview process is designed to assist clients in achieving new perceptions and meanings. It is directive in that it deliberately encourages clients to look at things differently, but it does not supply answers. Rather, it provides a context for clients to focus on "what's right" and other possible ways of being "right," rather than on complaints of "what's wrong." A problem arises and a couple seeks therapy when the partners view their situation in such a way that they do not have access to what is needed to achieve what they consider reasonable satisfaction. By directing clients away from the problem-saturated narrative (story) that has embroiled them, the therapist attempts to create a context for the clients to develop their own, more useful ways of looking and responding.

The solution-focused therapist serves as a skillful facilitator, assisting clients to better utilize their own (perhaps overlooked) strengths and competencies, with a recognition that how clients conceive their situation—the way they "story" their lives—will either empower them or cut them off from existing resources:

> Our attention is focused primarily in the here and now, and even more importantly, on the future, since the future provides a blank canvas on which the couple can paint a picture of the pair's wishes and hopes. (Friedman & Lipchik, 1999, pp. 325-326)

The solution-focused therapist assumes a posture of "not knowing" (Anderson & Goolishian, 1992; Hoyt & Berg, 1998), allowing the clients to be "experts" rather than the therapist telling the clients what is "really" wrong and how to fix it.

The therapist-couple alliance is evolving and dynamic. In his now-classic paper, "The Death of Resistance," de Shazer (1984) noted that traditional theories of resistance were tantamount to pitting the therapist against the client in a fight that the therapist had to win in order for the client to be successful. In contradistinction, de Shazer suggested shifting the focus of therapeutic activity to the study of how people *do* change. As de Shazer and Berg (1985, p. 98) explain:

> In our view, the therapist needs to set the stage for the "cooperating" of client and therapist. The therapist needs to assume that the client is also interested in cooperating and, consequently, to build the therapeutic stance on the assumption that changing is inevitable, rather than difficult, as many models built on the concept of resistance assume. Of course, the particular way of cooperating can differ from session to session with the same client (de Shazer, 1982).

From this perspective, clients could be seen as having unique ways of *cooperating with* rather than resisting the therapist in their mutual efforts to bring about desired changes (see Hoyt & Miller, 2000). While therapists may know that they are helpers—or at least think they are—clients may not be ready for the kind of help the therapist wants to offer. Imposition tends to produce opposition (Hoyt, 2000a). Appreciating and working *with* clients' sense of their situation—including their theories, language, motivations, goals, and stages of change (Berg & Miller, 1992; Duncan, Hubble & Miller, 1997)—maintains therapist-client cooperation and vitiates the concept of *resistance*.

Solution-focused therapists (see Berg, 1989) conceptualize three types of therapist-client relationships, which can (and do) alternate within sessions: *customer, complainant*, and *visitor*. As Shoham et al. (1995, p. 153, italics added) explain:

> Here the distinction between customer, complainant, and visitor-type relationships offers guidelines for therapeutic cooperation or "fit" (de Shazer, 1988; Berg & Miller, 1992). If the relationship involves a *visitor* with whom the therapist cannot define a clear complaint or goal, cooperation involves nothing more than sympathy, politeness, and compliments for whatever the clients are successfully doing (with no tasks or requests for change). In a *complainant* relationship, where clients present a complaint but appear unwilling to take action or want someone else to change, the therapist cooperates by accepting their views, giving compliments, and sometimes prescribing observational tasks (e.g., to notice exceptions to the complaint pattern). Finally, with *customers* who want to do something about a complaint, the principle of fit allows the therapist to be more direct in guiding them toward solutions....
>
> Both de Shazer (1988) and Berg and Miller (1992) emphasize that the customer-complainant-visitor categories represent dynamic, changing attributes of the therapist-client relationship, not static characteristics of the clients themselves. Visitors and complainants can become customers and vice versa. In fact, one of the main reasons to cooperate with clients in this way is to increase possibilities for customership.

As Hoyt and Miller (2000) have written, therapists may also find it helpful in enhancing therapist-client "fit" and cooperation to recognize where the client-couple may be in terms of *stages of change*. In Prochaska's (1999) *transtheoretical model*, for example, change unfolds over a series of six stages of motivational readiness. Some differential intervention stategies are suggested if one combines Prochaska's transtheoretical model of stages of change with some ideas from solution-focused and strategic therapy (de Shazer, 1985, 1988; Miller, Hubble & Duncan, 1996), as discussed at length by Miller, Duncan and Hubble (1997, pp. 88-104; see especially Hoyt & Miller, 2000):

Precontemplation:	Suggest that the client "think about it" and provide information and education;
Contemplation:	Encourage thinking, recommend an observation task in which the client is asked to notice something (such as what happens to make things better or worse), and join with the client's lack of commitment to action with a "Go slow!" directive;
Preparation:	Offer treatment options, invite the client to choose from viable alternatives;
Action:	Amplify what works—get details of success and reinforce;
Maintenance:	Support success, predict setbacks, make contingency plans for relapse prevention;
Termination:	Wish well, say goodbye, leave an open door for possible return as needed.

As discussed in the next section, the solution-focused therapist maintains activity to keep the couple moving toward solution rather than engaging in extended blame talk and escalation of negative affect (see Table 6.1). As I heard Michele Weiner-Davis (2000) succinctly put it, the emphasis is on "What will be happening" rather than on "What isn't happening."

Table 6.1 Solution-Building Vocabulary

In	Out	In	Out
Respect	Judge	Forward	Backward
Empower	Fix	Future	Past
Nurture	Control	Collaborate	Manipulate
Facilitate	Treat	Options	Conflicts
Augment	Reduce	Partner	Expert
Invite	Insist	Horizontal	Hierarchical
Appreciate	Diagnose	Possibility	Limitation
Hope	Fear	Growth	Cure
Latent	Missing	Access	Defense
Assets	Defects	Utilize	Resist
Strength	Weakness	Create	Repair
Health	Pathology	Exception	Rule
Not Yet	Never	Difference	Sameness
Expand	Shrink	Solution	Problem

TECHNIQUES OF SOLUTION-FOCUSED COUPLE THERAPY

While support and encouragement can be given and specific skills sometimes taught, the hallmark of solution-focused therapy is the use of questions to invite clients to organize and focus their attention, energy, and understanding in one way rather than another. Questions are asked and selected responses explored and elaborated to direct clients toward the realization of their desired outcomes. The therapist functions like a special kind of mirror that can become convex or concave and swivel this way or that. Rather than providing a "flat mirror" that simply "reflects and clarifies," the solution-focused therapist purposely and differentially expands and contracts the reflected image, so to speak—opening parts of the story and closing others, making "space" for discourses that support the realization of clients' goals (Hoyt, 2000a, p. 67). As discussed in the following sections, highlighting and amplifying clients' past successes and their agency in bringing about preferred outcomes helps empower couples to construct more self-fulfilling realities.

<u>The Structure of Therapy Sessions: A Guide for the Perplexed</u>

In his book *Clues: Investigating Solutions in Brief Therapy*, de Shazer (1988, p. 86—reproduced in Hoyt, 2002c, p. 342; also see Walter & Peller, 1992) offers a schematic map of solution-focused interviews. de Shazer and Berg (1997, p. 123) have also outlined the formal characteristics of a "classic" solution-focused brief therapy (SFBT) session:

> Characteristic features of SFBT include:
>
> 1. At some point in the first interview, the therapist will ask the "Miracle Question."
>
> 2. At least once during the first interview and at subsequent ones, the client will be asked to rate something on a scale of "0 > 10" or "1 > 10."
>
> 3. At some point during the interview, the therapist will take a break.
>
> 4. After this intermission, the therapist will give the client some compliments which will sometimes (frequently) be followed by a suggestion or homework task (frequently called an "experiment").

Following this outline, we will first discuss a variety of questions typically asked in solution-focused couple therapy, providing numerous examples; will then discuss the use of a short break or intermission during the session; and will then consider the post-break portion of the session, including the use of directives or "homework" assignments.

Sessions, which usually last 50-60 minutes, typically begin with a brief period of *socializing and joining*. As expressed in the title of the book by Ben Furman and Tapani Ahola (1992), *Solution Talk: Hosting Therapeutic Conversations*, the solution-focused therapist attends to creating ("hosting") a comfortable, collaborative therapeutic situation.[6]

Various types of questions may then be asked. In what follows, a sampler of typical solution-focused therapy questions is provided. Many have been drawn (with some paraphrasings) from Ziegler (2000; also see Ziegler & Hiller, 2001); with additional sources including Berg and de Shazer (1993), Berg and Miller (1992), DeJong and Berg (1997), de Shazer (1985, 1988, 1991a, 1994a), Hoyt

---

6. Even if a couple as a unit has not been mandated to treatment by the legal system, one partner may, in effect, be under mandate if he (or she) has come only under the insistence or threat of the other. With clients who are not there voluntarily, it is especially important to develop goals that appeal to each client (see Friedman, 1993a; Rosenberg, 2000; Tohn & Oshlag, 1996). "What would it take to get your partner off your back?" may not sound very elegant, but for some clients it may be a more engaging and effective starting place than "How would you like to improve your marriage?" or "Let's look at ways you and your partner can enhance your relationship."

and Miller (2000), S. Miller (1994), O'Hanlon & Weiner-Davis (1989); Walter and Peller (1992, 2000), and Weiner-Davis (1992, 2000).

A Sampler of Solution-Focused Therapy Questions
Before the Session: Eliciting Pre-Session Change
It is useful to recognize that the roots of change exist before the first session. On first contact, usually when there is a phone call requesting an appointment, the solution-focused therapist will make a request that helps direct clients' attention toward *exceptions* to the problem, times the presenting complaint isn't present:

> Between now and next time we meet, I would like you to observe, so that you can describe to me next time, what happens in your [*pick one:* family, life, marriage, relationship] that you want to continue to have happen. [de Shazer, 1984; de Shazer & Molnar, 1984; see de Shazer, 1985, p. 137]

This "Skeleton Key Question" (a generic "key" that can fit any lock) helps shift perspective—it implies (presupposes) that something positive is happening to be observed and recruits the clients' cooperation. Discussing at the session what was noticed (*Eliciting Pre-Session Change*) can help consolidate and amplify useful new awarenesses (see Adams, Piercy & Jurich, 1991; Weiner-Davis, de Shazer & Gingerich, 1987).

Initial In-Session Questions
These are intended to build rapport, make space for partners' views and theories, and establish a team (therapist-couple alliance) framework.

> *What brings you here today?
> *How can I be helpful to the two of you?
> *What changes have either of you noticed since you first made the call to set up this appointment?
> *How do you see the situation—what's your understanding (theory) of what would be helpful?
> *What needs to happen here so that when you leave you will think, "It was good that we went to see (the therapist)?"
> *What can I do that would help you two work better together at getting beyond these troubles and turning your relationship around?

Goal-Building Questions

These are intended to identity, in operational (achieveable and observable) terms what the clients desire from therapy.

> *Miracle Question:* Suppose when you go home tonight and go to sleep a miracle happens and the problems that brought you here are solved. But, because you are asleep, you don't know this miracle has happened. So tomorrow, when you wake up and go through your day you notice things are different between you but you don't know the miracle happened. What will be the first things you notice are different? What will you notice your partner doing differently that will tell you something has changed? What will your partner notice you doing different?
>
> *From General to Specific:* How will the two of you know you have solved the problems that bring you here (or have reached your goals)? How will things be different? What specifically will tell you that you have solved your problem or reached these goals? What will be the first signs (smallest steps) that will tell you that you two are moving in that direction? What else?
>
> *Getting Specific Details—Painting the Picture:* What will tell you that you are on track? What else? What will that look like? What else will be different? When you are on track, what will you notice, what will be different to give you the confidence that you two will keep heading in that direction even after we stop meeting?
>
> *Ends and Means:* How will it make a difference to you when these changes have happened? How will these changes change the way you feel about your partner and your relationship?
>
> *Relationship/Outside Perception Questions:* When your partner is being more the way you want him/her to be, what will (s)he see you doing differently that will tell him/her that his/her changes are having a meaningful effect on you? What will your partner notice different about you when…? How do you suppose this will make a difference to him/her? What will tell him/her that you are on track to solving your marital problems? What will your children notice is different? Friends? Other family members?

Exceptions Questions

These are intended to identify times the presenting problem has not been present. A hallmark of solution-focused therapy, they seek a kernel or "germ" that can be expanded into an alternative view that elevates awareness of clients' abilities to make a positive difference and opens the gateway to a new couples story, one not saturated or dominated by problems. The search is for "symptoms of solutions" (S. Miller, 1992).

*When in the past might the problem have happened but didn't (or was less intense or more manageable)?
*When have you managed not to____?
*What is different about those times when the problem does not happen?
*When (in the recent past) have you experienced some of the things you say make a difference (tell you that you're heading in the right direction)?
*When have you noticed that the two of you do better with this problem?
*How have you let your partner know when he/she does something that makes a positive difference to you?

Agency (Efficacy) Questions

These are intended to call attention to clients' self-efficacy, that it, their abilities to make a difference in the desired direction (see Ziegler & Hiller, 2001).

*How did you do that?
*How did you get that to happen?
*What was each of you doing differently when you were doing better (or when there wasn't a problem, or when the exception happened)?
*How did each of you decide to do that?
*What would you say you (your partner) need to do to get that to happen more?
*What needs to happen first?
*What would your partner say you could do that would encourage him (or her) to do more of the things you think he (or she) could do to make a difference? Would you agree, even though it might be hard to do it or go first?
*What do you know about (your past, your self, your partner, your situation, other people) that tells you that this could happen for you (that you can make it together)?

Coping (Endurance) Questions

These are intended to acknowledge the difficulty and painfulness of some situations while also highlighting the clients' contributions to their resiliency.

*How have the two of you managed to cope (survive, endure, keep going)?
*Given the terrible situation (how bad the [*pick one*]: arguing, grief, worrying, lack of communication, etc.) has been, how come things aren't worse (how have you managed to avoid it getting even worse)?
*What have you been doing to fight off the (*pick one*: arguing, grief, etc.)?
*How did you know that would help?

*If you hadn't been through this experience personally, would you have ever thought you had the strength to survive?

Scaling Questions
These are typically asked "to make numbers talk" (Berg & de Shazer, 1993):

> Our scales are used to "measure" the client's own perception, to motivate and encourage, and to elucidate the goals and anything else that is important to the individual client....Scaling questions are used to discuss the individual client's perspective, the client's view of others, and the client's impressions of others' view of him or her. (Berg & de Shazer, 1993, pp. 9-10)

They go on to elaborate:

> Scales allow both therapist and client to use the way language works naturally by agreeing upon terms (i.e., numbers) and a concept (a scale where 10 stands for the goal and zero stands for the absence of progress toward that goal) that is obviously multiple and flexible. Since neither therapist nor client can be absolutely certain what the other means by the use of a particular word or concept, scaling questions allow them to jointly construct a way of talking about things that are hard to describe, including progress toward the client's goal(s)....Here the scales give us a way to creatively misunderstand by using numbers to describe the indescribable and yet have some confidence that we, as therapists, are doing the job the client hired us to do. (p. 19)

It is important to recognize that the positive direction and valence of a scale helps shift discourse toward a solution (not problem) focus. For example, asking a couple to rate themselves along the dimensions of how hopeful or motivated they are or how much progress has been made evokes a very different mind set than asking how hopeless or unmotivated or how stuck they are. Thinking about where one might be rated along positively-worded dimensions *is* much more hopeful, motivating, and likely to stir progress than the latter questions, which are not merely statistical inversions of solutions but entirely different constructions. Once clients give ratings, their responses are respectfully accepted and the question then shifts to "What will it take to move from a 3 to a 4 [or a 6 to a 7, etc.]?"

> *Hope: On a scale from 1 to 10, 1 being absolutely no hope and 10 being complete confidence, what number would you give your current level of hope?

What will tell you that your level has gone up one level? What number will be high enough to warrant your working hard to try and change things?

Motivation: On a scale from 1 to 10, 1 being no motivation and 10 being a willingness to go to any lengths to solve your problems, what number would you give your current level of motivation? What will cause that level to go up one level?

Progress: On a scale of 1 to 10, where 10 is the day after the miracle, and 1 is when this situation was at its worst, where would you say things are today? On a scale from 1 to 10, 1 being when the problems were just before you made the call and 10 being the problems are solved and a thing of the past, what number would you give your current level of progress (where you're at now)? What will tell you that you have moved up one level? What number will tell you that you have made enough progress in solving this problem so that you can consider it solved?

Self-Other Perception/Meaning Questions

These relationship questions are asked to bring forth and highlight competencies, positive qualities, strengths and successes, and to weave them into the interpersonal context (see Ziegler & Hiller, 2001).

*What does this say about you as a couple?

*What else would you want your partner to know (or have him/her notice) that would tell him/her how much you (care or love him/her, are working hard, want the relationship to improve, etc.)?

*As you continue to see yourselves this way, how do you imagine things continuing to change for the better? How do you suppose letting your partner know you see these positive changes in him/her will contribute to the two of you turning your relationship around (continuing to make progress)? How does his/her telling you that he/she notices and appreciates how you are changing affect you in your efforts to keep working for positive change?

*How will this (does this) make a difference that you want to see continue?

Timing of Interventions

The purpose of solution-focused therapy is to help clients build a solution they find acceptable. If the client couple is making progress that is adequate and satisfying to them, it is important to keep in mind the principle *"If It Works, Don't Fix It."* In these instances, it is helpful to "cheerlead rather than mislead" (Hoyt & Miller, 2000, p. 222), that is, elicit details of the clients' success, offer encouragement, highlight their role (instrumentality) in bringing it about—and not push.

If the couple gets stuck (or more likely, *when*—since they probably wouldn't be in the therapist's office if they didn't need assistance getting unstuck), the solution-focused therapist earns his or her fee by recognizing how the couple is getting bogged down in "problem talk" and then intervenes appropriately to redirect them toward "solution talk." Thus, as discussed above, the therapist needs to discern what type of therapist-client collaborative relationship (customer, complainant, visitor) is active and proceed accordingly. A couple may be stuck because of not having a sense of an achievable goal, or because one or both parties do not feel competent to make a positive difference. Good intentions need to be translated into specific actions. They may be ready to proceed as customers, but not know what particular steps to take (or not recognize what steps have worked for them in the past).

The solution-focused therapist intervenes, interrupting "problem talk" before it escalates into demoralizing bickering, cycles of blaming and defending, accusations, and unhappy crescendos. Instead, the therapist reminds the couple of what they want, and asks questions to redirect attention toward their role in achieving solutions past, present and, most important, future. The "Miracle Question" captures clients' imaginations and shifts the tone and flow of the conversation (see Nau & Shilts, 2000). Exceptions, coping, and agency questions evoke resources; relationship questions highlight cooperation and the bond between the partners.

Scaling questions, which can be used at any point during the session, are particularly helpful when complaints (or progress) are vague or nonspecific, as when couples refer to topics such as "communication":

> [A] couple's perception of how well they communicate with each other varies for each of them from time to time. With 10 standing for communicating as well as is possible for a specific couple to communicate, their joint progress and their different perceptions are simply depicted through their ratings. We frequently ask each partner to guess the other's rating, which again simply depicts progress and differences in perception as well as implying that such differences are both normal and expectable. The question is not "Who is right?" but "what does the one giving the higher rating see that the other one does not?" Thus, no matter how vaguely and nonspecifically the clients describe their situation, scales can be used to develop a useful way for therapist and clients to talk together about constructing solutions. [Berg & de Shazer, 1993, pp. 22-23]

Session Break: A Pause to Reflect and Plan

While many solution-oriented therapists may not take a formal break during a session, in its "pure" or "classic" form a solution-focused therapy session is characterized by the therapist taking a short (typically 5-10 minute) break or intermission about 30-45 minutes into the session. (The therapist will typically have prepared the clients for this at the beginning of the interview, when he or she indicates the structure of the session and gets the clients' permission to have a team, if available, observe the session.) When the time comes ("Let's take a short break so that I can talk with my colleagues"), the clients may be asked to sit in the interview room while the therapist goes next door to consult with a team of observers, or the clients may be asked to take a brief recess in the waiting room while the therapist talks with colleagues. Even if there are no colleagues observing, the therapist can use the break to organize his or her thoughts, to reflect upon what has occurred, and to plan a message (feedback and possible homework task) to be presented to the couple when the session is resumed.

The couple can also be asked to think about what task or post-session activity might be useful for them. Building on the solution-focused idea that it is the client who is "heroic" (Duncan & Miller, 2000) and whose therapeutic contributions should be kept foremost, Sharry, Madden, Darmody, and Miller (2001) describe an interesting variant in which the session break can be used in a more collaborative or client-directed fashion. They suggest this expectation can be established in the way the therapist describes the purpose of the consultation break:

> We're nearing the end of the session and I'd like to take a five-minute break. This is to give you time to think and reflect about what we have discussed; to pick out any important ideas that came up, or to make any decisions or plans. You might also like to think about whether this session has been useful and how you would like us to be further involved, if that would be helpful. While you're thinking, I will consult with my team for their thoughts. We will think together about what you said. When we get back together, I'll be interested to hear what stood out for you today. I'll also share the team's thoughts with you. Together, then, we can put something together that will be helpful. (Sharry et al., 2001, pp. 71-72)

This puts the emphasis clearly on the clients' thinking, reflecting, and planning. Clients are encouraged to participate in the evaluation of the session and the decision about further work. There is no "automatic" assumption that more sessions will be needed or desired, and it is the clients rather than the therapist who have primacy in making decisions about the length of treatment. As Sharry et al. (2001, pp. 74-75) write: "[C]lients as well as the therapist team are encouraged to use the break as an opportunity to reflect on the session, generate their own conclusions and even assign themselves a homework task....it helps clients build on their own strengths and resources, recognizing their central role in any therapeutic change....The responsibility for successful therapy is shared between therapist and client."

<u>Resuming and Concluding the Session: Feedback and Tasks</u>

When the therapist returns or brings the couple back into the room after taking a break, the session resumes. If one endeavors to utilize an especially collaborative or client-directed session break, as Sharry et al. (2001) suggest, it will be important that the therapist "first seeks the views and thoughts of the clients in evaluating the session and constructing a plan of action" (Sharry et al., 2001, p. 74). The break "punctuates" the session, and clients are usually keen to hear what the therapist has to say after studying the situation and perhaps consulting with other therapists. Hence, while giving primacy to the clients' ideas, the moment also may be ripe for the therapist to introduce a suggestion or a reframing (Erickson & Rossi, 1979; de Shazer, 1985, p. 91). Feedback and "homework" tasks, which flow from the preceding conversation, can be designed collaboratively to promote goal attainment by reflecting and reinforcing client competencies and any emerging "solution talk." The therapist works to amplify whatever the clients are doing in the direction they want to go. DeJong and Berg (1997, p. 107) distinguish solution building from problem solving:

> End-of-session feedback in solution building is not the same thing as intervention in the problem-solving approach. In the latter case, the practitioner uses assessment information about the nature and severity of client problems to decide on what actions would best benefit the client. The practitioner then takes those actions or encourages the client to do so. These actions—the interventions—are thought to produce the positive changes for the client.... In solution-building, by contrast, we do not regard session-ending feedback as any more important than any other component of the process. Instead....we think that solutions are built by clients through the hard work of applying their strengths in the direction of goals that they value. Clients, not practitioners, are the primary agents of change. In the course of the interview, clients disclose information about themselves and their circumstances; session-ending feedback merely organizes and highlights the aspects of that information that might be useful to clients as they strive to build solutions.

Compliments, a Bridging Statement, and the Task

In classic solution-focused therapy, there are typically three components to what the therapist says after the session break: *compliments*, which acknowledge and validate the clients' point of view, affirming what is important to them, their successes and strengths; a *bridging statement* that links compliments to the suggestion or directive that is to be offered; and the *task or directive* itself, often involving performance of an "experiment" or "homework."

> [Compliments] are statements from the therapist and/or team about what the client has said that is useful, effective, good, or fun. This helps to promote client-therapist fit and thus cooperation on the task at hand.
>
> With some frequency, the compliments (in the first session) will include statements about the difficulty of achieving the chosen goal and some statements, based on the exceptions, about the progress toward the goal and the general viability of the goal. In later sessions, the main focus of the compliments will often be on the progress toward the goal. [de Shazer, 1988, pp. 96-97]

An example of the use of compliments, acknowledgment and validation, and a bridging statement near the end of a solution-focused couple therapy session are illustrated in these comments excerpted from a report by Hoyt and Berg (2000, pp. 160-161; also see Berg, 1994b):

> *Therapist [Insoo Berg]:* I really have to tell you that I think your calling to set up this appointment was really good timing. It sounds like you both are very concerned about what's not happening between the two of you, and you want to do something about that. And I am very impressed, Bill, that you responded to Leslie's initiating this meeting and your willingess to take time from your very busy schedule and obviously this relationship is very important to you....And that's why you are here, to do something about this. Both of you really care about this relationship a great deal. But both in a very different way....[She goes on to describe each partner's stated values.] So there's no question in my mind that both of you care about each other in a very different way. And that gets misunderstood. And I think that both of you need both ways....And so I think that you two have a very good start because you're already thinking about right now as well as the future. So the next task for the two of you is to figure out how to fit your concerns together. [*bridging statement*] I don't think it's either your way or your way. It's the blending of the two. In order to do that, both of you have to work together to strike this balance. And I really like the way that you want to get started on this. You have lots of ideas of how to get started on that...

In this case, the therapist recognized that each member of the couple was in a complainant position, that is, felt aggrieved but not (yet) instrumental to make a difference. She thus suggested an *observation task*, one designed to shape viewing (and thus affect subsequent interaction) by having each partner notice what the other person was doing that was positive:

> *Therapist*: So what I would like to suggest to you between now and the next time we get together, is for each of you to keep track of what the other person is doing. For you [to the wife] to keep track of what Bill does, and for you [to the husband] to keep track of what Leslie does to make things a little bit better for the marriage. And it's important for you not to discuss it, but just keep track of them. And when we come back together we will discuss this more, the details of them. But I want you to sort of observe, file it away, and then when we get together we'll talk about it. OK? [Hoyt & Berg, 2000, p. 161; also see Berg, 1994b]

Having each partner notice the positive helped to shift the basis of their interaction from a problem-saturated to a more solution-saturated worldview. Seeing one's partner in a positive light makes one more likely to respond in kind; this may help produce a "virtuous" instead of a "vicious" cycle. Had the partners been in more of a "customer" position, the therapist might have more directly offered them specific suggestions or guidance on how to improve their interaction (as complainants, they would not have felt able to use this information); had they been in the position of "visitors," disavowing any problem or interest in a remedy, the therapist might have simply paid them courteous compliments and invited them to return (as complainants, however, this would not have resulted in their feeling that their complaints had been acknowledged and taken seriously).

de Shazer (1985, pp. 67-68; reproduced in Hoyt, 2002c, p. 349) provides a decision tree and some suggestions to therapists for how to respond to clients' responses to tasks in the best way for promoting cooperation (and thus, solutions). "Fit" is enhanced by attending to the basic solution-focused principles of *"Once You Know What Works, Do More of It"* and *"If It Doesn't Work, Don't Do It Again; Do Something Different."* de Shazer (1988, pp. 97-99, emphasis in original) also provides some general guidelines for designing tasks:

1. Note what sort of things the clients do that is good, useful, and effective.

2. Note *differences* between what happens when any exceptions occur and what happens when the complaint happens. Promote the former.

3. When possible, extract step-by-step descriptions of any exceptions.
   (a) Find out what is working, and/or
   (b) find out what has worked, and/or
   (c) find out what might work, then
   (d) prescribe the easiest.
   If some aspects of the exception (or of the complaint) are sort of random, then
   (e) include something arbitrary or make allowances for randomness in the task.

4. When necessary, *extract* step-by-step descriptions of the complaint.

5. Note *differences* between any hypothetical solutions and the complaint.

6. Imagine a *solved* version of the problematic situation by:

   a. making *exceptions* to the rule,

   b. changing the *location* of the complaint pattern,

   c. changing who is *involved* in the complaint pattern,

   d. changing the *order of the steps* involved,

   e. adding a *new element* or step to the complaint pattern,

   f. increasing the *duration* of the pattern,

   g. introducing *arbitrary* starting and stopping,

   h. increasing the *frequency* of the pattern,

   i. changing the *modality* of the problematic behavior.

7. Decide what will fit for the complainant/customer, i.e., which task, based on which variable (a through i) will make sense to the particular client. Which one will the complainant most likely accept? Which one will the customer most likely perform? For instance: If a couple has a joint complaint, give them a joint, cooperative task. If only one member of a couple presents the complaint like a customer, give the "customer" a task that involves doing something and the other person an observation task.

de Shazer (1994a, 1994b; also see his remarks in Hoyt, 1996b, pp. 61-63) also cautions the therapist to keep it simple and not get caught up in overly clever, complicated strategizing, which might have the untoward effects of both disempowering the client and overburdening the therapist.

Lipchik (1997, p. 170) also describes the importance of attending to cooperative "fit" and maintaining a collaborative set throughout the closing portion of the session:

I believe the summation message has an important function in creating a different reality for clients. I now structure this message to reflect what I believe I understand about the clients' reality ("What I heard you say today is…"); my perspective on what I heard ("My response is…"), which includes positives, reinforcements of what the clients are doing that they experience as helpful, normalizing statements and sometimes some information; and a suggestion about what they might think about, or do until the next session. I present "the task" as a choice, not an assignment. Then I ask the client[s] for a short response. This gives clients an opportunity to correct anything I reflected on or responded to that they do not agree with before leaving the session. I find this format more fitting a collaborative relationship than my former, more "expert" way of structuring the messages (Compliment: "I am impressed with…"; a clue, a task assignment).

Common Messages
In their excellent text, *Interviewing for Solutions*, DeJong and Berg (1998, p. 121) provide a number of guidelines for giving feedback, and identify various basic statements—called *common messages*—for recurring situations:

> [W]here you decide to point a client will depend on your assessment of: (1) the type of relationship in which your client stands to your services; (2) the degree to which the client has developed well-formed goals; and (3) the presence or absence of random and deliberate exceptions related to what your client wants.

As DeJong and Berg (1998, pp. 120-133, with some paraphrasings) describe, here are some typical common messages for different situations (it is important to remember that *compliments* and *bridging statements* would precede these):

Clients in a Visitor Relationship
"We are very impressed that you are here today even though this is not your idea. You certainly had the option of taking the easy way out by not coming.…I agree with you that you should be left alone. But you also realize that doing what you are told will help you get these people out of your life and you will be left alone sooner. Therefore, I would like to meet with you again to figure out further what will be good for you to do. So let's meet next week at the same time."

Clients in a Complainant Relationship
No Exceptions and No Goal
"Between now and the next time that we meet, pay attention to what's happening in your life that tells you that this problem can be solved."
Exceptions But No Goals
"Between now and the next time we meet, pay attention to those times that are better, so that you can describe them to me in detail. Try to notice what is different about them and how they happen. Who does what to make them happen?"
If the Clients Attribute the Exceptions Entirely to the Other Person's Actions
"Pay attention for those times when your partner (relationship) is more the way you want. Besides paying attention to what's different about those times, pay attention to—so you can describe it to me next time—what he/she might notice you doing that helps him/her/the two of you to be more ____. Keep track of those things and come back and tell me what's better."
If the Clients View the Problem as Existing Outside of Themselves
But are Able to Identify Random Exceptions
"I agree with you; there clearly seems to be days your partner (relationship) is more ____ and days when he/she/it isn't. So, between now and the next time that we meet, I suggest the following: Each night before you go to bed, predict whether or not tomorrow will be a day when ____ or not. Then, at the end of the day, before you make your prediction for the next day, think about whether or not your prediction came true. Account for any differences between your prediction and the way the day went and keep track of your observations so that you can come back and tell me about them."

Clients in a Customer Relationship
A Clear Miracle Picture But No Exceptions
"Pick one day over the next week and without telling anyone, pretend that the miracle has happened. And, as you live that day, pay attention to what's different around your house, so that you can tell me about it when we meet next time."
High Motivation But No Well-Formed Goals
"I am very impressed with how hard you have worked on your problem and how clearly you can describe to me the things you have tried so far to make things better. I can understand why you would be discouraged and frustrated right now....Because this is such a stubborn problem, I suggest that, between now and the next time we meet, when the problem happens, you do something different—no matter how strange or weird or off-the-wall what you do might seem. The only important thing is that, whatever you decide to do, you need to do something different."
Well-Formed Goals and Deliberate Exceptions
"I am impressed how much you want to make things go better between you and your partner, and that there are already times this is happening (give examples). I agree that these are the things you have to do to have the kind of

relationship that you want. So, between now and when we meet again, I suggest that you continue to do what works. Also, pay attention to what else you might be doing—but haven't noticed yet—that makes things better, and come back and tell me about it."

Other Useful Messages
The Overcoming-the-Urge Task
"Pay attention for those times when the two of you overcome the urge to (argue, return to the old problem, not look for positives in what the other is saying, etc.). Pay attention to what's different about those times—especially to what you are doing to overcome the urge.
Addressing Competing Views of the Solution (Without Taking Sides)
"I am impressed by how much both of you want to improve your relationship. I am also impressed by what different ideas the two of you have about how to do this—I can see that, coming from your different perspectives (backgrounds, families, etc.), you have learned different ways to do things….I (or, the team) am (are) split on which way to go: both of you have strong ideas. Therefore, I (we) suggest that each morning, right after you get up, you flip a coin. Heads means that day you improve things the way (Person A) suggests, and the other person goes along; and tails means you improve things the way (Person B) suggest, and the other person goes along. And also—on those days when each of you is not busy being in charge—pay careful attention to what the other does that is useful, and how you help with that, so that you can report it to me (us) when we meet again."

In her bestselling self-help guide, *Divorce Busting: A Revolutionary and Rapid Program for Staying Together*, Michele Weiner-Davis (1992), another former member of the BFTC group, draws on many solution-focused ideas. Under the heading (pp. 124-125) "Why Focusing on What Works—Works," she provides and discusses four answers:

1. Exceptions Shrink Problems

2. Exceptions Demonstrate that People Are Changeable

3. Exceptions Supply Solutions

4. Focusing on Strengths Strengthens.

Weiner-Davis (1992, pp. 127-140) then provides (with extended discussion and numerous practical suggestions for application) the following nine guidelines to help readers "analyze what works in your marriage and give you information you need to get your marriage back on track":

1. Notice What Is Different About the Times the Two of You Are Getting Along
2. If You Are Having Trouble Identifying Current Exceptions, Recall What You and Your Spouse Were Doing Differently in Years Past that Made Your Marriage More Satisfying
3. You Don't Have to Like It, You Just Have to Do It
4. Focus on What's Doable or Possible
5. A Problem that Recurs Doesn't Necessarily Require a New Solution
6. Pay Attention to How Your Conflicts End
7. If There Are No Exceptions, Identify the Best of the Worst
8. Notice What's Different About the Times the Problem Occurs but Something Constructive Comes from It
9. Notice What's Different About the Times the Problem Situation Occurs but Doesn't Bother You

In *Re-Writing Love Stories: Brief Marital Therapy*, Patricia Hudson and Bill O'Hanlon (1991; also see O'Hanlon & Hudson, 1994) also highlight many solution-focused/solution-oriented ideas, including the importance of moving from blame to collaboration, changing the couple's way of "viewing" and "doing" their situation, the use of task assignments, the value of humor, and the power of commitments and consequences. More recently, in their *Brief Couples Therapy Homework Planner,* Gary Schultheis, Bill O'Hanlon and Steffanie O'Hanlon (1999, p. 1) write:

> We use homework assignments for many reasons, including that homework:
> *Introduces change to the situation
> *Encourages a spirit of experimentation
> *Encourages clients to take an active part in therapy
> *Evokes resources
> *Highlights and allows follow-through on something that happened in the session
> *Encourages the client to put more attention on an issue
> *Encourages the client to take the next step before the next session
> *Enhances the client's search for solutions.

They go on (p. 6):

> We want to, at the very least, create some sense that the situation is not hopeless. That means we quickly move into making changes. So, in addition to validating, we immediately set about helping the couple make changes in three areas around the problem:
>
> 1. What are they paying attention to in the problem situation and how are they interpreting it? *(Changing the Viewing)*
>
> 2. How are they typically interacting with one another, including patterns of how each of them act during the problem situation and how they talk with one another or others about the problem? We are searching for repeating patterns and helping couples change those problem patterns. *(Changing the Doing)*
>
> 3. What circumstances surround the problem? That is, what are the family backgrounds and patterns, the cultural backgrounds and patterns, the racial backgrounds and gender training and experiences that are contributing to the problem? In what locations do the couple's problems usually happen? *(Changing the Context)*
>
> In each of these change areas, we have two tasks:
>
> 1. Recognizing and interrupting typical problem patterns
>
> 2. Seeking, highlighting and encouraging solution patterns.

Drawing upon solution-based (as well as other) ideas, they then provide many ready-to-use between-session assignments. When thoughtfully selected, proffered and explained to couples, these user-friendly "homework" tasks can help couples develop skills for healthier relationships.

<u>Subsequent Sessions</u>

When a couple returns for a second (or subsequent) session, the solution-focused therapist endeavors to co-create a comfortable, cooperative situation; then inquires about progress, seeking detailed descriptions of any movement toward the couple's desired outcome (solution) and their roles in attaining it; and then assists the couple to look forward to how they will take their next pro-solution steps. This process is nicely summarized (with some examples of opening questions) in the acronym *E.A.R.S.* (Berg, 1994c; DeJong & Berg, 1997):

E (elicit)—	"What's better?" or "What worked for you two? or "What happened that you liked?"
A (amplify)—	"Tell me more" or "Who/what/where/when/how?" or "Walk me through how the two of you did that"
R (reinforce)—	"Wow!" or "That sounds great!" or "What part did you especially enjoy?"
S (start again)—	"And what else is better?" or "So, what do you think the next step might be?" or "How can you keep this going?" or "On a scale of 1 to 10 you say your progress (relationship, communication, love life, etc.) is now at a 5—what would a 6 look like?"

Recalling the marital therapy case (from Hoyt & Berg, 1998) referred to earlier, consider these excerpts from the therapist's remarks at the beginning of the next session:

> *Therapist [Insoo Berg]*: It's been about 2 weeks since you were here the last time. What's been better for the two of you?....No kidding! Really? Wow! How'd you manage to do that?....No kidding?....Wow! That must have been hard....You did, really—without the kids? Some intimate time....You were willing to do that, this time—wonderful! ....Would you agree, was that fun for you, too?....Wow! That must have taken quite a bit of coordination to pull it off, with 4 people's schedules....Huh-huh....That's good!.... Right!....What did Leslie do to make things a little easier for you to do that?....Huh-huh....Great!.... Before we get to that, let me ask you: What did Bill do that was helpful?....Wow! Yes! It seems like that was very important to you— what does that mean to you?....Is that one of the things he did? Anything else you noticed to make things better?....Huh-huh....What about for you—what did Leslie do to make things better? What else? Say some more about that....Really!....How hopeful are you now, on a scale of 1 to 10, that this marriage will make it? A 9? And you?....This is a big change, isn't it? What would it take for you to stay on this track?....What needs to happen for the two of you to feel you are moving in the right direction?....So, how do you solve it—what's the next step for the two of you? [from Berg, 1994b]

If, even after careful inquiry, there has been a lack of discernable progress (including not doing homework that was discussed), *coping questions* ("How did you keep things from getting worse?") may be appropriate. The solution-focused therapist may also recognize "no progress" feedback as an opportunity to repair a possible mismatch. The therapist may have misgauged the clients' stage of readiness or the type of therapist-client relationship pattern (see Hoyt & Miller,

2000). Blaming the client is not useful in building cooperation and solutions. In such instances, questions such as the following may be helpful:

>*What's your idea about what would be useful? What do you think the next step should be?
>*Are we working on what you want to work on? How is this going for you?
>*I seem to have missed something you said. What can I do to be more helpful to you now?

Common Technical Errors and Criticisms

Solution-focused brief therapists focus on solutions. Many traditional therapists, however, are trained and oriented toward problems and pathologies. In addition to highlighting negativities, therapists (solution-focused and otherwise) can engender opposition by trying to take clients to where they don't want to go:

DE SHAZER: Well, if I were to use the word *resistance*—I wouldn't, but if I were—it would translate in my vocabulary as *therapist's error*. That would mean to me that the therapist's wasn't listening, and therefore he told the client to do something the client didn't want to do. That means he wasn't listening during the interview. Most of our stuff is based on the fact of something they told us about, that they did such and such and it worked in some situation, so it's just a matter of transferring that from situation A to situation B. So there's nothing new. Most of our interventions are nothing new for them [....].

HOYT: I think another advantage, then, to a solution-focused approach is that it doesn't stimulate noncompliance because there's nothing they have to non-comply with. It makes it more user-friendly for both the therapist and for the client. It's less likely to drive clients away.

DE SHAZER: Less likely. What I see sometimes is the amateurs, so to speak—the beginners, who somehow think more is better and, therefore, they give this endless stream of compliments and bore the client silly with them and, therefore, the client stops taking them seriously. That's one thing I see happen with beginners, in particular: There's just too damn many compliments, and that will drive the client away.

HOYT: [....] How do we separate the idea of "influence" from "brainwashing," to call it that? [That w]e're influencing but not imposing our values, manipulating them?

DE SHAZER: There's that line, all right. Clients hire us to influence them; that's why they come. The more you are using their stuff, the less danger you are in of moving into brainwashing. The more you are putting in your stuff, the closer you're getting to brainwashing. That's pretty clear to me. Those are the two ends of it, perhaps. I'm not sure if it is a continuum, but there certainly in a line in between. And, frankly, I see many, many of the psychotherapy models as being closer to brainwashing than to anything else.

HOYT: I think the respectful ethic is that it's truly informed consent. We're identifying what their goals are and helping them meet their goals, rather than imposing our agenda.

DE SHAZER: Right. You know, we have a saying around here [BFTC]—there used to be a sign made by somebody on the team (probably Gale Miller): "If the therapist's goals and the client's goals are different, the therapist is wrong." [in Hoyt, 1996b, pp. 63-65]

The approach should not be "model driven" or "technique driven" at the expense of the therapist/client relationship (see Lipchik, 1997, 2002; Miller & Duncan, 2000). Several commentators (e.g., Efran & Schenker, 1993; O'Hanlon, 1998) have suggested, however, that solution-focused therapy can be applied in a heavy-handed, formulaic manner that results in clients feeling "solution forced" (Nylund & Corsiglia, 1994) and "rushed to be brief" (Lipchik, 1994), and that solutions may be embraced that serve to perpetuate problem patterns (Fraser, 1998). de Shazer (in Hoyt, 1994b, p. 39) has made his view clear:

> I know what I don't want, and that's for anybody to develop some sort of rigid orthodoxies. I'm afraid of that. I'm always afraid of that. For me, it's a big point of concern. That there's a right way to do this and that. And to see my descriptions—and they've done this to me; I've probably done this to myself—to see my descriptions as prescriptions.

Critics have also suggested that emotion may be downplayed or ignored, and that recurring complaints and important social issues (e.g., oppression of women, domestic violence) will not be recognized unless clients explicitly raise them.

When done skillfully, clients in solution-focused therapy do not feel "forced" or "rushed," but assisted to go where they want to go.

> We do not believe solution-focused brief therapy encourages practitioners to force solutions on clients. However, because the approach is usually presented with a heavy emphasis on the idea that solution talk, not problem talk, leads to solutions, it is easy for those learning this approach to prevent clients from talking about their concerns and troubles. We have never heard or read anything in the solution-focused brief therapy literature that suggests clients should be forced to talk only about positive things. Watching de Shazer and Berg on videotapes, we have always noted their respectful attitudes and their skillful ways of "leading from behind." [Ziegler & Hiller, 2001, p. 222]

Emotion is not avoided, but it is also not sought or elicited as a therapeutic "royal road" or as an end in itself (see King, 1998; G. Miller & de Shazer, 1998, 2000). As Eve Lipchik (2002, p. 64) has written in her book *Beyond Technique in Solution-Focused Therapy: Working with Emotions and the Therapeutic Relationship*:

> Solution-focused therapists have traditionally guided clients toward behavioral descriptions of their goals so they can track progress better, even though most clients describe their complaints in terms of feelings. The therapist's response does not have to be in either a behavioral direction or an emotional one. We can cooperate with clients and use their feeling words in conversation without sacrificing the benefit of more concrete signs of progress (Turnell & Lipchik, 1999).

The solution-focused therapist is present as a real, genuinely concerned person, but does not engage in unneeded (by the client) personal self-disclosure. The therapist resists the temptation to be clever or to explore unnecessary topics, although therapists will respond appropriately to situations of obvious abuse and various solution-focused methods have been described (see Johnson & Goldman, 1996; Lipchik & Kubicki, 1996; Tucker et al., 2000; Ziegler & Hiller, 2002) for such situations.

<u>Termination</u>

Solution-focused (couple) therapy stops when the clients are satisfied that their goal(s) has (have) been adequately met or achieved, a situation that can be identified by their response to these questions:

* "How can we know when to stop meeting like this?" (de Shazer, 1991a, pp. 120-131)
* "What needs to be different in your life as a result of coming here for you to say that meeting with me was worthwhile?" or "What number [scaling progress] do you need to be in order not to come and talk with me anymore?" (DeJong & Berg, 1998, pp. 148-149)

In her book, *Family Based Services: A Solution-Focused Approach*, Berg (1994a) elaborates some criteria and methods for ending therapy, including goal achievement, designating a limited number of sessions, no movement in a case, and leaving things open-ended in response to outside restrictions. She writes:

> If you wait until *all* the client's problems are solved, you will never end treatment....What is important to keep in mind is that "empowering" clients means equipping them with the tools to solve their own problems as far as possible. When they can't do it on their own, they need to know when to ask for help and where to go for help. Termination can occur when you are confident that the client will know when and where to go to seek help, and *not* when you are confident that he [she or they] will never have problems. [Berg, 1994a, p. 163]

The solution-focused therapist endeavors to become obsolete and thus end therapy as soon as possible. The object is to get the client out of therapy and actively and productively involved in living his or her life (Dolan, 1985, p. 29). The approach is characterized more by an attitude than a particular length: "as few sessions as possible, not even one more than is necessary" is the way de Shazer (1991b, p. x) has put it. Hence, the approach is "minimalistic" in two related senses: (1) theoretical elegance, staying close to the clients' goals without introducing unnecessary and potentially distracting topics *and* (2) short-term, using the minimum of necessary sessions. When a couple feels ready and able to carry on without therapy—including having some strategies for managing future conflicts (see Carlson, 2000)—it is time for termination. Sometimes termination completes a process; other times a couple has gotten "unstuck" and back "on track" (Walter & Peller, 1994; Hoyt, 2000a) and they carry on their conversation about a situation—without the presence of a therapist. de Shazer made a remark at the end of a published conversation that might serve as good advice for therapists considering when to terminate treatment:

HOYT: How shall we close?

DE SHAZER: Wittgenstein [1980, p. 77e] has some tremendous advice for all authors: "Anything your reader can do for himself, leave to him." [in Hoyt, 1996b, p. 81]

Although "no more than needed" is a guiding desideratum, it is important to make sure that the clients' problems have been "heard" and addressed:

> I have occasionally worked with clients who describe their experience with their past solution-focused professional as he or she having been too positive and not providing opportunity for talking about things that really bothered them. Positive reinforcement alone can initally lead to clients feeling better about their situation and themselves. However, as they begin to feel better and talk more about their complaints, the specific goals may shift, and unless the collaborating professional is aware of this, the collaboration may be ended prematurely. When it appears that goals have been reached, it is important for the collaborating professional to become very curious about how clients have been experiencing the sessions, and what they think has been useful or not useful. "What else would you have wanted me to ask you, or talk about?" could prevent premature termination. [Lipchik, 1997, p. 167]

In keeping with the idea of intermittent or episodic therapy (see Cummings & Sayama, 1995; Hoyt, 1995b, 2000a), it is also important to leave the door open for possible return. Termination should be structured in such a way that a subsequent decision for more treatment will be seen by clients as an opportunity for further growth, rather than an indicator of failure.

<u>Opening the Lens: Some Useful Ideas and Techniques for Solution-Focused Therapists from Other Models</u>

A number of writers have suggested ways to integrate ideas and methods from seemingly related orientations into the solution-focused approach. However, while psychotherapy integration or the borrowing of techniques from different models is a laudatory endeavor if it better equips the therapist to assist clients, it is not without its perils. Neimeyer (1998, p. 62) warns about the "indiscriminate gallimaufry of deconstructive rules deriving from incompatible metatheories" that might result, for example, if a therapist switched from eliciting, affirming and celebrating a client's emerging self-awareness to suddenly challenging its logical or empirical basis. While one could explore with clients their intentions or even carefully offer another possible way of construing a situation ("Could that be a way he/she tries to show concern?"), solution-focused therapists are wary of the concept of therapist-provided *insight*, since it implies that there is a "right" or "true" psychological reality underlying clients' awareness and elevates the therapist to the role of The Expert able to interpret what is "real" and what is not:

HOYT: What I'm getting from what you're saying is it's best to accept that what the patient is communicating about is accurate. And it's our job to figure out what it's accurate about.

WEAKLAND: That's an interesting way of putting it, rather than converting them.

DE SHAZER: I'm not even sure about the last part…just, "it's accurate."

HOYT: It's accurate.

DE SHAZER: Yeah. It's accurate. And that's all there is.

HOYT: But if we're going to be of service to them, not just to take them seriously and listen, what do we add beyond listening?

DE SHAZER: The seriously. Taking them seriously. See, I think a lot of people listen, but they don't take them seriously. [in Hoyt, 1994b, p. 30]

Shoham et al. (1995, p. 156; also see Fraser, 1998) note that there would even seem to be core contradictions between MRI problem-focused brief therapy and BFTC solution-focused brief therapy models:

> This is no easy task, because despite similarities, there are also many ways in which specific tactics and the general therapeutic stance prescribed by the two models can be quite incompatible (e.g., investigating complaints vs. exceptions to complaints, offering optimism and encouragement vs. pessimism and restraint).

Saggese and Foley (2000, p. 59), however, note that "The SFBT [solution-focused brief therapy] and PFBT [problem-focused brief therapy] models are prime candidates for integration because they share a number of basic assumptions about both the nature and resolution of human problems." They go on to suggest ways of integrating the different pathways the two models use when seeking to resolve problems.

In practice, most clinicians influenced by solution-focused therapy do borrow from various models (e.g., see Cade & O'Hanlon, 1993; Eron & Lund, 1996; Fish, 1997; Friedman, 1997; Jordan & Quinn, 1994; O'Hanlon & Weiner-Davis, 1989; Quick, 1996), and such "technical integration" (Lazarus, 1995) can be consistent with the solution-focused metamessage of *Do What Works*. All therapists, however, more-or-less think that they "do what works" (why else would they do what they do?), so it seems reasonable to establish more specific criteria for what may be consistent with the spirit and intentions of solution-focused intervention. In their thoughtful review, Beyebach and Morejon (1999) refer to Michael Hjerth's (1995) idea that solution-focused therapy can be distinguished along the dimensions of its *philosophy* (or basic premises and assumptions), *use of language*, and *techniques*, and then go on to write:

> Provisionally, we would like to describe Solution-Focused Therapy therapy as an approach that includes as its *premises* the beliefs that clients have resources, that change is constant, that in therapy a small change is enough (as long as it is noticed), and that therefore there is no need to understand a problem in order to solve it. The *language* used in Solution-Focused Therapy is usually possibility and future-oriented, with the aim of creating cooperation and putting the client in control of the change process. This language creates a *stance* of cooperation on the part of the therapist, who tries to agree with her clients and is always alert to their use of language and to their changing goals during the process of therapy. This stance includes also an attempt to stay "behind" the clients, to carefully listen to them and to avoid pushing them in the therapist's direction. The therapist does not lecture to the clients or tell them what to do, but tries to help them figure out on their own what course of action to follow. Common, but not necessary *techniques* include goal-talk, exception-talk, and scaling questions, all of which could be described as solution-talk as opposed to problem-talk (de Shazer, 1994). [Beyebach & Morejon, 1999, p. 29]

In his book, *Time-Effective Psychotherapy: Maximizing Outcomes in an Era of Minimized Resources*, Steven Friedman (1997, p. 234; also see Friedman & Lipchik, 1999) draws heavily from solution-focused therapy as he outlines five major processes that define a time-effective, competency-based approach:

1. *Connection*: Listening, affirming, and acknowledging each partner's story while joining with both around a set of mutually agreed-upon goals;

2. *Curiosity*: Opening space for a discussion of multiple perspectives while attending to the couple's resources;

3. *Collaboration*: Working together with both members [of] the couple in the direction of *their* preferred futures. Highlighting successes ("exceptions") and generating hope;

4. *Co-Construction of Solution Ideas:* (a) Introducing novel ideas that emerge from the clinical conversations; (b) defining action steps ("homework");

5. *Closure:* Giving compliments; celebrating and applauding change; offering each partner an opportunity to acknowledge and comment on changes in the other; offering future availability.

Lipchik (2002, pp. 14-21) also describes a series of solution-focused assumptions:

1. Every client is unique.

2. Clients have the inherent strength and resources to help themselves.

3. Nothing is all negative.

4. There is no such thing as resistance,

5. You cannot change clients; they can only change themselves.

6. Solution-focused therapy goes slowly.

7. There is no cause and effect.

8. Solutions do not necessarily have anything to do with the problem.

9. Emotions are part of every problem and every solution.

10. Change is constant and inevitable; a small change can lead to bigger changes.

11. One can't change the past so one should concentrate on the future.

Looking through these "lenses," various competency-based, collaborative, and future-oriented ideas and interventions borrowed from strategic, narrative, and systemic frameworks can be integrated into solution-focused work. I cite a few here from my clinical experience as well as from that of Shoham et al. (1995), Beyebach and Morejon (1999), Ziegler and Hiller (2001) and others referenced above:

Motivational interviewing (DiClemente, 1991; W. Miller & Rollnick, 1991). Clients' goals are clarified and their motivation for change is enhanced by exploring with clients their reactions to their current experience and their reasons for seeking therapy (e.g., "How is what you've been doing working for you?" and "Is that a positive or a negative for you?"). If clients are dissatisfied, sometimes I find it helpful simply to quote the old saying, "If you don't change directions, you'll wind up where you're heading!"[7] While solution-focused therapists favor solution talk rather than problem talk, hearing some of a couple's woes allows the clients to feel heard and understood. We don't want to get stuck or bogged down, but they're going to tell us anyway, and talking about problems can also be used as a starting point to identifying times the problems are not present.

Externalization and relative influence questioning (White, 1989; White & Epston, 1990; Zimmerman & Dickerson, 1993; Roth & Epston, 1996; also see de Shazer, 1993b). These well-known narrative therapy methods place the "problem" outside the person/couple and identify both times the problem entraps them and times they are able to withstand or control the "problem." Times the couple successfully influences the "problem" may be thought of as "exceptions" (and "coping") within the solution-focused framework, providing a basis for solution development. As Michael White (in Winslade & Monk, 1999, p. 42) notes, these "unique outcomes" (to use the narrative therapy term) or "exceptions" (solution focus) may be nascent and manifest themselves as actions, intentions to act, moments when the effects of the problem don't seem so strong, areas of life that remain unaffected by the problem, special abilities or knowledge about how to overcome the problem, or problem-free responses from others that can be learned from vicariously. As I have suggested elsewhere (Hoyt, 2000a, p. 44), seeking a 'history of the present recovery' may be more salutary than the conventional psychiatric 'history of the present complaint'; rather than (or in addition to) the usual genogram (replete with divorces, suicides, and cut-offs), what useful information might a client and therapist gain from constructing a 'solution-focused genogram'?

---

7. "More of the same" does not make a change. Even a small pattern deviation can get things moving, as Bill O'Hanlon (1999) suggests in the title of his book, *Do One Thing Different*. In a chapter on "solution-oriented relationships," O'Hanlon (pp. 157-162) discusses "Nine Methods for Resolving Relationship Crises":
   1) Change Your Usual Conflict Patterns or Style
   2) Do a 180: Change Your Usual Pursuer-Distancer Pattern
   3) Catch Your Partner Doing Something Right
   4) Unpack Vague, Blaming, and Loaded Words; Instead, Use Action Talk
   5) Change Your Complaints into "Action Requests"
   6) Make a Specific Plan for Change
   7) Focus on How You (Not Your Partner) Can Change, and Take Responsibility for Making That Change
   8) Blow Your Partner's Stereotype of You
   9) Compassionate Listening.

* *"Go slow" messages and predicting setbacks.* Particularly with couples that have experienced a lot of difficulties and are hesitating to make changes, it may be helpful to compliment them on their taking a cautious approach and to remind them that the course ahead may not be smooth...but that their thoughtful, determined efforts will overall yield progress. Instead of looking at setbacks as failures, slips and relapses can be reframed as reminders that the couple is still improving and needs to remain vigilant about their process (see Berg, 1994a, p. 213; Norum, 2000, p. 15). It is also important for therapists, even those who describe themselves as "brief" therapists, to recognize that change sometimes is slow and that patience may be needed to allow couples the time and space to make and consolidate hard-earned gains.

*Role playing (especially in-session rehearsals of possible "solution" behavior). Suggesting to one or both members of a couple that they "pretend" or act "as if" a miracle has occurred or the problem is solved allows them a glimpse of a problem-free future; having them "try it on" makes it more "real" and more likely that they will see themselves differently and thus continue the pro-solution enactment. (See Roth & Chasin, 1994, for a good example drawn from narrative couples therapy.)

*Kindness, humor, faith, and love. These often assumed or taken-for-granted qualities provide the soil in which various techniques may take root. Solution-focused therapists operate from a deep, abiding belief that people, if treated right, are competent and capable. We are in search of *their* solutions and, while not always, I generally have found that the harder I listen, the smarter the client gets—often in ways that I would not have expected or imagined. This belief allows the solution-focused therapist "to look for the light instead of cursing the darkness," which is sometimes no mean feat when unhappy couples occupy our offices.

*Evoking a positive his/herstory. Asking about good times and happy memories helps people restore a positive sense of themselves, their partner, and their relationship. In his self-help book, *Why Marriages Succeed or Fail...and How You Can Make Yours Last,* couple researcher John Gottman (1994, pp. 224-227) recommends "finding the glory in your marital story" and provides questions to help couples focus on early favorable impressions of one another, identify ways they have overcome problems and made successful transitions, and highlight positive aspects of their marriage.

*Giving information, education and advice, and building skills. This is a particularly "slippery slope," since we don't want to interfere with a couple's own solution development. The "prime directive" of solution-focused therapy—that

clients' goals and resources be respected—encourages collaboration and purposeful intervention but does not encourage a "strategic" ploy of the therapist using techniques to manipulate or "do" something to the clients, even if it is intended for their own good. However, while respecting clients' capacities and adhering to Erickson's idea (1980, p. 540—see Footnote 2 on p. 71 above) that we may not know what's best, I find that particularly when we are in a therapist-couple *customer* relationship, couples often benefit from and appreciate receiving information about ways they may be able to improve their communication, their problem-solving, their sex lives, their parenting, and so on. Invitation, not imposition, is paramount ("Would you be interested in...." rather than "You ought to...."), but not providing new ideas and perspectives when asked and appropriate may unnecessarily constrain clients to working *only* with what they already have—a restriction that can result in their attempted solution becoming a more-of-the-same repetition of the problem (see Fraser, 1998). There is nothing in the theory or technique of solution-focused therapy that would contravene, say, addressing a client's depression or lack of relationship skills, especially if doing so would be likely to help them toward their therapy goal. Similarly, adjunctive psychopharmacology may sometimes support clients' self-empowerment by relieving suffering and allowing them to better participate by "restoring restorying" capacities (Hoyt, 2000a, p. 74).

Examination of various effective brief therapies, including solution-focused intervention with couples, suggests that they all share certain basic characteristics (Budman, Hoyt & Friedman, 1992):

> *Rapid and positive alliance
> *Focus on specific, achievable goals
> *Clear definition of client and therapist responsibilities and activities
> *Emphasis on client strengths and competencies with an expectation of change ("After the miracle....when things are better")
> *Assistance for the clients to move toward new perceptions and behaviors
> *Here-and-now (and next) orientation
> *Time sensitivity, making the most of each session with the possibility of intermittent return as needed.

THEORETICAL UNDERSTANDINGS (CURATIVE FACTORS/MECHANISMS OF CHANGE)

> *"Not invisible but unnoticed, Watson. You did not know where to look, and so you missed all that was important."*
> —Sherlock Holmes (Arthur Conan Doyle; quoted in Kendrick, 2000, p. 68)

Solution-focused therapy does not conceive of the therapeutic endeavor in terms of "curative factors" (which would imply the medical model of "disease" and "cure") nor in terms of "mechanisms of change" (which would imply an "objectivist" or "cause and effect" concept). Rather, solution-focused therapy emphasizes the human, interactional achievement of meaning-making. How we look influences what we see, and what we see influences what we do—around and around. Changes in perception lead to changes in behavior (and vice versa). This happens through language:

> As the client[s] and therapist talk more and more about the solution they want to construct together, they come to believe in the truth or reality of what they are talking about. This is the way language works, naturally. [Berg & de Shazer, 1993, p. 9]

In his book *Becoming Miracle Workers: Language and Meaning in Brief Therapy*, Gale Miller (1997, p. 183) elaborates:

> Solution-focused therapists....use their questions to construct mutually satisfactory conversations with clients. The questions are not designed to elicit information about worlds outside ongoing therapy conversations, but to elicit information in building new stories about clients' lives. Within solution-focused brief therapy discourse, then, all questions are constructive. They are designed to define goals and to construct solutions that solution-focused therapists assume are already present in clients' lives.

As noted at the beginning of this chapter, solution-focused therapy is a "post-structural re-vision" (de Shazer & Berg, 1992; also see Riikonen & Smith, 1997); it is an anti-pathologizing, utilitarian view that emphasizes the use of language (or "conversation") in the social construction of reality. How we make sense of our worlds—the stories we tell ourselves and each other—does much to determine what we experience, our actions, and our destinies. When clients need a better story, they often come to therapy.

As I have described in *Some Stories Are Better than Others:*

> What makes some stories better than others? Ultimately, of course, the answer must come from each individual freely, lest we impose our own values or beliefs. In general terms, stories involve a plot in which characters have experiences and employ imagination to resolve problems over time....From this perspective, therapy can be understood as the purposeful development of a more functional story; "better" stories are those that bring more of what is desired and less of what is not desired....
>
> Aesthetics, effects, and ethics are all important. We like stories that are well told; that are vivid and eloquent; that involve the generation and resolution of some tension; that see the protagonist[s] emerge successfully, perhaps even triumphantly. A "good" story does more than merely relate "facts"; a "good" story invigorates. [Hoyt, 2000, pp. 19-22]

Some of the implications of "storying" for therapy with couples are elaborated by Phillip Ziegler and Tobey Hiller (2001; also see Atwood, 1993, 1997; Sternberg, 1998) in their book, *Recreating Partnership: A Solution-Oriented, Colloborative Approach to Couples Therapy:*

> It is a central tenet of our work that all couples live together, interact, and view each other and their relationship through the lenses of certain narratives—narratives that are either relationship supportive or destructive. These stories, some personal and private, others co-authored and shared by the partners, explain and give meaning to past events, shape each partner's perceptions of ongoing encounters and support their expectations about the future. Whatever their specific content, however long they have been influencing the partners' perceptions and interactions, certain stories, in the case of distressed couples, have woven themselves together into narratives destructive to the relationship—these constructs we call the *bad story* narrative. These *bad stories* have led to an ongoing and regenerating perception and experience of events on the part of the couple that result in an increasing loss of a sense of partnership. The couple no longer views itself as a team through good times and bad, a unit working together for the common good. People in this situation are becoming less and less able to draw upon what we call a couple's shared *good story* narrative. This is a co-authored story running both into the past and into the future which, in distinction to the effects of the *bad story* narrative, keeps good will and feelings of love alive even during times of trouble and struggle. This *good story* is, in general, one in which a couple views itself as uniquely lucky to be together, with a past pleasing to dwell on and a future full of hope and promise. Attention to the function of the *good story/bad story* narratives in couples' lives is very important in the therapeutic endeavor.

The solution-focused approach was developed inductively, by noticing what happened that preceded clients declaring their problems solved, and it is a tenet of solution-focused therapy that it is not necessary to know *why* (or even *how*) something works in order to be effective:

> For an intervention to successfully *fit*, it is not necessary to have detailed knowledge of the complaint. It is not necessary even to be able to construct with any rigor how the trouble is maintained in order to prompt solution....*any* really different behavior in a problematic situation can be enough to prompt solution and give the client the satisfaction he seeks from therapy. [de Shazer, 1985, p. 7; emphasis in original]

Still, it is interesting to speculate, and a good theory (like a good story) may point the way to something useful. Solution-focused couple therapy endeavors to help clients construct self-fulfilling ("good story") realities (Hoyt & Berg, 1998), that is, views of themselves, their partner, and their relationship that will bring the couple more of what they want. Solution-focused therapists attend to working *with* clients to identify and amplify client goals and client perceptions of their abilities to achieve those goals. Entire stories need not be re-written ("re-authored"), however, since clients can often "take the ball and run" once they are "unstuck."

Clients in solution-focused therapy are assisted to develop new awarenesses—not "insights" of buried pains and sorrows, but of underappreciated, overlooked, perhaps forgotten hopes, skills and resources. The focus is on enhancing *"solution sight."*

> This process of solution development can be summed up as helping an unrecognized difference become a difference that makes a difference. [de Shazer, 1988, p. 10][8]

Clients are conceived as cooperative and competent, and behavior change is seen to flow naturally from changes in the partners' views and viewpoints. Stories and narratives transform and clients cooperate (with the therapist and each other) and move forward more readily when they are assisted to develop solutions that embrace their preferred views of self and other (Eron & Lund, 1996; Sluzki, 1998). As Gottman (1994) has noted, marriages are most likely to fail not when there is conflict, but when there is a lack of conflict resolution—specifically,

---

8. Hence the title of de Shazer's 1991 book, *Putting Difference to Work*.

when there is a lack of *reparative gestures*, or when one (or both) partners frequently ignore the other's attempts to repair whatever hurts have happened when conflicts have occurred. Gottman and Silver (1999, pp. 63-64) also highlight the importance of what they term a *fondness and admiration system*, the therapist needing to help the couple "unearth those positive feelings even more and put them to work to save their marriage." By focusing on solutions and exceptions to the problem, solution-focused therapy emphasizes these repairs and positive elements, and avoids iatrogenesis.[9]

Solution-focused therapy is prospective, not retrospective. There is usually a "future focus," with the therapist drawing attention toward what the clients will be doing differently when they have achieved a desired outcome or solution. Questions are designed to evoke a self-fulfilling map of the future (Penn, 1985; Tomm, 1987). The language presupposes change ("After the miracle..."), the focus being on what *will* be different when the solution is achieved. Indeed, the language is sometimes hypnotic, collapsing time, conflating present with future. As a picture of a positive future develops (or a positive past is reevoked), the couple begins to see themselves differently, and they respond to what they see. They begin living in the solution, not the problem—once this "virtuous cycle" gets going, the couple is "unstuck" and moving toward where they want to go.

TREATMENT APPLICABILITY

There is nothing inherent to solution-focused therapy that would preclude working with any particular problem or group. Indeed, the strong emphasis on identifying and working with clients' own goals, motivations, language, and theories of change makes the approach widely applicable. Solution-focused therapy considers each person, each couple, and each case as unique and potentially cooperative. As Evan George, Chris Iveson and Harvey Ratner (1999, pp. 22-23) write in *Problem to Solution:*

> Like de Shazer, in recent years we have adopted the assumption that *all* clients are motivated for *something*. What we assume is that if, under any circumstances, a client has agreed to speak with us then they are doing so for a good reason, and one connected with our professional role. If we believe otherwise

---

9. Also see Glasser and Glasser (2000, p. 15) regarding the importance of avoiding the "Seven Deadly Habits" of criticizing, blaming, complaining, nagging, threatening, punishing, and bribing. For a more tongue-in-cheek view that uses satire and absurdity to emphasize the value of solution language, see Greenberg and O'Malley (1983), *How to Avoid Love and Marriage*.

then we are acting on an assumption about the client which is potentially offensive: that they do things without a good reason. Not a good start to what should be a working relationship! [emphasis in original]

Clients who are too psychiatrically impaired to participate in talking therapy would not be expected to do well in solution-focused or any other approach. Clients with so-called "chronic and persistent severe psychiatric illness" may find benefit, however, in that solution-focused therapy works in the here-and-now (and next) toward achievable goals rather than getting bogged down by long psychiatric histories (see Kreider, 1998; Rowen & O'Hanlon, 1999). Mandated clients—who usually arrive as visitors or complainants—can be productively engaged if a goal can be identified that appeals to the client. Situations involving severe sociopathy and/or domestic violence may require partners to be seen separately until safety can be assured (see Johnson & Goldman, 1996; Lipchik & Kubicki, 1996; Uken & Sebold, 1996; Ziegler & Hiller, 2002).

CASE ILLUSTRATION[10]

> *"Hey, Dad—that's good! Instead of letting them fight, she's getting them to talk about ways they could be happier!"*
> —Alexander Hoyt (then age 7), after watching a videotape of Insoo Berg (1994b) working with a couple (quoted in Hoyt & Berg, 1998/2000, p. 166)

Keeping in mind that a case report is a gloss, a few brush-strokes that can only suggest (or obscure), I will attempt to summarize or sketch some of what characterized the "solution-focused" nature of the therapy with a particular couple. It is important to realize, particularly in the spirit of the post-structural perspective informing the work to be reported, how little (including tone, timing, and nonverbal communication) can actually be conveyed through a single case presentation. Restraints of space only allow a few excerpts.

---

10. Additional case examples of couple therapy based on solution-focused or solution-oriented principles can be found in Berg (1994b), Beyebach and Morejon (1999), de Shazer (1982, 1985, 1991, 1994), de Shazer and Berg (1985), Friedman (1992, 1993b, 1996, 1997), Friedman and Lipchik (1999), Gale and Newfield (1992), George et al. (2000), Green & Flemons (2004), Hoyt and Berg (1998/2000), Hudson and O'Hanlon (1991), Iveson (2003), Norum (2000), O'Hanlon and Hudson (1994), Johnson and Goldman (1996); Lethem (1994), Lipchik (2002), Lipchik and Kubicki (1996), Nunnally (1993), Quick (1996), Walter and Peller (1988), Weiner-Davis (1992), Ziegler (1998), and Ziegler and Hiller (2001, 2002).

From Session 1

I had not had a chance to call the couple. The receptionist's intake appointment note had the clients' names ("Frank" and "Regina"), indicated that he was 29 and she was 30 years old, and simply read "Pregnant—not getting along." When I went to the waiting room, I introduced myself and we walked the few steps into my office. Once seated, I remarked:

> "Welcome. The purpose of our meeting is briefly to work together to find a solution to whatever brings you here today. What's up?"
>
> The couple looked at me, then at each other. Finally, Frank spoke:
>
> "Why don't you tell him. It was your idea to come here."
>
> Regina paused, then launched: "I'm tired of this crap! Like I told him [rolling her eyes toward Frank], if it doesn't get better, I'm through. I've raised my 13-year-old daughter by myself, and I can raise this one, too. [She gestured toward her belly.] I'm almost 4 months pregnant—we had talked about having a baby, but it wasn't exactly planned. We've known each other for a couple of years, and have been together for around 7 months. At first it was OK, but now I'm pregnant, and the last 3 or 4 months it seems like all we do is fight. I don't need this! Either things are going to get better, or else! It's Frank's baby and I would never deny him seeing the child, but if he's not going to change his attitude and get off his ass and help, then he can just forget it!"
>
> "Everything's all my fault, huh?"
>
> "I get mad, too, but I'm just tired of all this fighting. We never seem to have a good time, or even just get along. And we're barely able to make ends meet. I was making more money than Frank, and I'm on disability now [due to a work injury], and I'm not sure I'll even be able to go back to work before I'm supposed to go out for maternity leave. And when he comes home, the first thing he does when he walks in is ask me when dinner will be ready! There's no 'How was your day?' or 'I love you,' just 'Where's the food?'"
>
> "It's always about me, isn't it? How about *your* attitude?" Frank responded.

The bickering continued for a couple of minutes. Finally, I got a word in edgewise:

> "Wait a minute! You came here because you want things to be better, don't you?" They nodded affirmatively. "That's why you're here. You used to get along, so you know *how* to—it seems you came here because you want some help figuring out how to get back to being happy, right?"
>
> "Well, yeah…"

"Then let me ask you, each of you—and don't get into an argument over this—on a scale of 1 to 10, how would you say your relationship is now, where 1 is 'Horrible—it sucks' and 10 is 'Great—couldn't be better'?"

"A 2."

"Yeah, like that—a 2."

"OK. That gives us some room to work. Without getting into complaining, what would it take for you to think things have moved up to a 3, or even a 4? What will each of you, and the other person, be doing differently when things are getting better?"

"I don't know."

"I don't know, either."

"Oh. OK. Let me ask you this: Suppose tonight, while you're sleeping, a miracle happens…and the problems that brought you here are solved! But you're sleeping, so you don't know it…until you wake up. Tomorrow, when you wake up, what would be some of the things you'd notice that would tell you that, 'Hey, things are better?'"

Regina laughed, and then Frank laughed. They then sat there, looking dumbfounded, then laughed again, together. Regina spoke first: "We'd be getting along, not hassling."

"Yeah, we'd talk, and she wouldn't get so mad at me."

Before the window of opportunity closed, I quickly asked: "You'd be getting along—what will you be saying and doing? How about you, Regina—what would you be doing if you and Frank were getting along? And you, Frank—how would you respond to Regina, and what would you be saying to build on the positive?"

Much of the ensuing discussion expanded this theme. With numerous questions being asked to elicit and elaborate details, Regina and Frank described their initial meeting and courtship, a fun vacation they had taken, and some hopes they shared for raising their child together. When they began to slip back toward arguing, I twice gently interrupted them and redirected the discussion toward their positive stories. With some additional prompting ("When was the last time you got along OK, even for a few minutes?"), they also identified some more recent moments (albeit lately more rare than common) when they had bits of what they desired. Again, numerous questions expanded those "exceptions." They began to see one another more beneficently, slowly shifting figure and ground, moving from problem to solution. Drawing upon both their recall of happier times in the past and their imagination of a positive future, they seemed to be discovering and remembering—and began using—important relationship skills they already knew.

As the session drew to a close, I asked if the meeting had been helpful, and if so, in what ways. They both remarked that it helped to talk about things without arguing, and to keep some perspective and to be reminded about how to get along. I complimented them for making the appointment to come in, connotating it as "an indication of your caring for each other and your both being committed to making a happy home for your child."

I then asked if they'd like to make another appointment. They accepted for 2 weeks hence. Finally, I offered a homework suggestion:

> "You've come up with some very good ideas about how to make things better. Between now and when we meet in a couple of weeks—and even after that—please pay attention and notice whatever you do and whatever the other person does to make things better. It may not be perfect, but try to keep track of whatever positives you or your partner do or attempt to do. When we meet, I'll ask you about what you noticed."

From Session 2

It wasn't particularly sunny out, but Frank was wearing sunglasses—and didn't remove them—when he and Regina re-entered my office.

> "Well, how'd the two weeks go? What did you notice about things getting better?"
>
> "Ask her" was Frank's reply.
>
> "Things were really good for a couple of days. We were talking and not fighting and were actually having a good time."
>
> "That sounds like a positive—how'd you do that?"
>
> "I was careful about what I said, and Frank was doing better, too. Then we got into an argument."
>
> "What happened?"
>
> "Frank came home late, later than he said he would, and..."
>
> "Right. So it's my fault, again."
>
> Recognizing that we weren't headed where the clients wanted to go, I intervened:
>
> "Oops! I made a mistake. Sorry."
>
> "Huh?"
>
> "Well, you know, if you go to a lot of counselors, they sit there and try to figure out what you're doing wrong, and then they kind of bust you and point out what you should do. Sometimes it helps, but a lot of times people already know what they need to do. I used to do that, but I got tired of it. Now I've got a great job—I sit here and try to help you figure out what you're doing right, and then try to get you to do more of it. I think it works better, and I don't have to spend all day battling and fighting with people who just want to get along and be happier."

Frank removed his sunglasses and put them on the sidetable. He then spoke:

"You know, after we had the fight, Regina called me the next day at work and apologized. I know I was wrong for being late, but it really hurt my feelings the way she yelled at me."

"She called and apologized?"

"Yeah. I really appreciated it, too."

"You called?"

"Yeah, I called him at work the next afternoon. I was still annoyed about his being late, but I knew I had gone too far. I said some things that were out of line. I don't want to be a jerk."

"You really care about Frank and about the relationship, don't you?"

"Yeah. Sometimes it might not seem like it, the way I complain about him, but he's really not such a bad guy."

"You love him."

"Yes."

"What are some of the positives you appreciate about him?"

"He's actually really kind. He puts up with a lot from me. He's also got a good sense of humor, and I know he's trying to make things better."

"How do you know that?"

"I can see how he's trying to be more responsible. And he made me breakfast Sunday morning. And he's been helping out more around the house."

"Frank, did you know Regina was appreciating what you've been doing?"

"Well, kind of, I guess."

"Had she told you?"

"No, not really."

This got us into discussing how they communicate their needs and appreciation to one another. Frank noted "We could use some help there," and Regina agreed. Frank then acknowledged that "Sometimes my feelings get hurt, and then I withdraw and she gets even madder." I asked their ideas about how to handle tense situations better ("You know yourselves and each other better than I ever could—what do you think would work for the two of you?"). Regina and Frank both suggested alternatives, and I also proffered a few ideas. We discussed back and forth what would make sense that they would be willing to try, and they playfully rehearsed a couple of options.

As the hour again drew toward a close, I complimented them and offered a suggestion: "You've been doing a lot of good work. Things may not go perfectly, of course, so keep track of the things that are happening that you want to continue to happen." I asked when they would like another appointment. They choose three weeks, saying that would allow them time to practice.

From Session 3

They reported that Regina had not been able to return to work, and Frank virtually beamed as Regina expressed appreciation for his increased help around the house and for his offering to work extra hours. Frank had also been helping more with Regina's daughter, working with her on a homework assignment and driving her to cheerleading practice. They each rated their relationship as "between a 5 and a 6."

Everything, however, had not been smooth sailing. As they talked about preparing for the baby, they described a tense moment that had erupted into an argument when they were out buying items for the baby's room. Regina had been frustrated, she said, that Frank had not been more enthusiastic about shopping; in turn, Frank described feeling awkward with "baby stuff" and complained about not getting much recognition for having to make endless compromises and adjustments to their new (and impending) lifestyle as parents. Frank's assistance with Regina's daughter was noted and discussed as an example of his wanting to be helpful. A long discussion then ensued about the changes required by family life, including my sharing a couple of brief stories about ways I had struggled to come to grips with parenting when my son had been born 13 years prior. Even during these "normalizing" self-disclosures, I was very careful to keep the focus (directly and indirectly) on the clients' goals and challenges, asking Frank and Regina questions ("What are some examples of ways you have compromised successfully?" "How did you make up?" "What did you do differently during those times you coped constructively with your frustration?") that would highlight whatever they were doing in the direction they wanted to go.

To help keep them pointed toward their goal of improved teamwork, at the end of the session they were asked to notice and keep track of whatever either of them did that showed they were working together. It was also suggested that they each pick and invite the other to go on one fun outing. They agreed to do so, and scheduled another appointment for 3 weeks later.

From Session 4

They reported having had "the best three weeks we've had since Regina got pregnant." I mostly listened ("How'd you solve that? Wow!") and asked for details—which they gladly supplied—that further "thickened" the account of their functioning well together. I asked how they would rate their relationship. Regina said "9" and Frank said "10"—they looked at each other and laughed, rather than arguing about the 1 point difference. Alluding to the baby, I commented that "Since you're going to be together for at least the next couple of decades, it's nice to see that you're working on the "Frank *and* Regina Story" rather than the "Frank *or* Regina Story." I again congratulated them on their good "teamwork." We scheduled a follow-up for three weeks later. They left smiling and actually holding hands.

From Session 5

Regina complained about feeling tired; Frank was also tired, from working overtime, but expressed sympathy and support. They indicated that they had continued to do well and had thought about cancelling the session, but felt it would be good to come in to review their progress and talk about what they needed to do to keep it going. We talked at length about what they had learned and accomplished. I complimented them for their commitment and foresight, and noted that "There's sure to be extra stress ahead with the baby coming." We discussed how to apply what they had achieved as a couple to the challenges of becoming new parents while also raising Regina's daughter:

> "Would it be OK if I ask you both a hard question?"
> "Sure—go for it."
> "I'm glad that you're doing so well and that you're working as partners, but imagine a time in a few months, after the baby's born, and you're both tired and stressed and your other daughter is being a difficult teenager. How are you going to remember then to work as a team?"
> "I'm sure that will happen."
> "Yeah."
> "So, how are you going to deal with it? It could be easy to get back into fighting a lot."
> "We'll have to remember why we're together."
> "How will you do that?"
> "We know we'll have difficulties, but we also know that we can solve our problems."
> "Now when we start to have an argument, we stop and remember that we're 'Frank *and* Regina,' and that helps us not get into 'Me *versus* You.' And sometimes we talk about what we've talked about in here, how to use what you called 'Solution Talk,' how we used to fight and how we know how to treat each other respectfully and how to take a time out if we need it and how to listen to each other, and stuff like that.

Near the end of the session I asked if they thought we should make another appointment. "Not now, but we'll be sure to call if we need one."[11] I wished them well and asked if it would be OK for me to write up their story and put it in a book chapter. "Sure," they said, "but only if you promise to tell people that we did most of the work, not you."

CODA

> *When the night has been too lonely and the road has been too long*
> *And you think that love is only for the lucky and the strong*
> *Just remember in the winter far beneath the bitter snows*
> *Lies the seed that with the sun's love, in the spring, becomes the rose.*
> —Amanda McBroom (1979, from "The Rose")

Solution-focused therapy is a constructivist, collaborative, competency-based, future-oriented approach. The basic premise is deceptively simple: *Increase what works; decrease what doesn't work.* What are the "exceptions" to the problem? What is the patient doing differently at those times when he/she/they are not anxious or depressed or quarrelling? What has worked before? What strengths can the patient apply? What would be a useful solution? How to construct it?

Behind these apparently simple questions is a profound paradigmatic shift: competencies, not dysfunctions, are the focus; the quest is to access latent capacities, not latent conflicts. The orientation is toward the future, with the guiding belief that with skillful facilitation, people usually have within themselves the resources necessary to achieve their goals. Without obviating the idea of a physical universe, solution-focused therapy operates from the radical assumption that clients' experience of psychological problems is part and parcel of their language-based social construction of reality. As I heard my haiku muse whisper (Hoyt, 2000a, p. 47):

> Focusing language
> On solutions, not problems
> Miracles happen.

Therapeutic intervention, therefore, is construed as a process of assisting clients to play better "language games." While new information and relationship skills training may be provided—if they support the clients' worldview and movement toward their desired goals—solution-focused therapists primarily

---

11. As Cummings and Sayama (1995) have written, "brief, intermittent psychotherapy throughout the life cycle" is often precipitated by developmental challenges.

endeavor to help clients envision and realize solutions by assiduously calling attention to clients' strengths, resources, past successes, and ways of looking.

As therapists we are actively involved—whether we realize it or not—in helping clients construe a different way of looking at themselves, their partners, their situations, and their interactions. How we look influences what we see, and what we see influences what we do—and around and around the process goes, recursively. Even if one is unaware of it, one cannot *not* have an epistemology (Bateson, 1972, 1979). We choose what we use:

> Dear Reader,
> Suppose tonight, while you're sleeping, a miracle happens! You're asleep, of course, and you don't immediately know it has happened. But tomorrow, while seeing couples in your office, you begin to notice some things about your clients you haven't noticed or thought much about before. You can still see all the things that your training has allowed you to see, but as you look you begin to see some previously overlooked qualities: perhaps a love or a hope or a dream that somehow manages to survive, maybe some almost forgotten skill or ability, possibly a quirky interest or sense of humor, something. What might you see? What does the couple see that you don't? What does the couple think would help? What might happen if that could be used therapeutically? What difference might it make?

7

The Squeaky Wheel: Don't Let Managed Care Shortchange Your Clients

The Family Therapy Networker *(January/February 2001) asked me to respond to the question, "I'm on several managed care panels. Even though my orientation is toward brief, solution-oriented therapy, they are reluctant to authorize couples therapy. What do you suggest?" Here's what I said:*

Reviewers often tell therapists that couples therapy is "not covered"—that while perhaps helpful, it is generally mere "enrichment" (god forbid!) or simply "marriage counseling for problems in living," rather than a legitimate and necessary treatment for a specifically diagnosed disorder. Even given the bottom-line mentality of managed-care companies, such limits on coverage are short-sighted. A failure to resolve couples conflict often leads to more suffering, increased symptoms, and more expensive one-on-one therapy. Nevertheless, such short-sightedness is a fact of life for therapists today dealing with most managed-care companies. So it is important to recognize the steps to take that will increase the likelihood that conjoint therapy will be approved when you determine a couple needs it.

First of all, in all dealings with managed-care reviewers, it is crucial to understand their needs and expectations. *¿Habla usted managed care?* When you ask for authorization of couples therapy, phrase your rationale in terms they can understand, such as "brief," "cost-effective," "clear goals," "symptom reduction," "behavioral homework" and, of course, "time limited." For instance, the reviewers at one managed-care company I dealt with were reluctant at first to authorize marital therapy in one case, until I explained that the identified patient's depression and suicidal ideation were aggravated by on-going marital conflict and that the proposed time-limited, conjoint sessions would focus specifically on reducing this conflict via improved communication and assertiveness skills training. I added that we would know within 4 sessions if this approach proved helpful.

Since managed-care companies have a wide range of policies regarding working with couples, you should also check a client's "benefits" carefully. Most companies consider "couples counseling" as some form of psychoeducational instruction and do not cover it, while they view "short-term marital therapy" as a more specific treatment that they may cover. Some companies allow brief conjoint therapy, usually 4-8 sessions, if there is an identified patient. Sometimes a "Couples Communication Class," which actually can be very helpful for some couples, is covered and may even be a prerequisite to couples therapy.

Generally, to be authorized for treatment, a problem must meet the criterion of "medical (or clinical) necessity," which is usually defined as involving a combination of: likelihood of improvement with treatment, the need for treatment to avoid deterioration, and some cutoff score for the level of dysfunction. To make a case for couples therapy, you should document any symptoms (such as depression, suicidal ideation, or debilitating anxiety) that result from the couple's conflict and that are likely to improve with focused conjoint treatment. It is not enough to say simply that "the patient's problems are negatively impacting the marriage" or even that "the marriage is negatively impacting the patient's problems." While therapists know that the two are inextricably connected, the managed care reviewer needs to know what you specifically propose to do to ameliorate the situation. For instance, my saying "Jeff's suicide threats occur after he and his partner fight" got a "Too bad" response from a reviewer; but adding, "I think we can avoid more hospitalizations if we teach them conflict resolution skills," got couples therapy authorized.

One of the most difficult issues therapists must face in dealing with managed care is the degree to which we decide to adhere to the *DSM* system in order to obtain reimbursement for our clients. Under many policies, it is possible to get treatment covered if a *DSM* diagnosis is given to one partner while the other partner is included to "assist in treatment." Many therapists are reluctant, however, to assign diagnoses because they frown on the pathologizing effects of such labeling and dislike taking an "Expert" stance with their clients. But if one member of the couple qualifies for the *DSM* diagnosis of "Adjustment Disorder" or another disorder likely to benefit from conjoint therapy, this is a legitimate way to help clients obtain reimbursement. Clients may be glad if you can help them get their therapy paid for, but in such instances it will be important that the interactional nature of their problems be clearly established ("Her toes may be hurting more, but this is a two-person dance") and that conjoint treatment not be portrayed as some way to "fix" one person (lest the 'other' person say to the I.P., "See, dear, I'm only here because you have a problem"), or to (wink, wink) defraud the insurance company.

Managed-care companies often automatically decline couples therapy, banking perhaps on the fact that many providers will go away quietly. The "hassle factor" can be formidable, but I have found that being the squeaky wheel often gets results. If you can make a strong argument for treatment under the terms of the client's insurance, file an appeal of denied coverage in writing immediately. Here you should document the medical/clinical necessity for treatment thoroughly, explain symptoms clearly, estimate the length of treatment and its likely benefits, and make clear any risks (clinical, medical, and legal) if treatment is withheld. As reported recently in the *Networker* (Around the Network, November/December 2000; also see www.PsychotherapistsGuild.com), establishing a clear psychiatric diagnosis and medical necessity puts the company in the position of having to reduce the diagnosis ("downcode") to deny treatment, which cannot legitimately be done by a claims clerk. Spell out the fact that your clinical assessment is based on a face-to-face evaluation and that any proposed modification in your carefully considered treatment plan should also be based on a thorough, in-person assessment by a qualified mental-health professional. It is often helpful to develop a relationship with a particular reviewer (or two), so they get to know your skillfulness and don't need to question your recommendations. Let them know when cases go well, and especially when they finish early, to help establish your reputation as a preferred provider.

Even if couples therapy is not a covered benefit, I have heard of instances when a benefits or human resources department requested and got an exception for conjoint treatment for a good employee who was having a serious problem in order to help get the person back to work. Recent parity legislation (mandating equal levels of treatment for serious mental and physical conditions) may also help force some companies to recognize the cost effectiveness of including family members when treating problems such as depression, psychosis, and eating disorders.

Managed-care—which can be defined as various arrangements to regulate the costs, site, and utilization of services—now cover more than 160 million people in the United States. As long as case reviewers have a say in how we do therapy, we must, within ethical limits, be persistent and creative to get couples treatment approved. At the same time, we need to continue strongly advocating, as individuals and through our various professional associations, for the appropriate quality and quantity of mental health coverage.

To learn more about the managed-care world's perspective and what they are doing to improve review processes, visit the websites of the National Committee for Quality Assurance (www.NCQA.org) and the Utilization Review Accreditation Committee (www.URAC.org).

8

Early HMO Chart Note

(crisis log)

Jesus of Nazareth

Patient is 33-year-old Jewish male c/o anxiety and "holiday blues." Unemployed (has worked as carpenter), has delusional ideas about his birth ("My mother was a virgin") and magical thinking ("I've walked on water and raised the dead," etc.). Patient says he has "followers." Worries about possible attack, "especially around Passover." Unmarried, no steady partner, some contact with prostitutes and misfits. Denies ETOH/drug use. Now spends time wandering, attempting to speak to crowds. Note: Hispanic name, but claims to be Israeli.

DSM-IV Impressions:

I. delusional disorder, paranoid type; "holiday blues" (anniversary reaction? seasonal affective disorder?); r/o manic psychosis ("I can feed thousands with 5 loaves and 2 fishes")

II. personality disorder NOS (with prominent narcissistic features—refers to self as "Son of God," "The Christ," and "The Messiah")

III. denies medical problems but says he has laid hands on lepers and persons with fevers

IV. homeless, unemployed, conflicts with authorities

V. global assessment of functioning: unknown.

Treatment Plan:

1. Not commitable—no imminent danger to self/other
2. Patient refused meds or voluntary hospitalization
3. Patient offered crisis group—declined when told he can't preach there
4. Recheck patient's insurance—claims to have "unlimited benefits"

(see Gergen, 1994; Haley, 1969; Schweitzer, 1948; Tomm, 1990)

9

The Pros and Cons of Postmodernism in Psychotherapy: Stepping Back from the Abyss (with Phillip Ziegler)

"*It all depends on what the meaning of the word 'is' is.*"
—Bill Clinton[1]

Turning and turning in the widening gyre
The falcon cannot hear the falconer;
Things fall apart; the centre cannot hold;
Mere anarchy is loosed upon the world [....]
—William Butler Yeats (1921/1989, p. 187)

Over the past two decades, the term *postmodernism* has found its way into the vocabularies of a number of psychotherapy theoreticians and clinicians. Postmodernism has been portrayed as proffering a new paradigm, a new epistemology, which ostensibly provides a philosophical foundation for radically different and promising ways of thinking about and practicing psychotherapy. The term is most commonly used by family and brief therapists from three major schools—solution-focused, narrative, and collaborative language therapies. While

---

1. These parsing and prevaricating remarks were made during Clinton's 1998 grand jury testimony in response to the question of whether he had been in a certain place at a certain time with Monica Lewinsky.

not all of their developers embrace the label "postmodern," proponents of these schools frequently use the term in reference to their philosophical and metatheoretical assumptions.

We have become increasingly uncomfortable with the way in which some of our constructionist colleagues have rallied behind the banner of postmodernism—some, we think, without fully understanding its principal assumptions. We begin this chapter by identifying some of the basic principles of postmodernism; next we briefly describe the rise and fall of its influence as a general philosophy in contemporary intellectual discourse. We then identify and untangle some of the terms and concepts that have been too loosely lumped together under the rubric of postmodernism. Then, moving on to the heart of our concern, we examine the ostensible appeal of postmodernism in the psychotherapy field and point to some of the "slippery slope" problems and perils entailed by this perhaps well-intended but muddling and potentially destructive trend. We also discuss some ways that the related but distinct traditions of constructivism, poststructuralism, and social constructionism can provide a useful epistemological underpinning for the practice of collaborative psychotherapy.[2] We present our belief that what is more important than the modern/postmodern distinction is the distinction between objectivist and collaborative forms of therapy. We further propose that constructionist thought and collaborative clinical practices will appeal to a wider professional audience when their advocates present and emphasize existing empirical evidence about the common factors of effective therapy. These are emphasized in collaborative, constructionist therapies because these approaches focus on custom-tailoring treatment to the particular client and the particular problems being presented. Finally, we conclude with a summary of several of the major challenges that postmodernism raises for the practice of contemporary psychotherapy.

PO-MO—WHAT'S IN A NAME?

Postmodernism refers to a loosely-defined school of philosophy that posits that all knowledge is relativistic and that all "truth" is constructed. Neimeyer and Mahoney (1995, p. 407) provide the following description:

---

2. It may be noted that we are neither literary critics nor philosophers of science; but rather, we are both active clinicians (M.F.H., a psychologist; P.Z., a licensed marriage and family therapist) familiar with the theories and practices that often go under the rubrics of *collaborative, social constructionist, constructivist, solution-focused and solution-oriented*, and *brief therapy*. We appreciate the input of Tobey Hiller in the preparation of this chapter, as well as the encouragement of Nick Cummings.

Postmodern. That perspective in philosophy or worldview that acknowledges the complexity, relativity, and intersubjectivity of all known experience. Postmodernism accepts the lack of any ultimate foundation for the multiplicity of human belief systems and calls into question the idea of an essentialized self, in contrast to the modernist belief in a knowable world and in self-contained individualities having specifiable characteristics. Postmodernists also advocate that science is essentially an interpretive, rather than computational, enterprise, and they judge the adequacy of a position in part by whether it yields a useful critique of unquestioned dominant practices and ideologies.

Postmodernists claim, with some legitimacy, that the core assumptions of modernism include the belief that there are universal truths and that, through science and over time, those truths continue to be revealed. Whereas Church dogma provided Universal Truth in the Medieval Age, since the Age of Enlightenment, reason and the scientific method became the means for uncovering and understanding the nature of reality (and the reality of nature). Postmodernism, in its broadest sense, is a reaction against Enlightenment ideas such as the progress of humankind, the existence and discoverability of universal truth, and a reliance on science as the one legitimate method for clarifying and defining what is real and what is not. At its most extreme, postmodernism views science as just one way of viewing and making meaning of things that is no more or less valid than any other. As Bill Matthews (2002, p. 149) has described it:

> In its essence, postmodernism and its related concepts of constructivism (radical and social), poststructuralism, and deconstructivism can be characterized by a nonbelief in (1) the objective world and (2) meta-narrative explanations (e.g., the universal theories/explanations generated by science). Kvale (1992) states that in postmodern thought there is no foundation for a universal and objective *reality*. For the postmodernist, there is no pure, uninterpreted datum; all facts embody theory. Thus, in the absence of objectivity, reality is purely a function of social and, by definition, linguistic construction....Kvale (1992) further states that "there exists no standard method for measuring and comparing knowledge within different language games and paradigms; they are incommensurable" (p. 35). He further states that "a postmodern world is characterized by a continual change of perspectives, with no underlying common frame of reference, but rather a manifold of changing horizons. *Language does not copy reality.* Rather, language constitutes reality, each language constructing specific aspects of reality in its own way. The focus is on the linguistic and social construction of reality, on interpretation and negotiation of the meaning of the lived world" (p. 35, italics added)

The modernist idea that there are different legitimate ways of looking at a situation is common currency in a contemporary, pluralistic society. Postmodernism, however, asserts something else: that there is no way to know what the situation really is (or even, in some versions, that there is *a* situation). Matthews (2002, p. 147) is forthright in his assessment of these developments:

> [R]adical social constructivism and its equivalencies of cultural constructivism, deconstructivism, feminist discourse, poststructuralism, postmodernism and the like have become, in my opinion, a serious blight on the American intellectual landscape.

Even the term *postmodern* is somewhat curious and oxymoronic: if *modern* means contemporary or now, how can something be postmodern? How and why did postmodernism develop? Let's take a tour, and then see what sense we can make of its challenge in psychotherapy.

THE RISE AND FALL OF POSTMODERNISM

The last third of the last century was marked by a rapid technological shift toward information, not production; toward postindustrial consumerism; toward social movements; and toward globalization and the breaking down of boundaries between cultures (Lyon, 1994), all of which resulted in the sense that "reality ain't what it used to be" (W.T. Anderson, 1990). At the same time, as the 20th century neared conclusion, it was hard to look back on the last 100 years without noticing both the tremendous technological and scientific advances and the horrendous destructive forces and events that marked the period. It was not unreasonable to question whether humanity was progressing toward a brighter future or heading toward a dramatic end.

Within this context, a group of predominantly French theoreticians—including Jean-Francois Lyotard, Jacques Derrida, Michel Foucault, and Jean Baudrillard, among others—developed philosophical positions which they applied to cultural studies such as aesthetic theory and literary criticism as well as to sociopolitical analysis.[3] Against the backdrop of recent European (and world) history, there was a growing distrust of ideologies. They saw the Age of Enlightenment, modernity, and the hegemony of science, with their promises of progressively revealed Ultimate Truth, to have failed.[4]

Thus, in his signal book, *The Postmodern Condition: A Report on Knowledge*, Lyotard (1984, p. xxiv) wrote:

> Simplifying to the extreme, I define *postmodernism* as incredulity toward metanarratives.

and (pp. 25-26):

> [S]cientific knowledge requires that one language game, denotation, be retained and all others be excluded....Drawing a parallel between science and non-scientific (narrative) knowledge helps us understand, or at least sense, that the former's existence is no more—and no less—necessary than the latter's. Both are composed of sets of statements; the statements are "moves" made by the players within the framework of generally applicable rules....It is therefore impossible to judge the existence or validity of narrative knowledge on the basis of scientific knowledge or vice versa: the relevant criteria are different.

Derrida rose to prominence with a famous 1966 lecture in which he developed and used the idea of *differance* to challenge the underlying assumptions of Western philosophy. Publishing three groundbreaking books in 1967, he posited that "There is nothing outside the text" and developed the practice of *deconstruction* (which emphasizes *perspectivism* by focusing on exposing the assumptions underlying any given position) and explored (e.g., in *Of Grammatology*, 1967/1976; and *Writing and Difference*, 1967/1978) the way that knowledge is an ultimately interpersonal achievement, having no essential meaning except as constituted by the reading and understanding of the Other.[5] As Butler (2002, p. 16)

---

3. Additional important figures in the development of postmodernism include linguistic philosophers Mikhail Bahktin, L.S. Vygotsky, Ludwig Wittgenstein and Richard Rorty, plus others. Brockelman (2001) places postmodernism's origins in the collage practices of Piccaso and Braque; others see roots in Nietzsche and Hegel and Kant (see M.C. Taylor, 1986). For introductions to the history of postmodernism, see W.T. Anderson (1990), Appinnanesi & Garratt (1995), Butler (2002), Fillingham (1993), Kvale (1992), Lyon (1994), Palmer (1999), Powell (1997), and Rosenau (1992), plus the website www.pmth.com [Postmodern Therapies News].
4. As Pirsig (1974, p. 119) noted, it is ironic that science has contributed to this skepticism: "The purpose of scientific method is to select a single truth from among many hypothetical truths. That, more than anything else, is what science is all about. But historically science has done exactly the opposite. Through multiplication upon multiplication of facts, information, theories and hypotheses, it is science itself that is leading mankind from single absolute truths to multiple, indeterminate, relative ones. The major producer of the social chaos, the indeterminancy of thought and values that rational knowledge is supposed to eliminate, it none other than science itself."

explained, "Truth itself is always relative to the differing standpoints and predisposing intellectual frameworks of the judging subject." As Gergen (1999, p. 20) has noted, however,

> Such critique demonstrates the meaningless character of rational argumentation, but rests its case on exactly such argumentation. As Derrida was fully aware, his own arguments should also be placed "under erasure" (as he called it); they cannot sustain themselves. Descartes was moved to doubt his senses, all authority, all common opinion, but in the end could not doubt the fact of doubt. This left him with a center, a place to stand and to build. In the current debates we find that even doubt must be doubted. There is no center that can hold.

In addition to claiming that there is no underlying, universal reality, postmodernists—most notably Michael Foucault (1980; see Fillingham, 1993), and others—have been especially alert to dominant political and social forces that establish and promote certain reality-defining discourses and devalue and marginalize others. "History is written by the winners," as the saying goes, and certain voices are given (or more accurately, take) privilege and recognition—a situation that can result in imposition, "psychological colonization," and the denial of the experiences ("realities") of the disfavored. Such "reality battles" and the empowerment of the dispossessed are a hallmark of those therapeutic approaches usually placed under the postmodern rubric, especially narrative therapy (White & Epston, 1990; Freedman & Combs, 1996; also see Fish, 1993).

Baudrillard, a post-Marxist especially interested in popular culture, theorized about "hyperreality," "hyper-aesthetics," "simulacra" (a *simulacrum* is "a copy

---

5. Michael White (1993, pp. 34-36) elaborates some of the implications of *deconstruction* for narrative therapy: "According to my rather loose definition, deconstruction has to do with procedures that subvert taken-for-granted realities and practices: those so-called 'truths' that are split off from the conditions and the context of their production; those disembodied ways of speaking that hide their biases and prejudices; and those familiar practices of self and of relationship that are subjugating of persons' lives....Deconstruction is premised on what is generally referred to as a 'critical constructivist' or, as I would prefer, a 'constitutionalist' perspective on the world. From this perspective, it is proposed that person's lives are shaped by the meaning that they ascribe to their experience, by their situation in social structures, and by the language practices and cultural practices of self and of relationship that these lives are recruited into....This constructionalist perspective is at variance with the dominant structuralist (behavior reflects the structure of the mind) and functionalist (behavior serves a purpose for the system) perspectives of the world of psychotherapy."

without an original") and the postmodern replacement of depth with surface. In his book *Simulacra and Simulation*, he wrote (1981/1994, p. 6):

> Such would be the successive phases of the image:
> it is the reflection of a profound reality;
> it masks and denatures a profound reality;
> it masks the *absence* of a profound reality;
> it has no relationship to any reality whatsoever; it is its own pure simulacrum.

and, in the same treatise (1981/1994, pp. 160-161):

> I am a nihilist.
> I observe, I accept, I assume the immense process of the destruction of appearances (and of the seduction of appearances) in the service of meaning (representation, history, criticism, etc.) that is the fundamental fact of the nineteenth century. The true revolution of the nineteenth century, of modernity, is the radical destruction of appearances, the disenchantment of the world and its abandonment to the violence of interpretation and of history.
> I observe, I accept, I assume, I analyze the second revolution, that of the twentieth century, that of postmodernity, which is the immense process of the destruction of meaning, equal to the earlier destruction of appearances. He who strikes with meaning is killed by meaning.
> The dialectic stage, the critical stage is empty. There is no more stage. There is no therapy of meaning or therapy through meaning: therapy itself is part of the generalized process of indifferentiation.

In his perhaps most provocative book, *Seductions*, Baudrillard (1979/1990, pp. 6-7) wrote: "Freud was right: there is but one sexuality, one libido—and it is masculine....[The] strength of the feminine is that of seduction"; and then went on to describe a series of "Superficial Abysses" involving seduction via mirrors, images, effigies, displays, and so on.

In summary, the basic themes of postmodernism are (1) a strong stand against all metanarratives, including the so-called "narrative of science" and its efforts to develop methods for uncovering truth; (2) the belief that all knowledge is based in language, context, and perspective; and thus, (3) the rejection of the idea of a separate and individual self. In its rejection of so much, postmodernism seemed to offer the promise of a kind of liberation, a recognition of plurality and a freeing from (or at least an exposing of) the "dominating discourses" of "power/knowledge" (Foucault, 1980; see Holzman & Morss, 2000; Sarlo, 2001).

It is this invitation to look freshly at things, to challenge the dominant discourse of the culture and to make room for hitherto disenfranchised voices, we believe, that has attracted many intellectuals—including some of those who have been developing ideas and practices in the field of psychotherapy. In their article, "Welcome to the Postmodern World," Maureen O'Hara and Walter Truett Anderson (1991, p. 20) stated the challenge and possibilities:

> [W]e have moved into a new world, one created by the cumulative effect of pluralism, democracy, religious freedom, consumerism, mobility and increasing access to news and entertainment. This is the world described as "postmodern" to denote its difference from the modern world most of us were born into....We are all being forced to see that there are many beliefs, multiple realities, an exhilarating but daunting profusion of worldviews to suit every taste. We can choose among these, but we cannot choose not to make choices.

Kenneth Gergen (who in 1985 heralded social constructionism in psychology), also welcomed these postmodern developments in his book *The Saturated Self: Dilemmas of Identity in Contemporary Life* (1991, p. 49):

> It is my central thesis that....[increasing immersion in the social world] is propelling us toward a new self-consciousness: the postmodern.... What I call the technologies of social saturation are central to the contemporary erasure of individual self....There is a population of the self, reflecting the infusion of partial identities through social saturation. And there is the onset of a multiphrenic condition, in which one begins to experience the vertigo of unlimited multiplicity. Both the populating of the self and the multiphrenic condition are significant preludes to post-modern consciousness.

And, in *An Invitation to Social Construction* (Gergen, 1999, p. 19), he championed their postmodern advancement:

> While creating enormous controversy and resistance, these developments also form the beginning of a brave new dialogue, dangerous yes, but one both exciting and profound in consequence. The dialogue is variously called post-foundational, post-Enlightenment, post-empiricist, post-structural, and *postmodern*.

However, while some were relishing the possibilities of a more open and inclusive intellectual paradigm, others found the themes of postmodernism disorienting and disturbing, a shift toward chaos and *fin de millenium* hopelessness. Critics within the intellectual world expressed their discontent with postmodernism from a variety of perspectives. Norris (1993; also see Brockelman, 2001), for example, questioned postmodernists' reading of Kant. Kellner (1994) referred to the "schizophrenic" quality of postmodernism; Kroker et al. (1988, Kroker, 1989) cited "panic" as the key psychological mood of postmodern culture; M.B. Smith (1994) described it as "vertiginous"; and Jameson (1998) referred to its "commodity fetishism." Kellner (1994, p. 12) described an ultimate melancholy: "Baudrillard's nihilism is without joy, without energy, without hope for a better future." Macey (2000, p. 307) noted that Jurgen Habermas (1985) "argues that postmodernism is in fact an anti-modernism that betrays the promise of modernity by retreating into a wildly eclectic irrationalism." The humanistic psychologist Sigmund Koch (1992, p. 965; quoted by M.B. Smith, 2001, p. 442) wryly noted, "I think it is more important to be deeply conversant with a few great texts than to proclaim that human beings can be read as texts. Or that they *are* texts."

Postmodernism contends that everything is relativistic, that there are no universal truths, that all is context and perspective. Discussing the use of the term *deconstruction*, the sociologists Fuchs and Ward (1994, p. 483) pointed out that it is a two-edged sword: "The political implications of deconstruction are uncertain and controversial. There are those who think deconstruction is an ally of democratic social change, while others see deconstruction as part of a neoconservative reaction against the Enlightenment." Ian Parker (2000, pp. 36-37; also see Norris, 1992) raised the danger of extreme relativism and gave us a good example of just how far one postmodernist has gone:

> We can see how extremely unlikely and pernicious the postmodern story is if we look at how it corrodes realist accounts outside psychology....Postmodern relativism provokes irrational conspiratorial views of the world, mystifies our understanding of state power, and undermines historical narrative....[A] serious example is Baudrillard's claim that the Gulf War in Iraq did not *really* happen. Such a claim plays a profoundly ideological role. Postmodern celebration of irrationality and mystification also has disastrous consequences for the past and the present, and historical revisionists are all too ready to jump on the postmodern bandwagon to erase the past.

Although some feminists (see Nicholson, 1990) might welcome postmodernism because of its emphasis on social dynamics, others see it as just another form of power-tripping masculine neurosis masquerading as philosophy. For example, in her book, *Nothing Mat(t)ers: A Feminist Critique of Postmodernism*, Somer Brodribb (1992, pp. 19-20) wrote:

> Postmodernism is an addition to the masculinist repertoire of psychotic mind/body splitting and the peculiar arrangement of reality as Idea. [p. xvi]

and

> It is my contention that postmodernism is a masculine ideology based on a notion of consciousness as hostile, and an epistemology of negation which is one of separation, discontinuity and dismemberment. Narcissistic and romantic.... [t]hey are engaged in a process of disengagement....Postmodernism is the attempted masculine ir/rationalization of feminism. [pp. 19-20]

Brodribb (1992, p. 20) went on to recommend a "listening cure" and suggested individuals suffering from this "neurotic symptom" can be identified as exhibiting at least three of the following delusions:

1. Does not know how to listen. Cannot deal with narrative structure.

2. Is bored, fascinated and melancholic.

3. Thinks his word is God. Or at least, confuses his penis with a deity.

4. Is narcissistic, constantly gazing into mirrors, surfaces, looking glasses. Even when not looking directly into a mirror, sees his reflection everywhere.

5. Cannot make a commitment. Fears the political engagement of others.

6. Despises matter but appropriates its form in a contrary and fetishistic way.

7. Thinks any critique of sexism is easy, superficial, unfair, and cheap.

8. Worst feeling: connection to and responsibility for another.

9. Favorite feeling: exterior control and interior flux.

10. Favorite acts: repetition, sacrifice.

11. Favorite authors: de Sade, Nietzche.

In their book, *Fashionable Nonsense: Postmodern Intellectuals' Abuse of Science*, Alan Sokal and Jean Bricmont (1998, pp. 274-275; also see Gross & Levitt, 1994) debunked the pretensions of those who would attempt to gain authority by wrapping themselves in the mantle of science while, at the same time, denying the very existence of an observer-independent reality:

> Epistemological agnosticism simply won't suffice, at least not for people who aspire to make social change. Deny that non-context-dependent assumptions can be true, and you don't just throw out quantum mechanics and molecular biology: you also throw out the Nazi gas chambers, the American enslavement of Africans, and the fact that today in New York it's raining....[F]acts do matter, and some facts (like the first two cited here) matter a great deal.

In his concise book, *Postmodernity*, David Lyon (1994, p. 55) also discussed the postmodern vision and "the shape(lessness) of things to come":

> Not only are old institutions and authority centers—religion, royalty, tradition—criticized and contested. Even the metanarratives of modernity turn out to have limited shelf-life. Not only do truth and justice appear rather questionable concepts; but also the reduction of everything to exchange values seems to iron out all 'lasting' values. Will the postmodern condition leave us in a permanent flux of relativity, where all is subject only to the arbitrary machinations of the marketplace? [And, a few pages later....] Values and beliefs lose any sense of coherence, let alone continuity, in the world of consumer choice, multiple media and globalized (post)modernity....The vertigo of relativity, the abyss of uncertainty, are its results. But this also is a consequence of a world where choice reigns supreme; hesitation, anxiety and doubt seem to be the price paid for that sense of choice. The shift from fate to choice, or from providence to progress, that was supposed to be so liberating, appears to have a darker side, which veils the further spiral into nihilism. [pp. 61-62]

Over time, many in the worlds of philosophy and cultural studies have become disillusioned with the "narcissism and nihilism" (Wilbur, 1998) of postmodern excesses. In her book, *Nothing Remains the Same: Rereading and Remembering*, Wendy Lesser (2002, pp. 13-14) remarked:

> And postmodernism always entails a certain level of strain—an embarrassed self-consciousness, an effort to blatantly entertain or just as blatantly alienate, a nostalgic longing for the real even as the patently fake is seen as the only acceptable result of an artistic undertaking.

A recent newspaper article by a humanities and sciences professor at an art college, appearing under the banner "The 'New Realism' Takes Over," heralded the shift (which Held, 1995, would call "Back to Reality"):

> We have, it turns out, managed to survive the postmodern era (1960-2000), an era in which, as such eminent French theoreticians as Jean Baudrillard argued, images replaced reality and the media replaced the world, in which the whole Earth became Disney World and even we ourselves became fabrications. The great pop stars of the postmodern era were born in 1958: Madonna, Michael Jackson, and Prince. They were shape-shifters, people who actually tried to have no self outside a series of video images. They made perfect pop music: music largely without guts or roots but at its best providing a perfectly crafted, utterly mediated pleasure....Folks like Bill Clinton and Al Gore were postmodern politicians, concerned almost exclusively with polling and image making, and living in a realm well beyond quaint notions like authenticity or belief.
>
> "The Matrix" was an interesting moment in the genesis of the new reality. The attraction of the movie was largely in the glamour of its virtual reality, in which many of the limitations of our physical bodies could be suspended. One could dodge bullets or spin through the air like a supernatural Baryshnikov. Nevertheless, the movie was a New Realist manifesto, in which rebels waged a guerilla war on behalf of reality. The reality they were fighting for was gritty and dangerous compared to the state's artificial world. But it was precious simply because it was real. And "The Matrix" was, like almost all science fiction, a parable of the present....
>
> [The New Realists] embody our exhaustion with the virtual, our disillusionment with illusion, our yearning toward reality, and the perverse, stupid, beautiful persistence of our humanity. [Sartwell, 2002, p. D4]

In their introduction to *After Postmodernism: An Introduction to Critical Realism*, editors Jose Lopez and Garry Potter (2001, pp. 3-4) wrote:

> It is the best of times. It is the worst of times. It is a time for the celebration of diversity. It is a time of fear of the Other who is different. It is a time of technological marvel and a time of feat and distrust of science. It is a time of unprecedented affluence and a time of the direst poverty. It is a time of nostalgia for the old and enthusiasm for the new. It is a time of optimism and hope for humanity's possibilities of freedom and happiness and yet grim pessimism and fears about the future.
>
> It is the year two thousand, [a time] to pause and attempt to reassess the role of reason, philosophy and the sciences. In so doing, it is impossible to avoid considering postmodernism. First, because it was one of, if not *the* most significant of the intellectual currents which swept the academic world in the

last third of the twentieth century. Secondly, because it was an intellectual current which seriously bruised the self-confidence to which reason, objectivity and knowledge had become accustomed. It was most influential in the social sciences and humanities, though it had plenty to say about the natural sciences as well. Most significantly as far as the latter were concerned, postmodernism presented the most radical challenge to its epistemological foundations since the Enlightenment. One could say uncharitably that unfortunately it presented an ultimately intellectually incoherent challenge to those foundations. On the other hand, the claim could also be justified that it served to problematize the very notion of philosophical 'foundations' and to critically uncover a host of very real problems concerning humanity's relationship to knowledge, rationality, science and 'modernity.' The claim could be made that, for all its contradictions, postmodernism served to capture the spirit of the contemporary age. At any rate, postmodernism managed to escape the confines of the academic world and terms such as 'postmodernity' and 'deconstruction' have passed into journalism and popular discourse.

Postmodernism not only affected each of the different disciplines to quite varying degrees but it made its impact upon them at earlier and later times. Some, perhaps, are only now beginning to come to terms with it. That said, however, the single most significant fact about postmodernism in the year two thousand is this: it is in a state of decline! It lingers on, its influence for good or ill continues, but postmodernism has 'gone out of fashion.'

We want now to turn our attention to how postmodernism found its way into the field of psychotherapy and how postmodernism has been confounded with other philosophical traditions; this will serve as a prelude to considering the pros and cons of these developments.

THE INFILTRATION OF POSTMODERNISM INTO PSYCHOTHERAPY

> [N]arrative therapists assume that knowledge is socially constructed and that there are many valid, diverse ways of understanding ourselves and others. These ideas are seen as culturally informed and situated in ever-changing local contexts and relationships. Professional, social science ideas about human behavior are viewed as potentially useful ways (among many others) of thinking about clients' concerns, rather than as objective, empirically verified truths. Social constructionism, with its emphasis on partial, perspectival knowing, shifts conventional therapy's emphasis on objectivity and therapeutic certainty to an emphasis on intersubjectivity and therapeutic curiosity. [Craig Smith, 1999, p. 3]

Postmodernism entered the world of psychotherapy through a related but distinct and much older development in the philosophy of knowledge called *constructivism*. The importance of meaning making in human affairs has long been recognized. In the East, Buddhism and various meditation practices have emphasized the role of mind. In the West, this awareness can be traced through ancient Greece and Rome (Epictetus, Seneca, Marcus Aurelius); through Rene Descartes, Immanuel Kant, and Giambattista Vico; through the Enlightenment and even in all but the most objectivist elements of the world of science and its reliance on the scientific method. Indeed, appreciating the integral role of perception and mentation, the recognition that the experience of reality is mediated by subjective processes, is an honorable tradition that is the very stuff of psychology. As Carlos Sluzki (1998, pp. 80-81) has noted: "Constructivism is a way of *talking about* therapy, rather than of *doing it*. Being a theory of knowledge rather than a set of techniques, constructivism offers us not a particular way of helping clients, but a way of understanding how we use our clinical tools and the interplay between practitioners' beliefs and their practice." Along with its cousin, *social constructionism* (more about that later), constructivism is central to many schools of psychotherapy, including personal construct theory (Kelly, 1955) and cognitive-behavioral therapy (Meichenbaum, in Hoyt, 1996c; Ellis, 1998), as well as the various forms of therapy—influenced by Gregory Bateson's (1972) "ecology of mind" and Milton Erickson's (Combs & Freedman, 1994; Lankton & Lankton, 1998) "emergent epistemologies"—that are usually identified as "postmodern": solution-focused (de Shazer, 1988, 1991a), narrative (White & Epston, 1990), collaborative language systems (H. Anderson, 1997), and some aspects of strategic interactional intervention (Watzlawick et al., 1974).

In his paper, "Postmodern Thinking in a Clinical Practice," William Lax (1992, pp. 69-70) elaborated some of the implications,

> Writing on postmodernism frequently focus on ideas regarding text and narrative, with attention to the importance of dialogic/multiple perspectives, self-disclosure, lateral versus hierarchical configurations, and attention to process rather than goals. In addition, such writing is often characterized by the following emphases: the self is conceived not as a reified entity, but as a narrative; text is not something to be interpreted, but, is an evolving process; the individual is considered within a context of social meaning rather than as an intrapsychic entity; and scientific knowledge or what would be considered undeniable 'facts' about the world yields to narrative knowledge with emphasis placed more upon communal beliefs about how the world works....
>
> This transition incorporates several significant changes. Universal truths or structures give way to a multiverse or plurality of ideas about the world....The

> view of families as homeostatic systems yield to one of social systems being generative and states of disequilibrium as being productive and normal....Families are conceptualized as social systems composed of meaning-generating, problem-organizing systems (rather than systems in which symptoms serve functions) with problems existing in and mediated through language....Additionally, hierarchical, expert-orientated models of therapy are shifting to ones of lateral configuration, with both clients and therapists having a more equal responsibility for the therapeutic process....These shifts call for a re-evaluation of much of our traditional thinking about family therapy. The family no longer becomes the object of treatment, viewed independent of an observer or as a source of problems, but as a flexible entity composed of people with shared meanings....

In addition to the pursuit of trendy fads borrowed from academic literary criticism, there are several more substantive reasons for the appeal of postmodernism in psychotherapy. In his article, "Family Therapy Goes Postmodern," Doherty (1991) observed that there had been no new comprehensive theories about the family since Salvador Minuchin's and Murray Bowen's work in the 1970s. As Held (1995; also see Held in Hoyt et al., 2000/2001) has posited, therapists struggle with how to get from *generality* to *particularity*. Eschewing any grand ("totalizing") narratives and treating "the client as expert" (Anderson & Goolishian, 1992) are attempts to stay respectful of the individual specifics of a case and not to impose a predetermined system of therapy.[6] Martin and Sugarman (2000, p. 398) also noted that

---

6. In their paper, "Milton Erickson: Early Postmodernist," Gene Combs and Jill Freedman (1994) review some of Erickson's case reports and writings to support their contention that his work prefigured what is now considered "postmodern." As they show, Erickson favored flexibility and recognition of the individual's capacities rather than any preset notion of what is "normal" or a rigid adherence to standard procedures. As Erickson said (quoted in Zeig & Gilligan, 1990, frontispiece; also see Zeig, 2002): "Each person is a unique individual. Hence psychotherapy should be formulated to meet the uniqueness of the individual's needs, rather than tailoring the person to fit the Procrustean bed of a hypothetical theory of human behavior." It is important to note that while he carefully selected what he would attend to and emphasize, Erickson based his work *on* the capacities of his patients. As his daughter, the therapist Betty Alice Erickson (2002, pp. 288-289) has written, "'Observe, observe, observe,' he would say. The therapist must learn to set aside personal perspectives and really see and hear from the client's point of view."

At the same time as psychologists and educators resonate to postmodern themes of difference, plurality, peculiarity, and irregularity as refreshing changes from past adherence to sameness, universality, and strict rationality, they actually maintain many time-honored views of themselves and continue to believe in some version of progressive, warranted enlightenment as afforded by their developing, changing understanding. In effect, having labored within the straightjacket of modernity, they enjoy the ludic romp of postmodernism's radical problematizing without really believing its full social constructionist and deconstructivist implications for themselves and their everyday and professional practices.

On the surface, constructivism and postmodernism would seem almost identical: both emphasize the role of language and discourse in the individual and social construction of meaning, experience, and reality (see Freedman & Combs, 1996; Friedman, 1995; Held, 1990; Shawver, 1996). There are constructivists and there are constructivists, however. In the glossary of *Constructivism and Psychotherapy*, Neimeyer and Mahoney (1995, p. 403) provide useful distinctions:

> *critical constructivism* asserts that the individual is synergistically interdependent with his or her environment and that there are, indeed,"external" (extrasystemic) constraints (call them physical, material, or whatever) that importantly constrain and influence each person's continuing constructing.
>
> *radical constructivism* asserts that the individual is self-sufficient in these processes and that his or her physical environment or medium of existence is a relatively insignificant factor in the construction of experiences. However, some radical constructivists strongly emphasize the role of language in shaping the constructions of human individuals and groups, even to the point of shaping their most basic sense of self and relations.

When so-called 'radical constructivists' (e.g., von Foerster, 1984, 1985; von Glaserfeld, 1984)—who argued that language is the territory, not just the map—joined hands with postmodernism, a dangerous conflation occurred:

> Over the past few decades, the progression of constructivist thinking in psychotherapy has been more rapid and, in some respects, more turbulent as well. Like any stream of thought, the course that constructivism has taken has been responsive to the broader contours of the intellectual landscape that surrounds it. In this instance, the landscape has been shaped by the influence of postmodernism, with its iconoclastic penchant for celebrating the multiplicity of belief systems, resisting methodological prescriptions, and undermining faith in the "timeless truths" embedded in our social charters, cultural mores, mas-

terworks of literature, and even science itself....In this cultural context, contemporary constructivist psychotherapy has gained momentum—deepening, broadening, and occasionally being buffeted by contradictory crosscurrents originating in rather different disciplinary terrains. (Neimeyer, 1995, p. 12)

Efran and Fauber (1995, p. 276) threw down the gauntlet:

> The sophisticated epistemologist may regard objectivism as naive and antiquated, but everyone else still relies on it to get through breakfast. Tamer variants of constructivism, such as critical constructivism (Mahoney, 1991), permit objectivists a certain amount of elbow room, but radical constructivism does not—it insists on an all-out epistemological battle, with no prisoners taken. The major distinction between radical and critical constructivism concerns their respective assumptions about an underlying reality. Critical constructivists tend to be realists who assume that there is a definite reality that people increasingly approximate in their constructs, even though they may never be able to "access" it completely. In contrast, radical constructivists are idealists who do not concern themselves with the ultimate nature of a reality beyond the human experience.

Herein, we believe, lies the rub. Postmodernism goes too far when it joins with radical constructivism in asserting not just that language is important, but that language is *all* important; and when it asserts that there is no reality outside of the images created by language.

> If one were to select from the substantial corpus of postmodern writings a single line of argument that (a) generates broad agreement within these ranks and (b) serves as a critical divide between what we roughly distinguish as the modern versus the postmodern, it would be the abandonment of the traditional commitment to *representationalism*. By representationalism I mean here the assumption that there is (or can be) a determinant (fixed or intrinsic) relationship between words and world. [Gergen, 1994, p. 412]

While usefully reminding us of the possible multiplicity of competing belief and value systems, when taken seriously postmodern philosophy tends toward a solipsistic quagmire, mirrors within mirrors. Postmodernists may choose to use provocation to highlight their perspective, but when they argue that 'nothing is real' their purpose is not well served. "Truth" is an elusive critter and everyone can have his or her heartfelt beliefs and "take" on reality, but if we ignore the situation outside us, we are somewhere between autistic, ignorant, irresponsible, and psychotic. Come on, get real!

Hence, while cursing (radical) constructivism (for what we believe are really the shortcomings of postmodernism), Frank Pittman (1992) rightly decried those who would hide behind "It's all in your mind" or "That's just how *you* look at it" to use sophistry to change words rather than right wrongs:

> Postmodernism entered family therapy in the form of constructivism, espousing that reality is in the eye of the beholder, and that it doesn't matter what people do, only what story they tell about it. What a breakthrough! People don't have to change what they do! They can just use different words instead! Constructivism is fun intellectual masturbation, until we notice that the world constructivism is defining away is a cruel, unsafe, unfair place that hurts real people. [p. 58]

In his address at the 1990 Evolution of Psychotherapy conference, Salvador Minuchin (1992) also asserted:

> I am extremely concerned about the preservation of strengths that, I think, are vitiated by the constructivist framing [p. 5]....When the constructivists equate expertise with power....and develop a new technology of interventions that avoid control, they are only creating a different use of power. Control does not disappear from family therapy when it is renamed "co-creation." All that happens is that the influence of the therapist on the family is made invisible. Safely underground, it may remain unexamined. Therapy is a temporary arrangement. Hierarchies are mutually organized for a period of time and for a "more or less" specific purpose. Temporary as it is, this arrangement would be a sham if the therapist were not an expert—that is, a person of informed uncertainty—on the human condition, the variety of family systems, family and individual development, processes of change, and the handling of dialogues, metaphors, and stories....The bottom line is that the constructivist approach, by bracketing the idiosyncratic story, obscures the social fabric that also constructs it [pp. 7-8]....Constructivist practice, with some exceptions, binds the therapist to the procrustean bed of talking and meaning, robbing the therapist of human complexity. [p. 10]

In his paper, "The Seductions of Constructivism," Minuchin (1991, pp. 48-50) amplified this view:

> [T]he extreme emphasis constructivists place on language, and their distaste for more behavioral therapies geared to the way people act, seem to undermine one of the historic advantages of family therapy—its pioneering use of experiential and action-oriented techniques. The addition of these dynamic, interactional forms of therapy to the traditional mode of verbalization gave therapists

far more flexibility with families, who, after all, communicate in lots of ways besides talking......A more serious objection I have to constructivist therapy is its tendency to concentrate overmuch on the idiosyncratic "story" of the individual family and ignore the social context that may actually dictate much of the "plot" of their lives—the institutions and socioeconomic conditions that determine what they do and how they live....At the very least, I see no reason why a therapist cannot be a strategic constructivist *and* explore social norms *and* be an advocate for the clients *and* challenge the family story in a variety of ways, including passionate confrontation, without theoretical conflict.

Barbara Held (1995, p. 132) expressed a similar view:

[T]o see or treat people's actions, including their utterances, as literary texts to be deconstructed is to apply a metaphor that brings with it some danger than the therapist will be tempted to ignore or minimize the importance of the (extralinguistic) reality of the real person sitting before the therapist, with all her real life experiences. These include real psychological, social, and economic circumstances, for instance, poverty, oppression, abuse, and even, contrary to the narrative view, real mental illness, such as schizophrenia or depression. For if all we need to do to solve the client's problem is change her [antirealist] narrative/view of it, then we need not put any efforts and resources into trying to change the real circumstances of that extralinguistic reality.

William Doherty (1991, p. 42) saw both possible pros and cons:

At its best, postmodern family therapy, like postmodern culture, offers a rich blend of perspectives, a pluralistic approach to theory and therapy, in contrast to the narrow modernist focus on family micro processes. Transcending models and schools and orthodoxies, postmodern family therapy crosses disciplinary boundaries and allows a freedom of thinking and action not possible within the old paradigms ....But at its worst, postmodern family therapy is a pastiche of discordant styles, a mindless jumble of theories and fancy vocabulary. To structural family therapy, add a little psychodynamic theory, sprinkle with feminism and ethnic consciousness, try some paradox and circular questions, and see if the mix jells. Like some failed example of postmodern architecture—a disharmony of random historical styles—this magpie collection of therapies is the American triumph of technique over substance.

Held's 1995 book, *Back to Reality: A Critique of Postmodernism in Psychotherapy*, offers the most extensive criticism. Focusing on philosophical issues, she stated:

> It is my claim that a central, defining feature of linguistic philosophy and poststructural literary theory—and indeed of all postmodern theory itself—is the explicit adoption of a fundamental antirealism. Thus, if there is one position that unites the many manifestations of postmodern thought, I believe it is the rejection of a realist epistemology in favor of an antirealist one....The antirealist doctrine, which has also been called constructivism or constructionism in psychotherapy circles (e.g., Efran, Lukens & Lukens, 1990; McNamee & Gergen, 1992), states that the knower cannot, under any circumstances, attain knowledge of a reality that is independent of the knower; rather, knowers make, invent, create, constitute, construct, or narrate, in language, their own subjective realities or, in the usual terminology, antirealities or nonrealities....For antirealists, then, a theory, language, construct, or narrative always intervenes, or mediates, between the knower and the known—that is, between the knower and the targeted independent reality that is usually presumed to exist....For example, the therapist cannot know the true nature of the client and his struggles as they really exist, no matter what the therapist observes in the therapy sessions. Rather, the antirealist doctrine insists that the therapist's theories, language, constructions, or narratives about the client always determine just what the therapist observes, and so preclude any direct (i.e., theoretically unmediated), undistorted, or even any indirect (i.e., theoretically mediated), undistorted knowledge of the client's true condition.

and (pp. 8-9):

> For the postmodern narrative therapist, then, all experiences of the world are mediated by the (reality-distorting) theory, language, discourse, narrative, or story that clients and therapists, who inhabit *particular* (linguistic or discursive) contexts, adopt....Thus, according to the antirealist doctrine that postmodernists in general propound, one's view of, or discourse about, reality can never reflect the true or independent (of the knower) nature of that reality....These statements have important implications for the postmodern narrative therapist, because the anti-realist doctrine they reflect radically alters what is commonly understood to be the nature of truth. For the postmodern therapist in particular, as well as the postmodern theorist in general, there is no way of knowing that can give us *any* true, independent reality. All "truths," therefore, are *merely* constructions in language made by knowers situated in *particular* discursive contexts....But whether the antirealism is of the more or the less radical sort, it always precludes any access (direct or indirect) to an independent reality, and *that* is the point of all antirealist doctrines. So it is also the point of postmodern theory itself.

Matthews (2002, pp. 147-148), in his trenchant article, "Reality Exists: A Critique of Antirealism in Brief Therapy," similarly wrote:

> The argument, which I refer to in general terms as postmodernism, is fallacious logically, and on reasonably close inspection falls under its own nihilistic weight. In essence, the postmodern position is that truth is a mere construction created by a given context....Since truth is only relative and subject to various prejudices, the statement that all truths are relative and have no generalizability is itself simultaneously relative and absolute, and as such offers us no reason to accept....[Relativism] is, by definition, a direct attack on science, scientific method, and critical rationality. This view would offer us no way to distinguish between superstition and verifiable knowledge and as such is both nonsensical and intellectually dangerous (cf. Matthews, 1998).

There is much to recommend Held's book and Matthews' article.[7] However, although Held wrote

> I want to be very clear about the fact that the postmodern narrative therapy movement....already involves a modest, or limited realism. That realism is found (a) with respect to secondary rational awareness both of theories about narrative and of narratives themselves, and (b) with respect to the implicit reliance on primary rational awareness to make such general claims as the fundamental ones within narrative therapy, namely, that the way one narrates one's life affects the perception of options in life, and that this perception in turn affects the way life actually gets lived. These claims bring with them the realist imperative that we understand how language or narrative, as a *system*, itself works to produce maximum impact on clients' understanding and behavior. [Held, 1995, p. 192]

their repeated characterization of the works of several leading figures in the solution/narrative constructivist traditions as "antirealist," which would seem to imply a disregard for the actualities of clients' lives, is very much at variance with their practices—as based on our numerous direct observations and conversations, as well as a close reading of their writings. For example, in contradistinction, consider:

Paul Watzlawick, the chief constructivist theoretician of the Mental Research Institute's strategic-interactional approach, has described *reframing* as

> To reframe, then, means to change the conceptual and/or emotional setting or viewpoint in relation to which a situation is experienced and to place it in another frame which fits the "facts" of the same concrete situation equally well

---

7. See Held (1995), Larner (1995), and Matthews (2002) for informative discussions of the history of postmodernism in psychotherapy.

or even better, and thereby changes its entire meaning. [Watzlwick, Weakland & Fisch, 1974, p. 95]

Note that this definition does not deny the facts of the concrete situation, but offers a different way of understanding them. Watzlawick, although often considered a radical constructivist, clarified this further in a published interview:

HOYT: Is there something outside our consciousness [an external reality] that therapists should be attentive to?

WATZLAWICK: Yes, everybody's second-order reality, that differs from mine, is an external reality of which I may be totally unaware (to avoid the term "unconscious").

HOYT: Some theorists have been critical of constructivism and social constructionism on primarily philosophical grounds. Barbara Held (1995), for example, has argued for what she calls a "modest realism," a recognition that there is a *there* there, an external referent by which interventionists gauge their work. She writes (p. 173):

"Here I draw the reader's attention to what I consider to be a point of fundamental importance in understanding the confusion generated by the postmodern emphasis on the linguistic, and the postmodern linking of linguistic entities (including theories/propositions/stories/narratives/discourses) with antirealism. It is this: *All theories are constructions* [boldface in original]....But then to say, as social constructionists/ postmodernists say, that those constructed theories are the *only* reality we have—that is, that reality itself, or knowable reality itself, is *only* a 'social construction' (because we supposedly have no direct, theoretically unmediated access or even an indirect, theoretically mediated access to any reality that is independent of the knower/knower's theory)—is to confuse two things: (1)the linguistic status of the theory itself with (b)the (extralinguistic or extratheoretic) reality that the theory is attempting to approximate indirectly."

How do you understand and respond to this line of criticism?

WATZLAWICK: As far as constructivism is concerned, only the name is *modern*. That our views of reality are *subjective* and by no means an objectively "true" view, has been pos-

> tulated by philosophers (e.g., Vico, Kant, Schopenhauer, Jaspers), by physicists (e.g., Einstein, Heisenberg, Schrodinger) and even mathematicians. Regarding the last two lines in the above-mentioned quotation by Held: Constructivism does not "confuse two things"—it makes a clear distinction between reality of the *first order* (as conveyed to us by our sensory organs in terms of perceptions), and reality of the *second order* (i.e., the meaning, significance and value that every one of us inevitably attributes to the first-order reality—which remain totally subjective, unprovable, and, therefore, the cause of human conflict and misunderstandings). [Watzlawick & Hoyt, 1998/2001, pp. 150-151]

There is an interaction between our perceptual apparatus (attention, awareness, representation, knowing) and the outside world—a betwixt and between that Merleau-Ponty (1968) called the *chiasm*. As Watzlawick (1984, p. 9) put it in the book *The Invented Reality:* "if *what* we know depends on *how* we came to know it, then our view of reality is no longer a true image of what is the case outside ourselves, but is inevitably determined also [N.B.: *also*, not *solely*] by the processes through which we arrived at this view." Along related lines, Lois Shawver (1996, p. 379) quoted French linguistic philosopher Jacques Derrida:

> And Derrida chafes at interpretations of his work that make him sound as though he does not believe in the world beyond words....He says that his well-known phrase that there is 'nothing outside the text' merely means "that one cannot refer to this 'real' except in an interpretive experience" (Derrida, 1972, p. 148). [Shawver (1996, p. 379) explains:] [P]ostmoderns are most likely to sound as if they are saying that we have only words and nothing else, when they are trying to talk about the way language works to affect how we notice and perceive that which lies beyond our words....language creates categories that structure our understanding. Heidegger [1971, p. 62] says, "The word alone gives being to the thing."

Although Steve de Shazer (1993a, p. 81), the co-originator (with Insoo Berg) of solution-focused therapy, asserts that "there is no escape from language," he also recognizes that there are "misreadings"[8] and "creative misunderstandings." He writes:

> *There is nothing outside the session.* When I first started using the term "conversation" in regards to doing therapy (de Shazer, 1988), all I had in mind was

that the majority of time the simplest observation reveals that therapists and clients are taking turns talking together. And that's about all they do. Nothing mysterious is involved, nothing is hidden away. All I wanted to say was that therapy can be looked at as a conversation, that is, people taking turns talking together. There are no wet beds, no voices without people, no depressions. There is only *talk* about wet beds, *talk* about voices without people, *talk* about depression. There are no family systems, no family structures, no psyches: just talk about systems, structures, and psyches. When it comes to doing therapy, doing therapy is all there is and, therefore, there is nothing outside of the therapy session that can help us understand what is going on in the session. Even in our follow-up studies we are only having a conversation about results: We never *have* results, only depictions of results. As Wittgenstein says (in a different context), "You've got what you've got and that's all there is."

All I wanted to do, with my use of the term "conversation," was to point to something obvious, something that had been skillfully hidden away on the surface of things so that nobody saw it. Therapy involves the use of language. Therapy is in language and thus we need to look at the use of language in therapy....In my view, therapy is nothing but language, the client and the therapist are always using language. This, too, has been hidden away on the surface of things while therapists, influenced by their scientific frames, looked for something deep and hidden away. [de Shazer, 1993a, pp. 89-90]

He extended this theme in his next book, *Words Were Originally Magic* (de Shazer, 1994a), the title of which he borrowed from Freud's (1915/1961, p. 17) words:

> Nothing takes place in a psycho-analytic treatment but an interchange of words....the patient talks....the doctor listens....Words were originally magic and to this day have retained much of their ancient magical power. By words one person can make another blissfully happy or drive him to despair....Words provoke affects and are in general the means of mutual influence among men. Thus we shall not deprecate the use of words in psychotherapy and shall be pleased if we can listen to the words that pass between the analyst and his patient.

---

8. Long ago, Alfred Adler (1931/1968, p. 4) anticipated de Shazer's observation that we always "mis-read" as well as some of the ideas about narrative construction subsequently expressed by George Kelly and various cognitive-behaviorists: "Human being live in the realm of *meanings*....We experience reality always through the meaning we give it; not in itself, but as something interpreted. It will be natural to suppose, therefore, that this meaning is always more or less unfinished, incomplete; and even that it is never altogether right. The realm of meanings is the realm of mistakes."

Neither de Shazer nor anyone we know influenced by his thinking believes that the only reality is talk. Reading his comments in full, the point de Shazer is making is that what we can agree happens in a therapy session is that people are talking together—taking turns speaking (and, it may be hoped, listening) about certain subjects. There are no wet beds in the therapy room, just as there are not object relations or childhood sexual abuse *in the office*. Because, in the office there is only talk, therapy works, when it does (and doesn't, when it doesn't) because of the way the participants talk and make meaning together.[9]

DE SHAZER: ....History will always be rewritten in terms of who is writing it. History doesn't change; what you write about it changes.

HOYT: The event that occurred doesn't change, but the meaning we give it.

DE SHAZER: Right. [from Hoyt, 1996e/2001, p. 175]

In a recent paper, "Getting to the Surface of the Problem: The Bricks and Mortar of Our Constructions," de Shazer (2002, p. 250) elaborates:

> The idea that reality is constructed has become an answer when instead what is wanted are questions such as: "How is reality constructed? What materials are used to construct reality? What are the processes involved? Who constructs reality? What are the bricks? What is the mortar?" As a result of accepting this phrase as accepted truth, a concept useful for thinking, it has become a substitute for thinking (Weakland, 1993, p. 139)....[de Shazer, 2002, p. 257 concludes] Getting to the surface of the problem and simply describing what is going on (who?, what?, when?, where?), such as with problematic drinking, allows us to avoid the traps inherent in the concept of alcoholism and the grammar involved in our talking about it. Moving to the surface, and staying on the surface, allows us to see what it is that is going on in a particular case, and forces us to pay attention to details and not to generalize.

---

9. Gergen and McNamee (1997, p. viii), in their Foreword to Riikonen and Smith's *Re-Imaging Therapy: Living Conversations and Relational Knowing*, spell out something similar: "However, Riikonen and Smith extend these conversations in very important ways. At the onset, they inject into the literature a much needed emphasis on the pragmatic features of language, the capacity of words (as forms of action) to achieve consequences both in therapy and daily life. Language by their account is not a reflection of another world, but an implement of construction for the world we now occupy."

The title of Michael White and David Epston's well-known 1990 book, *Narrative Means to Therapeutic Ends*, also indicates that "story reauthoring" is the vehicle, not the destination. This was spelled out in *Experience, Contradiction, Narrative and Imagination* (Epston & White, 1992) when White (p. 81) wrote:

> Thus, the stories that we enter into with our experience have real effects on our lives. The expression of our experience through these stories shapes or makes-up our lives and our relationships; our lives are shaped or constituted through the very process of the interpretation of experience within the contexts of the stories that we enter into and that we are entered into by others.
>
> This is not to propose that life is synonymous with text. It is not enough for a person to tell a new story about oneself, or to assert claims about oneself. Instead, the position carried by these assertions about the world of experience and narrative is that life is the performance of texts. And it is the performance of these texts that is transformative of person's lives.

Although Held (1995) and Matthews (2002) do not discuss the seminal work of George Kelly, who was the first to develop a systematic clinical approach based on constructivist principles, Neimeyer and Bridges (2003) feature Kelly in their discussion of postmodern approaches. In this regard, it may be helpful to recall that in *The Psychology of Personal Constructs*, Kelly (1955, pp. 6-8; also see Raskin, 2001) wrote:

> We presume that the universe is really existing and that man is gradually coming to understand it. By taking this position we attempt to make clear from the outset that it is a real world we shall be talking about, not a world composed solely of the flitting shadows of people's thoughts. But we should like, furthermore, to make clear our conviction that people's thoughts also really exist, though the correspondence between what people really think exists and what really does exist is a continually changing one....Sometimes scientists, particularly those who are engrossed in the study of physical systems, take the stand that psychological events are not true phenomena but are rather epiphenomena, or merely the unreliable shadows of real events. This position is not ours. A person may misrepresent a real phenomenon, such as his income or his ills, and yet his misrepresentation will itself be entirely real. This applies even to the badly deluded patient: what he perceives may not exist, but his perception does. Moreover, his fictitious perception will often turn out to be a grossly distorted construction of something which actually does exist. Any living creature, together with his perceptions, is a part of the real world; he is not merely a nearsighted bystander to the goings-on of the real world.[10]

In *The Social Construction of Reality,* John Searle (1995) wrote:

> Strange as it may seem, realism has recently come under attack both in philosophy and in other disciplines. [Diverse thinkers]....are often interpreted (not always correctly, I believe) as challenging our naive assumption that there exists a reality totally independent of our representations of it....I would defend realism against the attacks made on it, but frankly I have trouble finding any powerful attacks that seem worth answering. Maturana [1980] rejects the idea of "an objective reality" in favor of the idea that nervous systems, as autopoietic systems, construct their own reality. The argument appears to be that since we have no conception of, and no access to, reality except through the social construction of realties in the "consensual domains," constructed by autopoietic systems, there is no reality existing independently of biological systems. Against this view I want to say, From the fact that our knowledge/conception/picture is constructed by human brains in human interactions, it does not follow that the *reality* of which we have the knowledge/conception/picture is constructed by human brain in human interactions. It is just a non sequitor, a genetic fallacy, to infer from the collective neurophysiological causal explanation of our knowledge of the external world to the nonexistence of the external world.

Neimeyer and Bridges (2003) also include Bruce Ecker and Laurel Hulley (1996) in their "loose confederation" of postmodern approaches. In their *Depth Oriented Brief Therapy*, which hydridizes concepts from both psychodynamics and constructivist brief therapy, Ecker and Huley (1996, pp. 6-11) wrote:

> A constructivist therapist assumes that there are any number of viable ways the client's view of reality could change that would dispel the presenting problem, and in a spirit of collaboration, the therapist and client consider and try out such possibilities. The differences among constructivist therapies are differences in how they select an alternative, symptom-free view of reality for the client to experimentally inhabit, and in how they invite the client to do so....This is a postmodern position in that it decenters any absolute, timeless truth about people's lives and instead recognizes a varying, local formulation of truth....Even in the midst of objective hardships, the difference between a triumph and a collapse of the spirit is the difference in how the ordeal is con-

---

10. Neimeyer and Mahoney (1995, p. 403) define Kelly's *credulous approach*: "[The] injunction for the therapist to treat the client's disclosures and formulations 'as if they were valid from that individual's standpoint rather than to treat client verbalizations as products of 'cognitive distortions' or 'unconscious dynamics.'" For some examples of working *with* the patient's beliefs, see Ziegler (1998) and Ziegler and Hiller (2001, pp. 200-208).

strued—the construction of meaning by which the individual relates to circumstances.

We might also comment here upon our own previous writings regarding postmodernism and psychotherapy. Ziegler and Hiller (2001, p. 218) made their view clear in their book, *Recreating Partnership: A Solution-Oriented, Collaborative Approach to Couples Therapy*:

> While a number of constructionist therapy developers (Hoyt, 1994a, 1996a, 1998) view their ideas as "postmodernist," we don't like to apply that term to our ideas and practices....Suffice it to say that, regarding human social behavior, constructivist and constructionist thought has had a leavening and often creative effect and made a substantive contribution to the practices of psychotherapy. We think, in the long run, that basing psychological theories and clinical models on the ideology of "postmodernism" is unnecessary and may in some cases weaken the case for constructionist therapies.

As noted, I may have contributed to the muddle (and thus especially welcome this opportunity for clarification) by my loose use of the term *postmodernism* to mean "multiple perspectives, multiple subjective realities" *a la* White's earlier comment (also see Coyne, 1982; Cade, 1986; Freedman & Combs, 1996; Held, 1990; Hoyt, 1994a, 1996a, 1998) quoted above. In the book *Some Stories Are Better than Others* (Hoyt, 2000a), the word *postmodern* appears in the title chapter, "Some Stories Are Better than Others: A Postmodern Pastiche." Although the importance of *storying* and *languaging* is central, numerous statements emphasize that it is changes in reality that count. For example:

> * "How we choose to conceive and pattern the present, the past, and the future—the stories we tell ourselves—profoundly influences our course." (p. 18)
> * "Our focus here is on the therapeutic, making a difference, and the sine qua non must be the ultimate effect or change in the patient's or client's life." (p. 20)
> * "Within this framework, the therapeutic endeavor can be understood as an attempt to construct and live within a more salutary reality." (p. 21)
> * "[I]t is important that some of the 'possible interactions' be realized." (p. 21)
> * "Life is not just lived 'in the head,' of course, so intrapsychic modification is seldom sufficient." (p. 22)
> * "A constructivist position may hold that we always are part of the equation, that there is no knowing without the knower; but there are extralinguistic forces to be reckoned with. One who ignores context, circumstances, conse-

quences, events, objects, and various social structures and systems risks ignoring a lot….Someone unmindful of traffic can still be run over—as Bill O'Hanlon and I quipped in a published conversation (Hoyt, 1996d, p. 106), 'My karma just ran over your dogma!' We may be meaning-makers only able to know approximately what's 'out there'….but there is a *there*." (p. 24)

* "We 'perform' (Omer, 1993) or 'enact' (Sluzki, 1992) our narratives in the world." (p. 24)

* "Constructive therapists know that *ultimately what counts are the real effects* of how people construe their 'reality,' the goal being to bring about positive consequences in clients' lives via attention to the social construction of preferred ('clinical' or 'therapeutic') realities." (p. 33, italics in original)

We agree that point of view and the making of meaning are important *and* that there is (of course) a reality external to the observer about which meanings are made. In a conversation published under the title "About Constructivism (or, If Four Colleagues Talked in New York, Would Anyone Hear It?)" Scott Miller offered a wise, pragmatic perspective:

> For me, I bring it back to the practical, what I actually do. I can tell you the constructivist thinkers have helped me in a very specific, measurable way. It's helped me pay attention to where our professional discourse has excluded certain populations of people in our clinical work. I feel very much informed by constructivist dialogue about work with people who have not been part of the empirical studies about psychotherapy thus far. So under-privileged populations, their voice has not been included. It's when the idea is taken one step further that I stumble. Practically speaking, I find constructivism very useful for opening my eyes, creating possibilities, but when it gets to the level of "Is it real, is it not?" I sort of glaze over and lose touch with reality—whatever that is! [Hoyt, Miller, Held & Matthews, 2000/2001, p. 209)

DISTINGUISHING CONSTRUCTIVISM, POSTSTRUCTURALISM AND SOCIAL CONSTRUCTIONISM FROM POSTMODERNISM

Although Held (1995) and Matthews (2002) lump them together, it is important not to blur the distinctions between postmodernism, constructivism, poststructuralism, and social constructionism. As Michael White, the co-originator of narrative therapy, has cautioned:

> I have never considered what I think and what I do to be "constructivist." I don't have much familiarity with constructivism, and I don't have an appreciation of the history of this tradition of thought….[I]t is not unusual these

days to see different traditions of thought and practice collapsed on to each other in ways that actually obscure what is being proposed in each of these distinct traditions. For example, in the literature I have read accounts of my thought and practices that represent me as "anti-realist," despite the fact that I have little sympathy for what is proposed in this tradition, and despite the fact that I believe the realist/anti-realist debate to be irrelevant to what I know of poststructuralist inquiry and narrative practice. I have also been represented as a social constructionist and a postmodernist. While I can relate to and appreciate many of the ideas that are represented as social constructionist, in this tradition of thought there is also much that leaves me unsatisfied. And I know just little fragments of the specificity of postmodernism, which has its roots in art and literature. Perhaps this specificity is now becoming lost, as the term *postmodernism* is now often employed to categorize any idea and practice that does not reproduce foundationist thought. But even the specificity of *this* description is at risk. I have recently seen postmodernism represented as a form of "anything goes" moral relativism, as the achievement of simultaneously holding multiple beliefs or views or theories about life, and even as a "new eclecticism." I think that this is an unfortunate turn, because in it postmodernism has come to represent what it contradicts.

On any account, this running together of distinct traditions of thought and practice is unhelpful. It leads to the false representation of the position of different thinkers. It destroys a climate of thought by manufacturing a soup that is so thick that it is indigestible, and one in which the different flavors can no longer be distinguished. As an outcome, discernable action in the name of therapy becomes impossible. And therapists are deprived of any clarity in regards to the development of proposals for the further exploration of specific ideas and practices. [White, Hoyt & Zimmerman, 2000/2001, pp. 270-271; also see Doan, 1997, 1998; Parry & Doan, 1994].

One of the hallmarks of modernism was the belief that behind all the apparent complexity and randomness of things, there is an underlying unifying Truth or Reality. Structuralism assumed that in order to know this underlying, unified reality, one had to develop a reliable method of establishing a correspondence between what could be observed on the "surface" and what was "really" going on at a "deeper" level. Thus, Freud, the psychoanalyst, studied his patient's dreams in order to understand what was in the patient's unconscious; Claude Levi-Strauss, the anthropologist, studied the observable behaviors of the natives and tried to develop models to establish the deeper, universal patterns they reflected; Noam Chomsky, the linguist, sought to clarify the universal "Deep Structure" of language by establishing a map to it from the "Surface Structure" of language. In short, like Platonists watching the shadows on the cave wall, the structuralists believed that there was a correspondence between the surface structure and the deep structure, and that methods could be developed for reliably establishing the nature of what could not be directly observed at the surface.

De Shazer (1991, p. 45; also see de Shazer & Berg, 1992), like White, talks in terms of poststructuralism:

> For the structuralist, meanings are stable and knowable through transformation, but for the post-structuralist, meaning is seen as known through social interaction and negotiation; meaning here is open to view since it lies between people rather than hidden away inside the individual.
>
> The traditionalists have inherited the legacy of Western thought that held that it was important to go deeper and deeper beneath the surface of whatever it was they were trying to explain. This approach is based on their belief that being puzzled by the surface of things means that there is something hidden and, therefore, that there is something very important that cannot be seen.
>
> As least some constructivists agree with Wittgenstein (1968) and say that "since everything lies open to view there is nothing to explain" (#126). Furthermore, "the aspects of things that are most important for us [appear to be] hidden because of their simplicity and familiarity. [That is], one is unable to notice something—because it is always before one's eyes" (# 129). [de Shazer, 2002, p. 244]

As do Gergen and McNamee (1997, p. vi):

> With the growing interest in social construction, narratives, metaphors, and the co-construction of meaning within the therapeutic community, we move into the domain of *post-structuralism*. In this case, we find that language is no longer an expression of manifestation of something else, but gains importance in itself. In the post-structuralist frame, language essentially constitutes the psyche, the family, the pathology, and the remainng family of therapeutic objects. The person is only such by virtue of the ways in which he/she participates in or is situated by language: families are what they are by virtue of their forms of communication; pathology is constituted in and through language.

Bill O'Hanlon (1999, pp. 145-146) provides a nice summary:

> Radical constructivists and quantum physicists suggest that what we call reality is constructed—fabricated by our beliefs and our neurology. There is no such thing as reality (or truth, either, which is another matter altogether and a compelling reason not to hire a radical constructivist to handle your cash).
>
> Social-interactional constructionists take a different stance. They (or I should say 'we," since I count myself in their numbers), hold that there is a

> physical reality out there but that our social reality, being influenced by language and interaction, is negotiable. This social reality can influence and be influenced by physical reality....This social reality is mutable, but within some limits—the constraints seem to be physical, environmental, and tradition/habits....The social reality created in therapy interviews is just that—social. It is cocreated by the therapists and clients, as well as by the culture and social system traditions that influence them. This stance is called social or interactional constructionism.[11]

We have to be careful that the model doesn't dictate what we can see. For almost 1500 years—from early in the 2nd century (Roman Empire) until the 17th century—astronomers tried to map how the planets revolved around the earth. Since Church dogma demanded that the Earth, not the sun, be the center of the universe, every astronomer from Ptolomy on had to work from that starting point, meaning that planetary movements, the seasons, and the calendar had to fit this fact. Now this created some problems when it came to designing a reliable seasonal calendar that would be accurate year after year. Under the Ptolemian system things sometimes didn't seem to work out—every 100 years or so it would snow in July, and the calendar had to be revised. July became January and the calendar would be right again. It wasn't until the 15th century that Copernicus challenged the idea of Earth being the center of the universe. Using mathematical formulations, he theorized that the earth and planets must all revolve around the sun. It took another 100 years before Galileo used a telescope to verify what Copernicus had only theorized. But, as we know, the Pope threatened to burn Galileo at the stake for daring to imply that the Earth was not the focal point of all Creation, and Galileo recanted (there was more at stake for him than losing his funding).

Today, social constructionists argue that psychosocial models of reality (and therapy) are just that—models—more or less useful depending on the context (see Blum, 1978; Cushman, 1995, p. 3; Mirowsky & Ross, 1989).[12] When we get to psychotherapy, the strong emphasis is on the human processes of relationship and meaning-making rather than on the physical (see Mahoney, 1991).[13] Yet we see psychotherapy often being described in terms that make it sound like

---

11. As Freedman and Combs (1996, p. 26) note, Lynn Hoffman (1990) initially assumed constructivism and social constructionism were synonymous but then, following Gergen (1985), shifted her alliance to the latter when she realized "that social constructionists place far more emphasis on social interpretation and the intersubjective influence of language, family, and culture, and much less on the operations of the nervous system."

an objectifiable medication treatment (e.g., studies of the dose-response effect relationship—see Hansen, et al., 2002) This mixes levels of analysis—the practice of psychotherapy is human meaning-making, while the scientific study of psychotherapy can count, for example, how many meetings occur on average before certain results obtain.

One can study psychotherapy scientifically from the outside, but from the inside it is largely a process of interpretation and meaning-making (see Bruner's [1986, 1987; also see Spence, 1982] distinction between *logico-scientific* and *narrative*). The *self* is not an objective "thing" but rather, a process, a capacity, an achievement in meaning (Taylor, 1989). Similarly, "marital problems," "poor communication," "passive-aggressive husbands," "hysterical wives," "co-dependency," and the like are interpersonally constructed concepts, not reified objects. Thus, Wilhelm Dilthey (1988; also see Chessick, 1990; Driver-Linn, 2003; Messer, Sass & Woolfolk, 1988) offered the distinction between *explanation* as the goal of the natural sciences and *understanding* as the goal of the human sciences. As Hans-Georg Gadamer (1960/1999) wrote in *Truth and Method*:

> The experience of a socio-historical world cannot be raised to a science by the inductive procedure of the natural sciences. Whatever science may mean here, and even if all historcial knowledge includes the application of experiential universals to the particular object of investigation, historical research does not endeavor to grasp the concrete phenomenon as an instance of a universal rule. The individual case does not serve only to confirm a law from which practical predictions can be made. Its ideal is rather to understand the phenomenon itself in its unique and historical correctness.

When solution-focused therapist Steve de Shazer says—paraphrasing that old modernist, Sigmund Freud—that all we have in the office is talk, he is more like Galileo than Ptolemy. He is saying, let us set aside all our ideas about what makes

---

12. Gergen (1999, p. 21) quotes Mikhail Bakhtin (1981): "We do not address inquiries to nature and she does not answer us. We put questions to ourselves and we organize observations and experiment in such a way as to obtain an answer." Even in the physical sciences, people continue to struggle with the question of whether they are working on the Hard Wiring of the Universe or whether they are working within paradigms (Kuhn, 1970), through lenses (Hoffman, 1990)—see Horgan (1996) and Appinnanesi (2002).
13. We were glad recently to read Cummings' suggestion (in Short, 2002, p. 23) that Rene Descartes be put in his grave; let's not resurrect discussions about mind-body dualism.

people tick, all our models of human personality development and learning theories, and really look at what goes on during a therapy session. What can be observed to go on between therapist and client can tell us enough to inform us about what's working and what isn't, and will minimize our making up or taking up a lot of ideas that in fact aren't necessary. One of the important features of effective therapy is that conversation turns to certain topics—what the client hopes to get out of therapy, whether those desires and goals are being advanced by our efforts, what strengths and resources the client has (or comes to believe she has, as a consequence of our conversations). Why do we believe these themes are important? Not because we believe that anything goes or that we can make things up wholecloth, or that there is no reality, or that we cannot know reality so any story will do. Rather, as social constructionists, we understand that in conversation people's subjective experience changes and that while therapeutic talk can't change the past events or current situations in the client's life, our conversations can influence how the client thinks about and makes meaning of past events, how they view and understand their current situations, and invites them to revise their imagined futures in ways that open up new possibilities of perspective and action outside the consulting room. As Gergen (2000a, p. 131) put it:

> For present purposes we may see social constructionism as a range of dialogues centered on the social genesis of what we take to be knowledge, reason, and virtue, on the one side, and on the other the enormous range of social practices born and/or sustained by these discourses. In its critical moment, social constructionism is a means of bracketing or suspending any pronouncement of the real, the reasonable, or the right. In its generative moment, constructionism offers an orientation toward creating new futures, an impetus to societal transformations.

In their influential text, *Family Therapy: Concepts and Methods* (1997, p. 347), Michael Nichols and Richard Schwartz agree:

> The best part of the postmodern revolution has been that by giving up our expert status and grand theories, we've been able to find our hearts. Family therapy has been humanized, with more attention given to qualities of the therapist-client relationship than ever before…Family therapy's bridge to the twenty-first century is collaborative social constructionism.

EMBRACING COLLABORATION: SOME STORIES *ARE* BETTER THAN OTHERS

Although postmodernism has morphed to mean many different things to different people (see Russell & Gaubatz, 1995; Gergen, 2001; Neimeyer & Bridges, 2003), its basis appears to be a belief in multiple "realities" and a distrust of overarching narratives. Gergen (1999, p. 30) himself notes

> It is in this soil of critique and dead-end despair that social constructionism takes root. For many constructionists the hope has been to build from the existing rubble in new and more promising directions. The postmodern arguments are indeed significant, but serve not as an end but a beginning. Further, it we are careful and caring in the elaboration of the constructionist alternative, we shall also find ways of reconstituting the modernist tradition so as to retain some of its virtues while removing its threatening potentials....We move then from a prevailing despair to more positive possibilities—from deconstruction to reconstruction.

While rejecting the idea that "nothing is real," we do embrace the social constructionist emphasis on collaborative relationship. Patients come to therapy when the way they are looking at a situation does not give them access to what is needed to achieve what they consider reasonable satisfaction. Assuming the problem is not totally biological, the skillful clinician endeavors to help clients to construe different ways of looking at themselves, their partners, their situations and interactions (Hoyt & Berg, 1998/2000, p. 144) and to make desired changes in same. Again, Gergen (1993, p. x):

> The various accounts brought to therapy by the client—tales of misery, oppression, failures, and the like—serve not as approximations to the truth, perhaps biased by desires or cognitive incapacities, but as life constructions, made up of narratives, metaphors, cultural logics, and the like. They are more like musical or poetic accompaniments than mirrors or maps. And their major significance lies not in their relative validity, but in their social utility. In this context a major aim of therapy becomes one of freeing the client from a particular kind of account and opening the way to alternatives of greater promise.

This is what Hoyt (2000a) means by the phrase "some stories are better than others" and what Ziegler and Hiller (2001) mean when they help couples "recreate partnership" by focusing on the "good story/bad story" narrative continuum. As Hoyt (2000a, pp. 21-22) wrote:

> From this perspective, therapy can be understood as the purposeful development of a more functonal story; "better" stories are those that bring more of what is desired and less of what is not desired.... Aesthetics, effects, and ethics are all important. We like stories that are well told; that are vivid and eloquent; that involve the generation and resolution of some tension; that see the protagonist emerge successfully, perhaps even triumphantly. A "good" story does more than merely relate "facts"; a "good" story invigorates.

This, and not postmodernism, is what unites the various approaches that Hoyt (1994a, 1996a, 1998) has termed *constructive therapies*: the emphasis on revising meanings and reorienting the clients' perspectives, based on the recognition that we are constructing, not simply uncovering, psychological realities. The term deliberately connotes activity that is positive, productive, and creative (Hoyt, 2000a, p. 139).

Although education, skill instruction, and support can be used, of course, constructive therapists particularly concentrate on talking with clients in ways that will evoke the clients' strengths and competencies and thus help the clients to alter the way they see their situation and the options and resources they have to change it. Thus, the solution-focused therapist asks the "miracle question" (de Shazer, 1988) and pursues instances ("exceptions") when the presenting problem isn't present; the narrative therapist engages in "deconstruction" and "externalization" and helps the client "reauthor" by bringing forward and giving voice to submerged capacities; the Ericksonian and strategic therapist offers reframing and problem-solving metaphors and suggests interactional directives to help guide clients into new experiences and awarenesses. In Harlene Anderson's (1997, p. 50) collaborative language systems approach, therapy is conceived as "a process in which client and therapist become conversational partners who mutually explore familiar narratives and explore new ones." In this latter approach, it is the therapist's open-minded willingness to witness and honor multiple perspectives that serves as her primary contribution to the transformative medium of dialogue. By rejecting a meta-knowing role for the therapist, Anderson serves in the role of Hermes, who was the guide to—but not the keeper of—secret knowledge. In practice, her model is more of a stance than a set of interviewing techniques. It is the conversation itself, she believes, carried out in a very non-directive way, which makes the difference. As she has written:

> Postmodern psychologies are not in search of true psychological knowledge or psychological knowledge as definitive reality, but, rather, invite the multiple interpretations of any psychological phenomenon.... I think of myself as being

in *conversational partnership* in which understanding comes from within and in which we construct knowledge together through *collaborative inquiry*. When involved in this kind of collaborative or shared inquiry, the inquiry is shaped and reshaped as we go along with each other; and likewise, we are shaped and reshaped as we go along with each other. Thus these kinds of conversations are relationships that entail uncertainty and ambiguity. [Anderson, 2000, p. 203, italics in original][14]

A (POSTMODERN) TEMPEST IN A PSYCHOTHERAPEUTIC TEAPOT

Postmodernism may have served a useful purpose by heightening sensitivities about power and perspective, but the realist/antirealist debate soon becomes a tiresome exercise in scholastic pedantry. Of course there is an external reality, and of course there are subjective awarenesses (so-called "realities"). So what else is new?

Much more valuable—and interesting—is the question *what makes therapy effective?* And here, the empirical evidence is clear: cutting across different schools and specific methods is the finding that the therapeutic alliance and client variables (more than therapist techniques or nonspecific factors) account for the majority of the variance in psychotherapy treatment outcomes (Duncan et al., 1997; Hubble et al., 1999; Miller et al., 1997). This is why we are advocates for social constructionist, collaborative forms of psychotherapy—without tying them to the tired shibboleth of postmodernism—because so-called constructive therapies place greater importance on the clients' theories, perceptions and desires than on the therapists' preferred psychological theories and clinical techniques. Expertise is shared—clients are assumed to be experts (although they may need help in identifying and using their expertise) about their lives, about what changes will signify successful therapy, and often about the means of change that will suit them best; and the therapist is expert in psychology and psychotherapy, including knowing how to guide and participate in interactions with clients in ways that have the potential of facilitating the clients' efforts and creativity.

---

14. By dint of her extreme attention to the conversation rather than external realities, Anderson's work is probably the most postmodern of the postmodern. Scott Miller (in Hoyt et al., 2000/2001, p. 221) comments: "Actually, Harlene Anderson [e.g. 1997] is probably the closest to someone....whose work I can't figure out what it's about....I love to watch her, but I can't figure out what the heck she's doing."

THE CHALLENGES OF POSTMODERNISM FOR PSYCHOTHERAPY

Many who had their hopes excited by postmodernism, including mental health workers, have increasingly found themselves confused, frustrated, and disappointed. In our opinion, postmodernism has promoted a number of potentially destructive trends in the fields of psychology and psychotherapy.

1. Lack of coherent theory to guide practice. "[A]ll therapists, those from these 'postmodern' perspectives included, regulate their engagement with clients on the basis of *some* conceptualization of human distress, whether implicit or explicit" (Neimeyer & Raskin, 2000, p. 3). As Held (in Hoyt et al., 2000/2001, p. 216; also see Held, 1995, 1999) has said:

> [I]t seems to me it's very hard to have a method of therapy that doesn't have at least implicit within it some predetermined idea of what the problem is and what are its causes, because even to say 'the method is deconstruct the patient's text or give them a new narrative' implies that you think the problem is in the way they're linguistically constructing their experience. It's a very general implicit notion, so there's lots of wiggle room for the particularities compared to traditional, conventional, complete systems of therapy....

We all need our polestars and lodestones, lest we become awash in a sea of deconstruction. Although we like very much the respectful attitude of Anderson and Goolishian's (1992) phrase, "the client is the expert," the therapist is also an expert—but about what? Doan (1998; also see Hart, 1995) notes the danger of focusing exclusively on social construction and disregarding other (e.g., genetic or biological) factors, as well as the paradox of some postmodernists erecting a new grand narrative that excludes or marginalizes accounts other than theirs. He quotes Nichols and Schwartz's family therapy text:

> The fervor and chauvinism of some followers of the newer models, like narrative and solution-focused, seems anachronistic in this postmodern era.....[I]t is important to remember that while the postmodern, constructionist revolution has been the headline story for the past decade, family therapists practicing less trendy approaches (behavioral, psychoanalytic, structural, strategic, Bowenian, experiential, and integrative) have continued their work....[T]hese models haven't remained static. Exciting developments coming from these traditions receive less attention because they're not in step with the hot new movements, but they are no less significant. [Nichols & Schwartz, 1997, pp. 347-348]

There is a body of psychological literature, including theories and empirical results. Even if we conceive our role as therapists largely as "conversational partners" *a la* Harlene Anderson, and even if we prefer to guide clients to their own discoveries via the skillful asking of questions (see Bohart & Tallman, 1999; White, Hoyt, and Zimmerman, 2000/2001), as therapists we do have various models and ways of thinking that may be useful for clients (see Minuchin's remarks quoted above). Indeed, not to offer new information might have the untoward effect of constraining the client to the existing problem (Fraser, 1998; Hoyt, 2000a). Matthews (2002, p. 161) makes a cogent argument:

> From the antirealist/postmodernist perspective, there is no objective truth, but only local truths. The accumulated empirically based knowledge of psychology and psychotherapy are in that catgory, are particular to that community (i.e., scientists), and as stated by Gergen and Kaye (1992), carry no special authority or privilege. One local truth is as good as another. Thus, the research on psychopathology, its etiology, and its treatment has no special authority. For example, the American Psychological Association Task Force on Psychological Intervention Guidelines (1994) indicated that cognitive-behavioral therapy is a very effective therapy for a range of presenting problems (e.g., anxiety, depression, phobias, obesity). Said report, however, is only a local truth that need have no meaning for the antirealist therapist, who is free to construct any meaning or any narrative in whatever manner he or she chooses. There is only the uniqueness of the client and his or her story with which the therapist has to deal. Could one imagine consulting a medical doctor who dismisses the science-based practice of cancer treatment in favor of his or her own local truths?

There is no escaping therapist influence—indeed, that's what clients pay us for. As Hoyt (2000, p. 56) has written elsewhere: "'To intervene or not to intervene' is *not* the question....*How* is the question." In this regard, Larner (1995, pp. 194-195) suggests a *both/and* perspective that "allows therapists to step outside the modern *versus* postmodern dichotomy" into what he calls the *paramodern*, "where difference and variety are respected and celebrated....in a wide range of metaphors." He writes:

> What is relevant here is not what therapists *say* they do in terms of theory, but what they *do* in practice. And here a deconstructive reading of therapy helps us to see that, in practice, to escape power is impossible, whether we believe in the metaphor of power or not. To say that by not *believing* in the metaphor, change occurs more readily, is to believe in power, the power of the therapist to change others by not believing in such power. To believe that change

occurs from the therapist being non-influential rather than powerful is to believe paradoxically in the power of non-power. [Larner, 1995, p. 201]

We are also well aware of the problem of potential pathologizing, that is, of using diagnoses and treatments pejoratively (for further discussion, see Gergen, 1994b; Hoyt, 2000a; Neimeyer & Raskin, 2000). Still, as active clinicians we recognize conditions such as schizophrenia, major depression, bipolar illness, obsessive-compulsive disorder—even if only approximately described in the *DSM-IV*—are more than mere theoretical constructs. As a clinical strategy, we may choose to overlook or not confront or even to utilize or "work with" a blatant symptom. We can use "psychojudo" and "humor the resistance" (Cummings & Sayama, 1995) without gainsaying the pathology. When Milton Erickson (see Haley, 1973), in his famous case of the mental patient who thought he was Jesus, put the patient to work in the hospital carpenter shop, he may have "accepted" the patient's delusional thinking but didn't come to believe it himself. "Invitation, not imposition" (Hoyt, 2000a) is a good rule of thumb, of course, but when possible, mental illnesses should be recognized and treated. Indeed, from the perspective of narrative constructionism, appropriate psychopharmacology can be conceived of as "restoring restorying" (Hoyt, 2000a, p. 261).

2. *Lack of method to test propositions and understand what works, and how.* Without denying its many useful increases in knowledge, Gergen (1999, p. 239) argues for "abandoning the view of science as a march to the truth....the attempt to narrow the range of ideas to the 'single best' approximation of reality." There may be many ways of knowing and many "right answers" (Combs & Freedman, 1994), but how can we know which to choose? The strong constructivist focus on the particularities of individuals and the desire to avoid simplifying into broad categories or metanarratives—the emphasis on the "idiomorphic rather than the nomothetic" (Hoyt, 1995a, p. 315; see Chapter 6)—creates an "essential tension" (Neimeyer, 2000a, 2002; Neimeyer & Bridges, 2003). Moreover, postmodern therapists sometimes express the view that research may be conducted more to promote the power and prestige of professionals than to serve the needs of clients (Parker, 2000). Thus, Gergen (1994b) laments the therapeutic professions' "diffusion of deficit" and (in Hoyt, 1996d/2001, p. 193) stated, "Personally, I think outcome evaluations are no more than window dressing for a given school of therapy, and the entire concept is misleading."

In her introduction to a special section on "Antiscientific Attitudes within Psychotherapy" that appeared in an issue of the *Journal of Clinical Psychology*, Held (2001, p. 3; also see Held, 2001b) wrote:

> Since the birth of psychoanalysis, the question of whether—and in what way—psychotherapy should be seen as a scientific enterprise has been debated. The debate has recently intensified, as proponents of social constructionist, constructivist, narrative, hermeneutical, and other postmodernist or postpositivist approaches to psychotherapy have challenged the application of a natural science methodology to the so-called human sciences, including the disciplines of psychology in general and psychotherapy in particular. Some who set forth this challenge offer a different conception of what a discipline of psychology and/or psychotherapy might or should be....a conception that is in some (but not all) cases so radically different from the disciplines of conventional science that we may question whether that conception should be considered scientific at all or whether it is radical enough to be considered antiscientific.

In addition to attacks against "placebo insight" (Jopling, 2001), the "dangers of anecdotal reports" (Spence, 2001), and "when scientists are unscientific" (Beutler & Harwood, 2001), the special section contained an article on "The Rejection of Natural Science Approaches to Psychotherapy: Language and the World" by Edward Erwin (2001). He wrote:

> If truth is not correspondence with fact, and if worlds are constructed, then what becomes of the idea of scientific discovery? [p. 10]

and

> There are many examples of this sort where the introduction of new diagnostic categories or theories has an impact on the way psychotherapists view their clients. Nevertheless, to make a causal claim about how the introduction of concepts and theories affect people is not to support the thesis that there are multiple worlds, or that worlds are constructed rather than discovered, or that worlds are not independent of mind and language. Nor does the causal thesis lend any support to the idea that we need a new kind of epistemology, or that it is not useful to employ natural science methods in psychotherapy....We create classifications and theories about such things, but what we do not create are the phenomena: expressive language disorders, schizophrenia, depression, alcoholism, and so on. Whether the categories we employ are useful, or apply in particular cases, are obviously empirical questions, as are questions about etiology and therapeutic effectiveness. [pp. 15-17]

Thus, Bill Matthews (in Hoyt et al., 2000/2001, e.g., p. 218 and p. 222) correctly and repeatedly noted "It's a scientifically-based argument" or "It's an empirical question" when discussants would make assertions about the effects of one reality construction versus another. Indeed, by the very terms of postmodernism, it would be incorrect (nay, impossible) to attempt research that would demonstrate the truth of postmodernist concepts, because this would involve using a methodology postmodernists would argue could only prove what empirical research can prove, not what's necessarily true. In science, a claim of truth normally requires both *theoretical coherence* and *empirical correspondence* (see Messer & Warren, 1995, pp. 112-113). Abandoning the latter requirement vacates "reality testing" concepts such as *right* and *accurate*. But facts are stubborn. Is science "just another way of knowing," a voice among many with no special claim in the "Tower of Babel" (see Miller, Duncan & Hubble, 1997)? Is it true, as Lewis Carroll's (1887/1946) Dodo Bird declared, "that all have won and all must have prizes?" Hence, M. Brewster Smith (1994, p. 408) writes:

> What I see as most unfortunate, however, is the tendency, abetted by Gergen, to give up the conception of science—natural or human, historical or ahistorical—as an evidential, public, self-critical social enterprise, an enterprise that has successfully sought progressively more adequate and comprehensive understandings of the phenomena in its domain—an enterprise committed to an ideal of truth, the approach to which can be evaluated pragmatically. I find little justification in the postmodernist literature for the claim that scientific constructions, fallible as they are and always subject to disconfirmation and revision, are simply operational myths on all fours with religious or political dogmas and ideologies.

And, in his 1995 (p. 393) reply to Gergen:

> [A]lthough empiricism may be dead as a theory of truth, it is very much alive as a method of discovery and finding evidence. As a result, scientific theories are not just "'stories' that scientists like to tell (White & Wang, 1995, p. 392)....I therefore cannot accept Gergen's (1994) politically correct rejection of a universalizing psychology as inherently "totalizing" and imperialistic. It makes a vast difference whether we seek to correct the ethno- or androcentric biases that the postmodern critics have called to our attention, or in defeat take such biases as disqualifying the entire scientific enterprise. I see perceptical bias as inevitable but corrigible. "Dialog" between perspectives is valuable not just for keeping the conversation going: It allows for the correction of perceptival limitations and their transcendence.

To which Gergen (1995, p. 394), true to his postmodern sensibilities, replied back:

In effect, by multiplying the voices engaged in the colloquy we have added significantly to the range and depth of understanding. The discussion expands, its laminations and nuances are augmented, and the arena of concern is enriched. This discursive option stands in contrast to foundationalist attempts—both in the realm of scientific metatheory and in the philosophy of ethics—to replace variability with univocality and dialogue with monologue.

3. Challenges to a coherent sense of self. Postmodernism depicts the self as "empty" (Cushman, 1990; Rosenbaum & Dyckman, 1996), only existing tenuously in context. As David Lodge (2002, pp. 89-91) has written:

> "Postmodern" is sometimes used in a very broad sense to include a whole range of cultural styles, attitudes, and arguments: deconstruction, post-Industrialism, consumerism, multiculturalism, quantum physics, cybernetics, the Internet, and so on. Most of these phenomena and ways of thinking deny the existence of universals in human nature. They regard the concepts of "soul" or "spirit," and even the secular idea of the "self" which humanism developed from the Judeo-Christian religious tradition, as culturally and historically determined....One must concede that the Western humanist concept of the autonomous individual self is not universal, eternally given, and valid for all time and all places, but is a product of history and culture. This doesn't, however, necessarily mean that it isn't a good idea, or that its time has passed. A great deal of what we value in civilized life depends upon it. We also have to acknowledge that the individual self is not a fixed and stable entity, but is constantly being created and modified in consciousness through interaction with others and the world. It may be, therefore, that every time we try to describe the conscious self we misrepresent it because we are trying to fix something that is always changing; but really we have no alternative, any more than the physicist has any alternative to bringing about the collapse of the wave function when he makes an observation, or the deconstructionist has any alternative to using language which she claims is bound to undermine its ostensible claims to meaning.

Neimeyer (2000b, p. 199) similarly notes, "[C]ritical voices, drawing on a myriad of literary, philosophic, political, and feminist sources, have offered an image of deindividuated selves buffeted by the cross currents of multiple discourses in which they are embedded," but then adds, "these embattled subjectivities are also sustained by the relational engagements through which they find meaning, direction, and the prospect of mutual development. I hope that this same postmodern vision, and the spirit of performance and resistance to which it gives rise, continue to infect and inform the practice of psychotherapy."

Postmodernism's rejection of individualism and the idea of a separate and individual "self" has raised some hackles. Martin and Sugarman (1995, p. 405) prefer to avoid the horns of the dilemma, however, and call for a both/and (not either/or) position: "Such a perspective should chart a middle ground between suffocating fixtures of modern certainty on the one hand and postmodern erasures of self and any possibility of progressive understanding of the human condition on the other." They quote Donald Polkinghorne (1999, pp. xiii):

> The postmodernists' commitment to reality as flux has led them to remove personhood or self from the philosophic conversation and to replace it with talk of neurology or sociology. What is currently needed....is a recovery of personhood; that is, a recovery of the psychological realm....The question is how one talks about and understands a nonstatic, changing personhood; that is, a reflective and purposive self that is open to its own inner emotions and thoughts, to other selves, and to the flux of nature.

Held (1995, p. 243; also see Kegan, 1994) expresses concern about encouraging patients who don't already have a good sense of reality to further loosen their grip. This was taken up in the following conversation between Hoyt and Gergen:

HOYT: Some cultures, such as the traditional Balinese....create or construct "selves" that in some ways resemble the condition we call "multiple personality disorder" [MPD]. Other writers, such as Glass (1993) in *Shattered Selves: Multiple Personality in a Postmodern World*, are very critical of postmodern conceptions of the self, arguing that true MPD is a fragmentation of self resulting from horrible childhood abuse and that such individuals suffer greatly for having to live without a firm identity. How do you see the relationship between a postmodern view of "self" and "multiple personality disorder"?

GERGEN: First, the assumptions embraced by Glass—that there simply are "MPD" persons in the world, and that they chiefly suffer from the lack of a firm identity—are exactly the kind of mentality I view as detrimental to the culture. Such presumptions not only serve to objectify the "illness," and to suggest that others may also possess this particular infirmity, but as well imply that there is something privileged in a state of "unified and coherent" being. In a certain sense, then, this kind of analysis is part of the problem.

> Now this is not to doubt that Glass confronts clients who are in deep pain, and that they can understand themselves in just the way he describes. But there are many other ways in which one's personality can be rendered meaningful—many alternative conceptions that can be generated of what he is authoritatively classifying as "MPD." And many of these alternatives would, in my view, be far more promising for the client (and society) as they move from therapeutic relations into daily life.
>
> There is also a certain genre of postmodern writing that provides just such a promise. If one feels split among selves, torn between competing tendencies, capable of multiple personalities, this literature suggests that such a condition may be the newly emerging cultural form. And it is not to be lamented—but explored for its potential riches. [in Hoyt, 1996e/2001a, pp. 193-194]

4. Shifting standards for ethics and morality. As Gergen (1991, p. 241) has written: "Under postmodernism, processes of individual reason, intention, moral decision making, and the like—all central to the ideology of individualism—lose their status as realities." Plato's ideals of *truth, good,* and *beauty* get replaced, as Mente (1995) has commented, with the questions *Whose truth? Whose goodness? Whose beauty?*

Mahoney (1991) cautions that the psychological demands of being a constructive psychotherapist are many and that a great deal of openness to self-evaluation and ambiguity is required. Held (1995; in Hoyt, et al., 2000/2001a, p. 215) cautions that the vagaries of relativism might provide "lazy license" for therapists to impose their own values and reality constructions upon clients. Beware the shoals and undercurrents: there are numerous perils potentially lurking when one forgoes the safety of the positivist or objectivist shore (Hoyt, 2000a, p. 61). In his critical article, "Selfhood at Risk: Postmodern Perils and the Perils of Postmodernism," M. Brewster Smith (1994, p. 409) wrote:

> In the face of the postmodern challenges, the crux of the matter is whether it is still possible to retain some toehold to sustain the old human struggle toward truth, goodness, and beauty as meaningful ideals. Putting it this way sounds very old-fashioned, but the shock these words evoke is evidence of the degree to which nihilistic relativism has permeated our perspective.

To which, it should be noted, Gergen (1994a, p. 413; also see 1985, 1998, 2000), in his response article, "Exploring the Postmodern: Perils or Potentials?" rejoined forcefully:

> It is insufficient in the face of the beast simply to chant the mantras of a science that will seek "progressively more adequate and comprehensive understanding of the phenomena in its domain," that is "committed to an ideal of truth"....It is of little avail to import the recondite writings of Tony Giddens (1991)—as if his authoritative call to "remoralizing" would sign the cross in the face of Satan. It is merely hortatory to resort to condemnation through catchwords such as *fashionable, resentful envy, libertinism*, and *fin de siecle gloom*. If psychologists truly wish to salvage the empiricist tradition or to claim a moral high ground, then it is essential to enter the dialogue with sterner stuff.

Prilleltensky (1997), in his discussion of the moral implications of psychological discourse and action, notes that different approaches vary in their values, assumptions, practices, potential benefits, and potential risks. Following Rosenau (1992), he distinguishes two distinct postmodern orientations: the *affirmative* and the *skeptical*. The former uses social construction and deconstruction to unchain from oppressive messages and to promote empowerment; whereas the latter casts doubt and distrust over all value systems and thus tends to freeze action in a miasma of uncertainty. Prilleltensky (1997, p. 528) writes:

> If the objection is to moral postulates that pretend to speak to and for all people, then the alternative is to create frameworks that are sensitive to context and to people's voices. Moral frameworks are forever partial, evolving, and embedded in subjectivity. But a metacriterion, the need to explore and to express our moral sense, should remain firm, for being passive or recondite in the face of injustice is a moral choice that is hard to defend.

Gergen (2000, pp. 147-148; also see Gergen, 1998) agrees:

> I do not wish to abandon the existing tradition of identity politics, the discourses of oppression, justice, equality, rights, and so on, nor the *in-your-face* activism that we have come to know so well. The point is not to eradicate existing vocabularies of action. Rather, my hope is that we are now participating in the generation of a new vocabulary, a new consciousness, and a new range of practices—a relational politics that will be incorporative, pervasive, collaborative, and unceasing. [Gergen, 2000a, pp. 147-148; also see Gergen, 1998]

Consensus about what constitutes *right* and *wrong* is necessary for the development of professional standards and guidelines (see Cummings & Cummings, 2000, pp. 1-19). When the unit of analysis moves past the monad, morality becomes based in *relational responsibility* (McNamee & Gergen, 1999). In this regard, the following exchange occurred between Hoyt and Gergen in a published conversation entitled "Postmodernism, the Relational Self, Constructive Therapies, and Beyond":

HOYT: Holy hermeneutics! If modernism gave us "ontological insecurity," postmodernism could produce a panic attack! As Sheila McNamee and you (1992, p. 2) have commented, "Little confidence now remains in the optimistic program of scientifically grounded progress toward identifying 'problems' and providing 'cures.'" With conventional standards of "what's right" no longer valid compasses, what suggestions do you have for therapists as we search for (and co-create) therapeutic realities with our clients? Any guides for the perplexed?

GERGEN: At the onset, I think we must all remain humble and interdependent in the face of the problem. This is not the time to look to a new guru who can remove our perplexities; we must work together toward new visions. With this said, my own preference is for a therapeutic approach that appreciates the force of local realities, but within an expanded context of connection. By this, I mean that the therapist would not begin with a single set of criteria as to what constitutes an effective intervention or a cure. Rather, he or she would be maximally sensitive to how such matters are defined within the local communities. What are the standards for judging satisfaction or dissatisfaction within the most immediate relationships at hand? At the same time, the therapist must remain concerned with the fuller range of relationships in which the immediate case is embedded. Meaning within the local condition is ultimately dependent upon broader cultural context. Again, this won't lead to a single standard. But the point is to allow the mix of standards into the therapeutic conversation.

HOYT: This gets at one of the challenges of a multicultural society, where different groups have different mores and standards. How do we steer between the Scylla of

	a Balkanized "anything goes" separatism and the Charybdis of a colonization by the dominant culture?
GERGEN:	It is in the mix of voices, it seems to me, that we find the answer—in the blending, appropriation, and paradox....In my view, the importance of social constructionism to current therapeutic theory and practice is that it enables many practitioners to articulate emerging beliefs and practices....I don't see constructionism as offering just another model of therapy, another "silver bullet" cure, a specialized vocabulary, or a new set of "musts." Rather, I see constructionism as inherent in a vast array of conversations taking place around the world—conversations that bring people together over pressing issues of common concern. To be sure, there are a circumscribed array of topics in these conversations, and in this sense constuctionist discussions cannot do everything one might wish. However, they do raise fundamental questions about long-cherished traditions in Western culture. Given the rapid changes taking place in meanings, values, and practices, and the enormous conflicts among meaning systems around the world, they are lilely to remain focal for some time.... Perhaps you can see again why I favor forms of therapy that enable people to speak in many voices, to comprehend the paradoxes in their own values, to appreciate the positive force of many local intelligibilities. The challenge here would not be to locate the one right position, ethic, or political ideal; nor would it be to suppress informed political action. Rather, it is to enable people to move with greater fluidity in the world, with a greater potential perhaps for coordinating the disparate as opposed to eradicating the opposition. [in Hoyt, 1996e/2001a, pp. 189-192] [15]

TOWARD A MEANINGFUL FUTURE

Postmodernism arose out of the *zeitgeist* of the last forty years, a time of burgeoning technology and exploding cultural diversity. Its initial appeal was in the area of art and literary criticism, and its application in science and human services has resulted in both a heightened awareness of social processes influencing knowledge and a critical attack on the validity of such knowledge. Although it may excite a sense of freedom and respect for different subjectivities, it has also contributed to a kind of fuzziness and sense of inherent meaninglessness when, taken to the extreme, it suggests that all views are equally valid and that only contextual utility, not truth, can be known.

> "When I use a word," Humpty Dumpty said in rather a scornful tone, "it means just what I choose it to mean—neither more or less."
> "The question is," said Alice, "whether you can make words mean so many different things."
> "The question is," said Humpty Dumpty, "which is to be master—that is all." [Carroll, 1887/1946]

Taken at its word, postmodernism risks promoting a relativist netherland that is potentially destructive, preventing people from knowing, from thinking clearly and critically, and from feeling that one is in a shared world with other people. We appreciate postmodernism's emphasis on the social basis of meaning-making and its challenges to taken-for-granted assumptions without accepting its invitation to step into a "Superficial Abyss" (Baudrillard, 1990). In this regard, we certainly agree with Matthews' (2002, p. 167) conclusion:

> Ultimately, the question regarding solution-focused/narrative therapies is simple, yet very important: "Do clients improve (change their behavior, beliefs, attitudes) as a function of solution-focused/narrative therapies when compared with some other form of therapy and no treatment? Psychoanalysis, as created by Sigmund Freud, was never interested in such a question, and became merely a form of literary criticism in which its practitioners engaged. If solution-focused and narrative approaches have something to offer as systems of therapy (which I believe they do), then these therapies must be evaluated systematically and compared with other approaches. Antirealist epistemology serves only to detract from a systematic understanding of these

---

15. Some of this appeal was anticipated by Carl Rogers (1978/1989, pp. 424-426) in his paper, "Do We Need "A" Reality?" in which he wrote: "I, and many others, have come to a new realization. It is this: The only reality I can possibly know is the world as *I* perceive and experience it as this moment. The only reality you can possibly know is the world as *you* perceive and experience it as this moment. And the only certainty is that those perceived realities are different. There are as many 'real worlds' as there are people! This creates a most burdensome dilemma, one never before experienced in history....Because of this change, I want to raise a very serious question: Can we today afford the luxury of having '*a*' reality? Can we still preserve the belief that there is a 'real world' upon whose definition we all agree? I am convinced that this is a luxury we *cannot* afford, a myth we dare not complain."

methods of therapy, is inherently contradictory, and can be abandoned without detriment to the commitment to its individualized practice.

We have attempted to recast the discourse not in terms of modernist/postmodernist (or realist/antirealist), but rather, in terms of objectivist/constructionist, and have preferred the related but alternative theories of *social constructionism* and *poststructuralism*, with their connotations of multiple perspectives, interpersonal coordination, relational responsibility, and therapeutic collaboration. While these evolving approaches are reflective of many of the themes loosely associated with postmodernism, there is no need to take on the "baggage" of the postmodern messages of unreality, anti-science, and alienation. Constructive psychotherapy, viewed as a relational and conversational process involving collaboration oriented around the clients' theories and meanings as well as the power of language and imagination, does not need to be grounded in postmodern philosophy.

In their 1967 song, "Strawberry Fields Forever," the Beatles told us that since nothing is real there's nothing to worry about. Would that were true.

10

Interview II—"Burn In, Not Out!": A Conversation about Truth and Beauty in Brief Therapy (with Tapio Malinen)

The following conversation took place in Helsinki, Finland, on March 9, 2001. I had just finished teaching a two-day workshop on "Integrative Brief Therapy," sponsored by the Finnish Family Therapy Association. Tapio Malinen is a school psychologist, therapist, tai-chi teacher, and editor of the Finnish solution-focused therapy journal, *Ratkes*.

MALINEN: You told the workshop audience that you have a wonderful ritual in your family. When you are together having Sunday night dinner, you take the time for everyone to say what was good this week and what each person enjoyed the most. I would like to start this conversation by asking you to imagine that you are back to California with your family, sitting Sunday night at your dinner table and it comes your turn to tell what was the most exciting or sparkling moment during your Finland visit…So, what would you tell them?

HOYT: What was the *most* sparkling moment? There have been so many of them…but right now I'm thinking about two things. One was being in the sauna and going swimming in the sea in the ice-water. Seeing the color of the water and the color of the ice, as I climbed down the ladder and went into the very frigid water, was very invigorating and wonderful. Wow! That whole experi-

Interview II: "Burn In, Not Out!" 183

ence of going from sauna to the water and back and forth was very special and beautiful.

Another moment was in the end of the one-day conference I gave for the A-clinic on supervision earlier this week. Ritva Saarelainen persuaded me to sing a song. I've never sung publicly before. And I sung the song "The Rose." The lines at the end—"beneath the bitter snows lies the seed that with the sun's love, in the Spring becomes the rose"—touch me very much. They remind me of solution-focused therapy, that even when conditions are hard and cold, wonderful things can still come through. Sometimes, particularly with a therapist's support or love, wonderful things can come through; even when it's hard times, we shouldn't give up, because there's always hope. And there are some lines in the song about "those who won't take a chnace, never learn to dance." As I started to sing, I became self-conscious; for a moment I was going to stop, but I realized what the song was telling me and I listened to myself and that was my solution. It was O.K. to "take a chance and learn to dance." And there I was. I also have had many other wonderful moments—some very interesting exchanges at the conference and wonderful discussions with people, who have been so warm and kind; dinner that first night at the Lapp Restaurant; spending the day with Ritva and her friends at artist studios and visiting the lovely town of Porvoo (where I understand you live); looking at the Gallen-Kallela painting "The Myth of Aino" at the Atheneum; and others. But right now, the sauna and that song are at the top of the list.

MALINEN: During these two day that I've listened to you at the workshop, I've got some glimpses of what the title of your book, *Some Stories Are Better that Others*, might mean. But could you specify that a little bit more—why are some stories better than others?

HOYT: Some stories are better than others because they are more enlivening and encouraging, and help people get more of what they want. They carry wisdom and hope.[1] They open people's hearts and touch their feelings. They speak to the person's truth or their dream. The person feels free and invigorated in those moments and I think that's what really makes some stories better than others. They touch us and they move us. Louis Armstrong, the jazz musician, said that there are two kinds of music: good music and bad music. Any music that makes you tap your foot is good music. And to me, stories that are good stories are stories that make me tap my foot, that quicken my pulse, that make me lean in to life and make me feel more alive, richer and more involved. The theory has to do with narrative construction and building a worldview through the stories we tell ourselves. For other people, good stories might mean something else, but I think for most people "better stories" are the stories that bring them more of whatever it is that makes them feel good.

MALINEN: I get the image from this tapping your foot, that that's the moment when you are somehow more in contact with yourself or with your life-energy and your personal rhythm of life.

HOYT: It's a metaphor and kind of hard to talk about specifically, but many people—including myself—do have an experience of being "on" or being "in rhythm" or being connected to the "flow" or something. "Stories" or "narratives" can lead me there and describe it afterwards, but it is also important to remember that stories are not Life.[2] In my best moments I'm so involved that

---

1. Dennis Olson (1995, p. 6) writes in his beautiful book, *Shared Spirits: Wildlife and Native Americans*: "We are bound by physical bodies and countless other limitations, but we are transcended by the stories we carry and pass on to others, and by the risks we take in that process. We are not important. We are vessels carrying water in a desert and fire through a blizzard. Our importance lies in the thoughts we carry, and the sharing of water and fire with those who follow."
2. See the discussion by Maryhelen Snyder (1996; also see Hyde, 1983; Rukeyser, 1996) about ways that *poetic knowing* differ from *story* or *narrative*.

	I forget about myself and I'm not separate from the experience.
MALINEN:	And during those moments you somehow break the limits between you and everything that's around you. There's no clear boundary.
HOYT:	Yeah.
MALINEN:	Let's come back to this after a moment. I know that you have done a number of interviews with some of the remarkable people in our field, for example, with Steve de Shazer, Michael White, John Weakland, Bill O'Hanlon, Kenneth Gergen, Paul Watzlawick, and Karl Tomm. What kind of moments have these been for you? How have they affected you? What have you learned from those moments—about the therapy world and about the human being?
HOYT:	There is the personal pleasure of meeting very bright people, who are all very articulate and brilliant in what they do. They're also very decent, nice people. If one loved golf, it would be nice to play a round with Tiger Woods, or if you were into basketball, to shoot some hoops with Michael Jordan. So, being able to talk solution-focus with Steve de Shazer or narrative with Michael White or MRI strategies with Paul Watzlawick or social construction of reality with Ken Gergen or possibility therapy with Bill O'Hanlon is very exciting to me. Doing the interviews, I noticed how very thoughtful and articulate all of my different colleagues have been and how very careful and precisely they use words to say things. Sometimes they even wanted to edit what they said, not to change it, but to make it clearer and to be really sure that they conveyed what they wanted to express.

    I was moved greatly during the conversation with Michael White and Gene Combs that we did several years ago (Hoyt & Combs, 1996/2001). We were talking about creating the path as we go. That we are making our world, making our reality with our choices and what we do. When we were talking about it, something very magical happened for me. Suddenly I realized how much I have choice in how I look at my life and how I experience it. And it has stayed with me—many times I have thought about how I have this freedom. I also am much more aware that what is, is. This may sound a bit like California psycho-babble, but only what we are attending to and talking about is happening and is real—everything else could be a possibility, but we are making our lives and our worlds as we go, together. That's been an interesting effect for me.

I also saw—and that reinforced in me—the value of hard work and preparation. My colleagues are very hard workers and very smart and I take that as an inspiration. By the way, all these interviews are together in a new book called *Interviews with Brief Therapy Experts* to be published in May 2001.

MALINEN: When I read your books and found so many interviews, I started to think that it's probably your preferred method to work, to explore things by having dialogues with your colleagues.

HOYT: The "conversation" or "interview" format allows a nice give-and-take that is congenial for talking about "talking therapy." The way I would do the interviews—and I hope to do more—is that I would approach someone and ask if we could come together and have an interview and then I would read most everything they have written. I would also attend their workshops and/or look at a couple of videotapes, and then would also read what people have said about them and ask some of my colleagues (including other interviewees), "What question would you like to ask this therapist or what would be interesting to explore?" I would prepare myself to get inside their thinking and attempt to grasp and understand what they were saying as well as how they were seen by others. So I would sort of develop these different "internalized others" in my head. When we would do the interview, I would have some questions ready to ask and a few backup-questions. I might also have some quotations where someone said something critical from a different angle. After the interview I would go through the transcript and add footnotes from my reading, to give some scholarly information and background to what we were saying, and would also invite my co-interviewees to make whatever additions they felt like making.

MALINEN: So your interviews are just the top of the icebergs. There have been lot of preparations before you meet your colleagues.

HOYT: Yes. You are Finnish, so you probably know more about icebergs that I do. But sometimes when I go back and look, I can see lots of levels of reading when I go into particular questions. A lot of it has come out of the conversation and I give credit to the people I interview, of course. But sometimes it's hard to know where ideas come from. They really bubble up from the interaction. Did I say it? Did they say it? Even when I said it, I said it in response to the context in the situation. So they are really very bipersonal or relational or collaborative or systemic. Together we are co-creating "inter-views." (My friend Don Meichenbaum once suggested calling them "inter-muses.") It's not just one person interviewing the other.

MALINEN: I just started to think: Just now we are doing an interview about the interviews!

HOYT: It's wheels within wheels, mirrors within mirrors.

MALINEN: You mentioned *words* and how precisely your colleagues talk. As I talk with you, I also can experience how precise your way of using the words is. I would like to ask you what's the difference in your dictionary between the words *eclectic* and *integrative?*

HOYT: The word *eclectic* generally means pulling or drawing from different areas. *Eclectic* to me sounds more like a collection, but the pieces are not necessarily organized synergistically or working together. I think lots of therapists who say they are eclectic may have a lot of techniques and ideas that sometimes contradict one another. It's very difficult, for example, to be doing solution-focused work but then also be questioning the client's underlying assumptions, the way they are viewing the world, be it via the making of psychodynamic interpretations or the cognitive-behavioral editing or correcting of the person's reasoning. If you are trying to tell them that their logic is valid and real, how can you also be challenging its validity at the same time? I tend to prefer the term *multi-theoretical,* because in English *eclectic* sounds like a cross between *electric* and *chaotic*! I think *integrative* has the implication that the pieces fit together and together they are more than the sum of the parts. They're multiplicative. So it's easier for me to integrate, say, ideas from Ericksonian and solution-focused and narrative therapy, because they all are based on ideas of competency and utilization of resources. Those are much easier to integrate than disparate ideas from traditions that are much different.

MALINEN: Could one say that real integration, as you put it, would be one of the roads for the development of psychotherapy? Something that is somehow emerging from these innovative and synergistic approaches?

HOYT: In the United States there is an organization called the Society for Psychotherapy Integration. They hold conferences and they try to look for "common factors" or what's similar in different therapies. What are the real factors that seem to make it work? Scott Miller and his colleagues (Miller et al., 1997) have talked about that at some length, about the big importance of the client's contributions relative to the therapist's contributions and the role of placebo effects. The difficulty, I think, with how to integrate different approaches *in practice* is that sometimes we wind up with mush; different approaches may not do what they do well with a little bit of this and a little bit of that. I think the concepts of social construction and narrative construction and the languaging of reality are ways for how to think about integration. It's interesting: the wheels within the wheels. We're trying to find a way to talk about talking, a language for languaging about languaging. In physics there are various forces and we go into a unified field-theory, some kind of concept that pulls it all together. For me, that's what social construction does. It's the idea of *building stories* and *language games* and *solution construction*.

MALINEN: Physicists are nowadays seeking for the so-called Big Theory.

HOYT: In brief therapy The Big Theory now is social construction. They used to think the Big Theory was The Unconscious; then, for awhile, it was Structure and Communication.[3] This is an interesting question: If anything is "The Unconscious," how is it useful to think about it and how is it not useful to think about? It's a concept and it may be a helpful concept, but everything we think about, every way we approach something, opens certain possibilities and closes certain others. So I am not necessarily for or against something as much as I'm asking, what do we gain or what do we lose by thinking in a certain way? Every model or theory opens doors and closes doors. What I gain by solution-focused approaches—whether it is specifically solution-focused therapy or some other variant (e.g., solution-oriented or possibility therapy or some other competence-based or even some of the language-system ideas)—is a sense of freedom. The client and the thera-

---

3. This is far from a settled issue; see, for example, Salvador Minuchin's 1998 article, "Where is the Family in Narrative Family Therapy?"

pist are building something rather than tearing something down.

As I mentioned in the workshop, I'm interested in the *aesthetics* of therapy; is it attractive and interesting? I'm interested in the *ethics*; is it respectful, does it enlarge the person? And I'm interested in the *effects*; does it work, is it helpful? From what I have understood so far about competency-oriented and language-based approaches, they satisfy all three of these more than any other schools or theories I have met.

MALINEN: There are two things I'm thinking about right now: Steve de Shazer (2001) has said that there is no theory in solution-focused therapy. Theories don't explain reality, they rather organize our brains. Wouldn't it be nice if we would have a Theory with a big T, so we would be legitimized. But if we would have that Theory, all our minds would be clouded. The Big Theory would cloud that what is as it is.

HOYT: Yeah—we'd be theorists rather than therapists, more interested in our "lenses" than our clients. Bill O'Hanlon and Jim Wilk (1987, p. ix) have a funny line in their book where they quote a famous Irish scientist and wit who was reported to have remarked, "Well, it works in practice OK…but does it work in theory?"!

MALINEN: The other thing I was thinking about was what Ken Wilber (1998), one of the greatest philosophers in the field of transpersonal psychology, wrote in his book, *The Marriage of Sense and Soul*. He also talks about good, beautiful and true; ethics, aesthetics and knowledge; moral, art and science. He is arguing that the good thing in modernism was that it differentiated these three spheres from each other. They all have their different languages. In my mind, your way to evaluate psychotherapy reminds me of his analysis.

HOYT: I'm wondering if I borrowed my three concepts of aesthetics, ethics and effects from Ken Wilbur. I don't know exactly when I read that book of his, but I did read it, at the suggestion of Cloe Madanes. I'm wondering if I'm having what is called *cryptoamnesia*, which means you picked something up but don't remember doing so or where it came from. I surely want to give him credit, if I borrowed it from him. If so—Thank you, Ken![4]

Wilbur also said some other things in his book that had me concerned. He has a very strong argument in which he talks about the "nihilism and narcissism" of postmodernism. This whole topic has become a real bugaboo. The concept gets used so loosely nowadays; sometimes *postmodern* means nearly anything, that everything goes or everyone can have her own reality and there's no reality that is better than any other. [See Chapter 9, this volume.] That might be true inside people's heads, that everyone can have his or her own "Truth," their heartfelt beliefs and "take" on reality. *Truth* is an elusive critter, but there is an external reality that science looks at, and if we ignore the objective reality outside us, we are somewhere between autistic, ignorant, and psychotic.

MALINEN: There's a really interesting note in your *Handbook of Constructive Therapies* (Hoyt, 1998, p. 15) containing a list by Gail Shafarman of "Thirteen Ways of Looking at How a Poet and a Therapist Are One." She says that both the therapist and the poet recognize the beauty of the form—and the need to judiciously break it.[5] Could you say something about what *beautiful* and *aesthetics* mean to you in therapy?

---

4. On further checking, I first described my tripartite criteria in June 1996 at a panel discussion (Tomm, Hoyt, Anderson & Gilligan, 1996) held at the Therapeutic Conversations 3 conference in Denver, Colorado.

5. Jay Haley provides "A Quiz for Young Therapists" in which he poses the question: "When one thinks of therapy as poetry, does a skillful therapist write sonnets or free verse?" For the wise and witty answer to this and other questions, visit www.Jay-Haley-on-Therapy.com.

HOYT: I know it when I see it. Sometimes it's hard to explain, but *beautiful* in therapy means to me that it elegantly and eloquently captures the magic of the moment. It often has a certain simplicity or efficiency, it is nothing unnecessary, and in some lovely way it gets to the core, to the heart of whatever the topic is that is being discussed. I heard Robert Bly, a well-known American poet, once read a long, beautiful poem. And someone in the audience asked him, "What does it mean?" And Bly said, "If I knew what it meant, I would have written an essay, not a poem." I think beauty, like poetry, is not linear. It's not something where you say "A+B+C=Beauty." It's something about the way the pieces come together. It's hard to explain.

MALINEN: Isadore Duncan also answered, when somebody asked her, what's the meaning of her dance: "If I knew that, I wouldn't dance!"

HOYT: Isn't that interesting! Mayby Bly borrowed from her. *Beauty* connotes for me that we are in a *constructive* (positive, creative, choice-making) process. There is an infinity of good and an infinity of bad we can focus on. What we choose doesn't make all the difference, but it does make a big difference. I was reading an interesting book by Alex Kerr (1996) called *Lost Japan*. In one passage (p. 243) he describes being at a tea ceremony in which a participant accidentally spilled the whole tea container all over the tatami mat. Everyone was petrified, until the tea-master spoke: "What is the appropriate think to say at a time like this? You should say, 'Look how beautiful!'....You may never see this again in all your lives....Look, and admire!" I love that! Damn, I wish I could hold that consciousness.

Thinking about *beauty* evokes for me an aesthetic sensibility, the world of grace and proportion and creativity and appreciation, which I find very attractive.[6] I love well-turned phrases and picturesque, compelling language, but beauty in therapy (or elsewhere) does not just mean that something is clever or pretty or happy. Beauty is not just skin-deep. The early 19th century English poet John Keats (1988, p. 346) is often quoted for the famous lines:

Beauty is truth, truth beauty,
—that is all Ye know on earth,
and all ye need to know.

As W.H. Auden (1966, p. 337) pointed out, however, Keats used those lines to criticize as shallow or superficial a kind of work of art that deliberately excludes the problems and evils of this life.[7] A poet friend of mine back home[8] recently called my attention to a poem by her mentor, Phillip Levine (1999), called "Keats in California," in which he starts by extolling the natural beauty of California and tells us that he's been reading Keats "for the first time in my 69th year." He then writes (p. 161):

I can see fields of wildflowers on fire until
I have to look away from so much life.
I could ask myself, Have I made a Soul
Today, have I sucked at the Teat of the Heart
Flooded with the experience of a world like ours?
Have I become a man one more time?

MALINEN: I really like the way you move back and forth using personal experience and poetic imagery.

HOYT: Thanks.[9] Having read your paper (Malinen, 2001) on using *appreciative language*, I know you have similar

---

6. A main alternative, as Stephen Gilligan (1996) has written, is *fundamentalism*, which involves right-or-wrong rigidities and adherence to a single Truth.
7. In his *Selected Letters*, Keats (1819/1974, p. 162) made clear that he saw beauty in whatever made soul in this world: "Do you not see how necessary a world of Pains and troubles is to school an Intelligence and make a Soul? A Place where the heart must feel and suffer in a thousand diverse ways!"
8. Thanks to Sandra Hoben.

	interests. So, let me ask you, Tapio, how do you think about *beauty* in therapy?
MALINEN:	I think beauty is in the eye of the beholder. So, for me, beauty in therapy is a way to see or a way to be in the world. If I as a therapist succeed to co-create together with my client an open space, where our truths (what is truthful for us, what makes sense and works for us) unfold in a respectful atmosphere and we can recognize once again who we are, our suchness, then I often experience that there are also certain aesthetic dimensions to this particular moment. It often kind of takes my breath away, takes time away, takes myself away, all at once. This mutual space has often the characteristics of flow, unpredictability, wholeness, uncontrol, serenity, participation and a kind of elegance. Often both the therapist and the client will be touched and nourished by the beauty of the moment. To create this space you need to have some technical skills, but at its best the therapist meets his client as the wind meets the water. Then the technique and the encounter of the human beings are one. And that's beautiful.
HOYT:	Indeed—and well said! Hey, *Ratkes!!*

---

9. In light of Auden's remarks about Keat's criticizing a shallowness that excludes the pains of life, consider also these lines from Robinson Jeffers' (1932) poem, "Fire on the Hills":

> The deer were bounding like blown leaves
> Under the smoke in front of the roaring wave of the brushfire;
> I thought of the smaller lives that were caught.
> Beauty is not always lovely; the fire was beautiful, the terror
> Of the deer was beautiful; and when I returned
> Down the black slopes after the fire had gone by, an eagle
> Was perched on the jag of a burnt pine,
> Insolent and gorged, cloaked in the folded storms of his shoulders.
> He had come from far off for the good hunting
> [....]
> I thought, painfully, but the whole mind,
> The destruction that brings an eagle from heaven is better than mercy.

MALINEN: In your *Handbook of Constructive Therapies*, Ken Gergen has written the Foreword. He talks about how the entire therapeutic venture is fundamentally an exercise in ethics, and about the *spirit of cooperation* and the *inspiration of the incomplete*. And then he talks about something that personally interests me: the *blurring of boundaries between professional and client*. I have experienced many times as a brief therapist, that the roles of the client and the therapist are not the same as in the so-called "modern" therapies. There is not so much hierarchy. As you said a couple of minutes ago, you create meanings together, you and your client collaborate. Many people talk when they work, for example, solution focused, that from the therapist's point of view it's a hell of a lot lighter to focus on strengths and possibilities than on pathology and problems. You don't experience your work to be so heavy and there is even an aspect of playfulness in what you are doing. It prevents burn-out. Do you agree with this, that brief therapy has some beneficial effects on the therapist?

HOYT: I think very much that in the kind of work we do, as in everything, how we look greatly influences what we see. And if we spend our day looking at pain, pathology, resistance and cruelty or failure, we'll spend a very ugly day. And it has to have a negative feedback to the therapist (and the client). You feel that you have spend the whole day in the mud. It is encouraging to look more at strengths and positives. The issue of expertise is very complicated. Consider Anderson and Goolishian's (1992) well-known phrase, "the client is the expert." We talk about recognizing and respecting the validity and truthfulness of our clients and their perspective; we try to support that. The therapist's expertise becomes largely, but not completely, a matter of how to evoke the client's expertise. Much like a good movie director has to figure out how to get the best performance out of an actor or actress, we have to woo or coax the best out of the person. Sometimes it's like seeing a spark and blowing gently on the embers, or helping bring forward a latent photographic image.

Having said that, there are also many instances where as professional therapists we have knowledge or expertise that we should share with the client. For example—I'd rather not put anyone's name on this—I watched someone working with a patient who I thought would probably benefit enormously from a certain kind of medication. But the therapist did not mention medication to the patient, even as an option. And when we later discussed it and I said, "Why did you not bring up medicine?' he said: "The patient didn't mention it, so I didn't want to bring it up, because I wanted to work with his resources and competencies." I think, in addition to our expertise in bringing forth client resources, we do have some expert knowledge and I think it's important to offer it in a respectful way. I was very concerned. Sometimes if we don't do that, the client may be limited to developing solutions from their existing repertoire and not be able to borrow knowledge or skills from other people who have learned things they don't know about yet. So I think it's important that we don't go so far in trying to support the client's expertise that we forget that there are two experts in the room and that we can integrate their expertise.

MALINEN: One expert who knows how to direct an orchestra and another one who knows how to play his or her instrument?

HOYT: Yes. And one who knows how to play the instrument sometimes could be taught some new songs that they may not already know.

MALINEN: And maybe to tune his or her instrument in a little bit different way?

HOYT: And if the instrument is broken, it might be good to offer them some glue or a screwdriver or whatever it is to fix the instrument. Sometimes there's a role for medication. I have not heard many people talk about the use of medicine in a solution-focused frame. As a narrative constructivist, I think of the appropriate use of medication as "restoring restorying." It's restoring the person's capacity to continue constructing their story. But if they are too depressed or too confused or too scared, they may not be able to pull their thoughts together. So I think sometimes it may be helpful to consider medicine, although it's a slippery slope—we don't want to overmedicate or medicate prematurely, or use medication to control or manipulate people.

MALINEN: I have a personal experience of using anti-depression medication. And I really think it was a good experience for me and when I nowadays work with my clients it's quite easy for me to somehow remember their rights on this. But I have also asked myself, what would be the solution-focused way to use medication?[10]

HOYT: I have colleagues whom I respect greatly, but who are always battling against the pharmaceutical companies and acting as though patients taking medication is always some abuse of the patients. They act as if medication is always inappropriate. I have know many patients, however, that have found it very helpful. Let me give an example of someone I knew. I had a patient—we did so-called "brilliant" work...but nothing changed. It did not help the person. And then eventually, in desperation, I asked whether she would be willing to see a psychiatrist, to have some medication. A few weeks later she was feeling much better and beginning to make changes, and she said something that changed my way of looking at medication. What she said was: "Michael, the therapy we did was helpful. I thought I got a really good map. But when I took the medicine, I felt like I had some gas in the tank of my

---

10. Phil Trautman (2000) has written about this in his paper "The Key to the Pharmacy: Integrating Solution-Focused Brief Therapy and Psychopharmacological Treatment."

car and now I can use the map and go somewhere." Once I heard that, I began to think of particular people who were not moving their "cars" very far—that maybe the problem wasn't a lack of solutions, but it was a lack of energy. Invitation and information, not imposition, is a key.

MALINEN: Concerning the energy of the therapist, there's a lovely paper you have written together with David Nylund called "The Joy of Narrative" (Hoyt & Nylund, 1997/2000). It reminds me of our previous comments about how brief therapy effects the therapist. There's a nice exercise in it, too.

HOYT: Thank you. I very much appreciate how you have taken the time to read some of these things. As you know, being an editor and a writer yourself, we don't make any money writing articles and professional books. We do it for the joy of doing it and to contribute back to the field, so it's wonderful when someone actually takes the time to read and think about it. I remember one of the first times I published a paper and a few months later I received a request from Japan for a reprint of the paper. It thrilled me, that some idea that I had had in my head had meant something to somebody on the other side of the world and we were now in communication. My world became smaller and friendlier as a result of that. It was—and still is—very exciting.

The exercise David Nylund and I developed in our article involves being interviewed as though you are your client and talking about how the therapy went from the client's point of view. It uses an "internalized other interview," as Karl Tomm or David Epston might call it. And when we've used this exercise in many workshops both in the U.S. and other countries, it's remarkable what people come up with. If they let themselves really get immersed in how they think their clients experienced them, they make interesting discoveries that have been very helpful.

MALINEN: Now I want to direct this conversation to another issue. I have lots of thoughts about how the human potential movement in the 1960s and the ancient wisdom traditions have a similar picture of the essence of the human being as the social constructionists have nowadays.

HOYT: How so? In what ways?

MALINEN: In a way that somehow we have always already everything we need inside of us. Buddhism would say that we have the Buddhahood potential always already in us. Wittgenstein would say that since everything lies open to view, there's nothing to explain. What you have to do is just look. Nothing is hidden. But because of our different blinders we don't see what's always in front of us—that the fly-bottle is always open for the fly to escape. In your *Constructive Therapies, Volume 2* there's a nice paper by Rosenbaum and Dyckman called "No Self? No Problem!" The authors show how the view of the human being in social constructionism and, for example, in Buddhism resembles one another. That, for example, there's no such "thing" as self, that everything exists only in relationship. Many postmodern writers also stress the inherent relational and contextual nature of self. Do you see any similarities between these ancient ways of thinking and the picture of a human being as it shows itself in the background theories of brief therapy, especially in social constructionism? Does this question have any personal meaning for you?

HOYT: That's a big, wonderful question. I have some personal interest in this area, but I don't know enough about ancient traditional teachings to say anything well-informed. I agree with you about what you were saying, that there's a belief in people's resourcefulness. Sometimes there's a belief that "liberation" or "enlightenment" comes from realizing your true self that is different from your perception-making ego. There's also often a belief that we are connected to something outside of ourselves and that we are part of the larger

MALINEN: reality. I think we have become very atomistic, very cut off and separate; one from the other, us from our past, us from the environment.

MALINEN: You from your client?

HOYT: We are separate people, and sometimes it's good to have the space to work, but sometimes we talk about therapy as "Person A treats Person B," as though they were objects (not people) and that influence only flows in one direction. There are resonances and reverberations between people. Even without evoking ideas of spirituality or mystical states of mind, I've tried to articulate a few ideas about this in a recent paper called "Connection: The Double-Edged Gift of Presence" (see Chapter 2, this volume).

MALINEN: Besides being a psychologist, I'm a tai-chi teacher. Maybe that's why I find your paper "A Golfer's Guide to Brief Therapy" (1996f/2000a) so living and personal for me—to think of golf or dance or martial arts as a metaphor of therapy. In your paper you wrote that a game plays itself through the player and that therapy plays itself through the therapist. What meaning does that have for you?

HOYT: I used to be Michael Hoyt doing therapy, then I was a therapist who was Michael Hoyt, and now I'm back (sometimes) to being Michael Hoyt doing therapy. I find that when I'm at my best during the day, all I'm doing is being myself and talking with people. People come in and we have a conversation—we make a language game together, do a dance together, or whatever you want to call it. And I disappear! "How can we know the dancer from the dance?" as Yeats (1928/1989, p. 217) put it. I become part of the process. In Zen they would say: "Burn clean and leave no ashes." When I get fully involved, I don't have an observing sense of my self; I'm not in the corner watching myself, saying "Oh, this is good," or "That's the right tech-

	nique" or "I wonder what doctor so-and-so would think of this?" In the golf paper I quote someone who said that when you're really playing, golf becomes a verb, not a noun. You are *in* golf, you *are* golf. I'm not an excellent golfer, but I have had moments when I was in the flow. I didn't have to think— there was "no-mind," as they say in some Eastern traditions. You trust your unconscious and let it go and it is happening.
MALINEN:	In studies of so-called "peak experiences" in sport, it has been reported that players somehow experience a kind of altered state of consciousness during those moments.
HOYT:	Yes. Michael Murphy has talked about it in *The Psychic Side of Sports* (Murphy & White, 1978) and *Golf in the Kingdom* (1972).
MALINEN:	Yes. And in *The Future of the Body* (1992).
HOYT:	He lives a couple of miles from my house and our sons at one time were in the same school and I knew who Michael was, because I had read his books. One day I took my son to the local park and his son was there, too, and they were playing and the two fathers, Murphy and I, were sitting on the bench and we had one of the most remarkable conversations I have ever had. Neither one of us said anything about our backgrounds or interests or identified our names. But I felt like I was hanging out at the park with Shivas Irons (the protagonist in Murphy's *Golf in the Kingdom*) or with Don Juan from Castaneda's books!
MALINEN:	That flow is something you have experienced in your therapy work, too. That you just do your work and somehow you forget the time and you are in kind of timeless space and everything is running very smoothly and you are doing an excellent job.
HOYT:	Sometimes it last for couple of hours. There have even been a couple of times when I have walked down the hallway between appointments and said jokingly to one

of my colleagues: "I'm hot, I'm hot! Quick, do you have any problems?" And we laughed. And the other side is true, too. There have been many moments, too many, where I was just stuck and couldn't get it going. Maybe I could try to be competent in a general way, but I didn't have any of that sort of magic.

MALINEN: Suddenly I started to think that if it would be possible to learn to do therapy in the kind of mindful way, that would burn you more *in* than *out*. Especially in solution-focused therapy, you have the outer form that focuses on strengths and the good powers of life. Is it possible to think that it could kind of trigger in some therapists these altered states of consciousness or these flow-moments? And, if so, how to use them ethically during the therapy process?

HOYT: I think that being in the positive mind-set that solution-focus encourages helps, as does having an active sense of humor. I also find it helpful to try to approach each client with love in my heart.[11] We can all visit that "on" place occasionally or rarely and some people, the masters, can hang out there longer. But I think it takes a lot of talent and skill and a lot of disciplined training. I cannot just pick up a musical instrument and perform as a professional can without spending years and years of learning. It's important that we have a lot of discipline, and I'm saying this because I don't want to suggest that whatever we do is "therapy" or therapeutic. I think the ultimate test of it is, does it work? We have to look at, are the clients getting what the clients want? That's the honest, accountable approach. And if what we are doing works for the person we are serving, then it's good. But if what we are doing doesn't work for them, we have to figure the way it would work better

---

11. See Karl Tomm's discussion (in Tomm, Hoyt & Madigan, 1998/2001) about *therapeutic love* and *ethical postures*.

	for them...and not blame them. That's what we are supposed to be doing.
MALINEN:	In your book, *The First Session in Brief Therapy* (Budman, Hoyt & Friedman, 1992, p. 81), you were asked how you became a brief therapist, and you answered: "I was born to be a brief therapist. My mother, a loving and wonderful woman bless her soul, was a major-league worrier. I often consoled her, and soon learned to do it quickly." If you think about your dearest and most influential people when you were a kid, for example, at five years old, who among them knew that some day you will become a brief therapist and how did they know that?
HOYT:	I think my grandfather Ben Bernstein knew I would do something with language. He used to say how much he loved to listen to me. And I loved when he would come to our house. He was a salesman and he travelled a lot and he would spend hours telling stories about people he had met and things that had happened. I learned something about storytelling from him. My mother, who did worry a lot, also had the biggest heart I've ever known anyone to have. She loved to make friends and talk with all sorts of different people. My father had a great intellectual interest in things and was an avid reader.[12] I don't recall my parents ever telling me specifically that they wanted me to be a psychologist, but

---

12. I love the story my father told me (recounted in Hoyt, 1995a, pp. 331-332) about the time he was at a baseball game at Wrigley Field in Chicago, and a drunken and belligerent fan in the bleachers was verbally abusing one of the ballplayers. The man let it be known that he was packing a gun, and it became alarmingly possible that he might use it. My father—who was a salesman by trade and something of a strategic therapist by nature—got involved. Dad was also a gun fancier. He got the irate fan engaged in a discussion by asking about the type of gun, showed some interest, and wound up bargaining for and buying the gun on the spot. (The police never came.) When I asked my father what he had done with the weapon, he said he had taken it to a shop the next day and sold it, for a profit. When I asked why he had done that, he replied, "Hey, you've got to get paid for this kind of work."

they were very happy when I did well in school.

I also had a friend when I was a teenager (we're still friends) whose mother had been a social worker and she talked to me about how good it would be to become a social worker or a psychologist or somebody that would help people. The ear doctor I consulted during college when I was looking for medical excuses to avoid the Viet Nam war also steered me toward the clinical helping professions (and away from being a lawyer). Some of my college professors were also inspirational.

While all of these were influences, in some ways I think it was "meant to be." When I was a child I was always interested, from the beginning, in why people did what they did and how they talked about it. When my parents' friends would come to visit, I would ask my parents afterwards questions like: "When Mrs. Goldberg starts to talk about her daughter, why does Mr. Goldberg always get up and go outside to have a cigarette?" or: "When Mr. Goodman wants to have a drink or say something, why is Mrs. Goodman always interrupting him?" I never had an interest in mechanical things or how cars work. I still don't like computers. I can't hook up my own stereo equipment very well. But I always had this interest in things like stories, comedy, sports, poetry, art and literature, anthropology, folklore, human relations. So when I said I was born to be a brief therapist, I didn't just mean because I was born to my nervous mother, but I also meant that it seems to me an enormous wonderful thing, that we get to go into small rooms with people, talk to them and at the end of the day get paid for doing it. What a wonderful way to make a living![13]

TM: It's a privilege.

---

13. For further discussion, see Chapter 14, "I've Always Been This Way—Thanks to Them!"

Interview II: "Burn In, Not Out!" 205

HOYT: Yes. It's a privilege to make a living in that way. I can hardly imagine anything more enjoyable than being with people and sharing stories.

TM: And being in a real context. For example, in business life the contexts are much more manipulative and more inauthentic than in the therapy world. Or are they?

HOYT: I know a businessman, who I respect, and he told me that he likes business because there are few rules and you keep score with money. I like therapy, because there are few rules and you keep score with happiness.

TM: If I would be a lucky man and we would meet somewhere, let's say after eight years, and we would have a couple of beers and I would ask you: "How are you, Michael?" and you would answer: "I'm fine, thank you." And something you have dreamed many times would have come true. And you would be 60 years old then and you would share your dream come true with me. So, what would you tell me?

HOYT: When you asked the question, what came to my mind was that my son and my wife would be happy and healthy. That would make me very happy. And if that can be, everything else will be great!

TM: Yes. And as far as professional activities are concerned?

HOYT: I'm waiting for my next inspiration. I'm waiting to see what's going to catch my interest. One thing that has been very exciting is this trip to Finland, and some contacts I have made with friends in Ireland and in the U.K. and in Japan. I'm realizing how narrow my American perspective has been and how much bigger it could be. I'm interested in learning more from people from other places. On the airplane coming here I was reading the book *Smilla's Sense of Snow* by the Danish author, Peter Hoeg (1993). I've got it right here. I resonated with what he seemed to be saying when he wrote:

The moment you grasp what is foreign, you will lose the urge to explain it. To explain a phenomenon is to distance yourself from it....I feel a connection to the Inuits. That is because of their ability to know, without a shadow of a doubt, that life is meaningful. Because of the way, in their consciousness, they can live with the tension between irreconcilable contradictions, without sinking into despair and without looking for a simplified solution. Because of their short, short path to ecstasy. Because they can meet a fellow human being and see him for what he is, without judging, their clarity not weakened by prejudice. (p. 193)

I want to live my life passionately and compassionately, with both truth and beauty. I'm hoping to have more of those opportunities in the next years.

TM: Thank you.

11

Interview III—"Snow and Sand": A Conversation about Culture, Alcohol and Empowerment (with Lotta Lehmusvaara and Tracey Powers-Erkkilo)

I also had the following conversation on March 7, 2001, after teaching a supervision seminar for the A-Clinic in Helsinki. In addition to conducting the interview, Lotta Lehmusvaara and Tracey Powers-Erkkilo, staff members at the A-Clinic, translated the interview for posting on their Finnish-language website, www.paihdelinkki.fi.

LOTTA: Many husbands here in Finland feel that it is necessary for them to have a couple of drinks each night after work to relax, and many women are desperate, concerned and/or angry about this behavior. Could you give them some advice how to deal with the drinking of their husbands?

HOYT: First, I should say that I don't know how much the person is drinking and how serious the problem is, so I would want to know *Why is she angry?* and *Whether there is truly a problem with alcohol?* What is the husband failing to do? Is he neglecting her or their children? Are there financial problems or health problems? Etc., etc. So I'm not sure how serious the problem is…but with that said, *if* there is a serious problem, *more of the same isn't going to help!* If she's already tried being angry, nagging, and complaining and all he's continued to do is drink, her continuing to be angry may in his mind even justify his drinking more. If it's time for him to come home and he thinks, "I'm just going to be yelled at and she's going to be angry," he may want to drink more. Her coming from a place of being angry is not going to be helpful for her or him.

What to do different? If there are days or times when he is not drinking, what are he—and she—doing differently then? Even if these exceptions are infrequent or rare, they may offer opportunities to build upon. It may also be helpful to *try to understand why the husband is drinking.* (This doesn't mean accepting it or excusing it.) What could she do to help him feel better or boost his self-confidence? She may want to talk with him when she's not angry. Sometimes it is difficult to talk and it works better to write a letter to the person because then they can't deny the words because they've seen them. If you see it in black and white, sometimes it stays with you more and is harder to forget. She might also want to consider seeking the help of someone close to the husband that he would respect, such as another family member or a close friend.

Sometimes heavy drinkers may have a physical dependence or addiction, and may need a lot of support and encouragement (and sometimes even medical assistance) to stop drinking.

Just continuing to get angry or depressed isn't going to help. There's a saying, "If you don't change directions, you're going to wind up where you're heading!" If you don't do something different, you are going to get more of the same.

TRACEY: What kind of advice would you give to those living with addicts to help them separate the problem from the person?

HOYT: You can love the sinner but hate the sin. For example, one could think and say, "I care about you as a person but I don't want to be with you while you're poisoning yourself and affecting the rest of the family. I love the healthy part of you and I would like to help you take care of the unhealthy part." If she doesn't want to stay in the situation, she has to consider her options and make choices. Thinking about whether to leave is often very difficult, and it may be helpful to seek some counseling and professional support. There are well-known organizations that can help her consider what to do, to stay with him or not, and how to take better care of herself regardless of the decision. Here in Helsinki, for example, she may want to contact the A-Clinic. Alcoholics Anonymous (A.A.) and Al-Anon have also helped many drinkers and their families.

LOTTA: Many Finns drink because we are not satisfied with our lives. Someone else seems to be in control and "the captain," so to speak, but not us. How could we encourage ourselves?

HOYT: What you said is a broad generalization. I certainly don't know enough about Finnish culture to even speculate about to what extent people may drink because they feel they lack control and are not satisfied with their lives. I do think it is important to find ways to be satisfied by learning to pay attention to those things that you can be proud of in yourself. Often times I think people are taught to be too "modest" about their strengths and not to value themselves. They learn to pay more attention to what they haven't done than to value that which they have accomplished. When they do something well they say, "Oh, it's not important" or "It's just my duty to do it." Self-esteem means how you feel about or rate yourself. Positive self-esteem seems to begin from when we are children and how our parents treat us. It also comes from whether we believe in ourselves and trust in and appreciate our abilities. You can't feel very empowered if you don't take credit for what you do. Perhaps some cultures don't do enough to promote healthy self-satisfaction of this kind.

I'd like to say a bit more about that in terms of the needs of children in their early years. I think there are five things that are very important for children to learn. One is that they are lovable, good, attractive, etc. *just because they exist*. Second, that other people are basically good. Although there are some troublesome people out there, children need to know that people are generally trustworthy and it's healthy to interact with them. So once they learn that "I'm okay" and that the other person is okay, they've got some of the basics. The next is that it's okay to have feelings: sad, mad, glad, excited, curious, frustrated, sexy, happy, etc. They need to learn that they can have a full range of feelings. Children also need to learn how to feel good about their bodies. Knowing that their bodies are okay and can support them contributes to their sense of being empowered, of being competent and able, and also serves as a basis for enjoying sensuality and pleasure. Children also need to be encouraged to learn to trust their brains; that they are smart enough to solve problems, that they can figure things out on their own. They should be able to say: "I'm able to use my judgment, I'm able to reason. I'm able to see reality and figure out what is what."

When they feel okay about themselves and other people, when they feel okay about having feelings, when they know that they can think, and that they can use their bodies…then the rest becomes how to solve problems and live life. I think that a lot of the difficulties people have with low self-esteem and not being satisfied may have to do with some interference in one or several of these areas in their personal development.

LOTTA: Finns are often times categorized as "melancholic." Is it okay to be in this state?

HOYT: Another big question! I would think of it in this way: I would wonder why it is that some people, and maybe some cultures, seem to specialize in melancholia—why they have so much experience and practice and are such experts in sadness, grief, depression, misery…

TRACEY: *[jokingly]* the weather in Finland…

HOYT: Some of it may very well be the weather and that life is hard. A certain amount of melancholy is normal and perhaps even healthy. If you have grief because some sad thing has happened, dealing with a death or a loss, etc., being depressed for a while is normal because it gives you time to think and deal with the emotions associated with the loss. Sometimes particularly in a colder climate where it is dark for many months you may need something that makes you go inside your mind because you can't go outside the house very much. So there may be some relation between the weather and what happens internally.

I think it's important, however, to have a good balance. I wonder if there are certain stories in the culture that emphasize melancholia to the point where people are becoming too expert at melancholia and not expert enough at happiness or curiosity or pride? Is this what people really prefer? Again, I don't know enough about Finnish culture but it would be interesting to see if people get indoctrinated into a melancholic worldview and lifestyle. Ritva Saarelainen (the Director of the A-Clinic) was telling me the other day that there was some research done where they presented positive words to Finns such as joy, happiness, love, etc. and they would get very little reaction. But when they would show them words like sad, suicide, trouble, suffer, and so on, they would have a big response. It was like they had developed receptor sites that were highly attuned to these particular emotions and ideas. They resonated with these words so much that they had a finely differentiated vocabulary. In the U.S. we say about the Inuit people in Alaska that they have 42 different names for snow. People in sunny California and Hawaii don't know all these "snow" words, but we do have an extensive vocabulary for beach sand. To extend the metaphor, I think perhaps the people that you are talking about who know 42 types of "melancholia" might—with some encouragement—enjoy learning to recognize 42 varieties of other emotional states.

LOTTA: In your writing and lecturing you have said, "How people look influences what they see, and what they see influences what they do." What do you mean?

HOYT: There is a reality outside our minds, of course, but what we're seeing is also influenced *by the way we look*. To return to your first question, if a woman is expecting her husband to be drunk and gets angry, when he comes home she's already going to have in her mind certain ways of reacting and relating to him. And if he's five minutes late, she is going to be angry and conclude that he's been drinking, even if he hasn't. If looking at him through the eyes of an angry wife could be replaced by seeing him through the compassionate eyes of a concerned partner—even if he has been drinking—she wouldn't be so angry when he came in but might be worried, or glad to see him, and then maybe he'd want to come home and not want to be drunk or half-anesthetized when he got there.

The theory that I'm talking about when I say "how we look influences what we see" is called *constructivism*, which is the idea that we're not just discovering the world but that we're constructing our image of it. Of all the different ways we look at a situation, we tend to look at it certain ways rather than others (usually based on things that have happened to us in the past that have taught us to expect certain things or to look in certain ways). Sometimes when people want to change, or want their relationships to change, they would like others to change but they do not realize that they may have to change the way they act and the way they look at things as well. The way people look helps determine what they will see and what they see influences what they do in a situation.

There is not only one way to look. When you travel from one culture to another or one country to another or one family to another or even from one person to another you realize how differently people look at the world. Speaking more than one language also helps you realize that there are differences. Some ways of looking are more encouraging than others. I wrote a book called *Some Stories Are Better than Others* (2000a). Some stories are more invigorating and encouraging. If you look in certain ways you'll get more happiness out of life. Some stories are not so encouraging. They lead to melancholia or despair, to having little hope or energy. If you see life through those eyes you will not enjoy what's happening because you'll be mostly noticing negative things and telling yourself depressing stories. If you believe something is likely to happen you tend to act in ways that bring it about. So I would wonder, are people acting in ways that would bring them happiness or are they not?

TRACEY: It seems from what you're saying that one needs to be responsible for their own actions and lives. Do you find when you're doing this kind of counseling that often times people blame others for what's happening to them? That the hardest part is looking at oneself?

HOYT: They say that when you point a finger at someone else there are three fingers pointing back at you. *[illustrates by pointing a finger]* I think it's sometimes very difficult to take responsibility. Often we say "you made me angry" or "my boss makes me angry which affects my work." In some situations, most normal people would feel scared, disappointed, or angry, of course, but still we have some choice about how scared or angry we choose to be. Even if we're angry—if we have the feeling—what we do with this feeling is still up to us to decide. Do I walk away? Do I try to make a joke? Do I turn the other cheek? Do I ask them to apologize? Do I argue, or fight? Even the word "responsibility" means the ability to respond. We still have some choice as to how we will respond to whatever situation we are in. We all—including me, and probably whoever is reading this—sometimes forget that ultimately we still have some control.

I want to make clear, however, that there are some events that are terrible and cause great hardship in people's lives. I'm not trying to pretend that child abuse doesn't exist or that drunken husbands don't exist or that the wars with Russia and the Nazi Holocaust didn't happen. There really are social forces and hard realities that need to be paid attention to. With that said, though, I've known some people that a tragic thing has happened to, such as a rape or a death or a great loss, and they say, "My life is spoiled. I'm now ruined forever"; yet other people who have had similar disasters happen to them will respond by saying, "It hurt terribly and left a mark on me but it's not going to be the entire definition of my life." It's an ugly chapter, a tragedy, a bad year or a bad marriage, etc., but the person is bigger than the problem.

TRACEY: For those working in the helper capacity, could you go through the steps of empowerment when working with addiction that you find useful or aspects of empowerment that you would recommend?

HOYT: The American-English dictionary I have at home defines *empowerment* as "giving authority to or to give power." What someone in the helper capacity could do is help the addict acknowledge or feel like they have some control or role that they can play. Help them see that they have some power to change their current state. From the perspective of the addict, I think to empower yourself you need to recognize ways that you can and do make a difference. You also need to recognize the situation you are in. You can't pretend it doesn't exist. Denial will not help. If you hide your head, your butt will still be sticking up. Once you recognize that there is a problem then you have to ask, "Am I myself about to take care of this problem?" You need to be honest with this answer. If you're able to take care of it, then what are you waiting for? You're not enjoying the problem. It is causing misery and suffering in your life and those around you, so it would seem to make sense to start doing something different. If you're not able to take care of the problem, and it's continuing despite everything you're trying, then you should acknowledge that it's more than you can deal with on your own. You need to ask for help, possibly utilize the services offered in your community, reach out to a friend or family member. It's not something you have to go through alone.

It also helps to recognize that you may have to avoid situations that lead you back into your problem. We say that you have to live one day at a time. The problem may trick one into thinking it's good to be using drugs, or it's good to be so thin that your body is starving, or it's good to be compulsively gambling. This confused thinking may mean that the person is not making clear judgments about their behaviors. If so, it's time for them to talk with someone they can can trust—a healthy friend, a good minister, a healthcare provider, or God—and to start making the changes that will bring health and happiness.

TRACEY & LOTTA: Thank you for sharing your thoughts. Before we stop today, is there anything else you want to add?

HOYT: I appreciate the opportunity to talk with you. I hope that people who read this who may be having personal troubles will remember, like the line in the song, that 'beneath the bitter snows lies the seed that, warmed by love, in the Spring becomes the rose.' Somewhere inside each person, in their heart or soul or memory, she or he knows that life can be better. Please don't give up that dream—make it real!

12

Road Trip

When I finished graduate school in 1976, my father flew East so that we could meet and drive back to California together. We planned to hook-up in Chicago and head West, taking our time, a father-and-son road trip. I filled my little Japanese-import stationwagon with my few belongings—a Persian rug, a bent-wood rocker, a couple of boxes of books, and a certificate declaring me a newly minted Ph.D., said goodbye to New Haven, Connecticut (where I had gone to school), and drove to the Windy City, where my father was spending a few days visiting old friends and family. After a night at my aunt and uncle's, Dad and I headed out for our big adventure.

Route 80 took us across Iowa and Nebraska, then south to Denver. A long conversation ensued as we motored along a concrete and asphalt ribbon of changing landscape, roadside motels, steak houses and truckers' breakfast spots. Small talk, jokes, family histories and mysteries, silences, discussions about school and my future, updates on family news, some sightseeing. Passing the Rockies, we entered Utah and decided to press on to Las Vegas.

Somewhere in southern Utah, somewhere along the way, somewhere in the night, a sign said "Construction Ahead" and the road diverted. We turned off and took the side road, and then another. It was late and dark, and a sign directed us toward another detour. We were moving slowly on a dry scrabble dirt road. We passed fires in open oil drums and abandoned heavy equipment that looked like eerie dinosaurs in the shadows cast by our headlights. We slowly drove on for what seemed a long time, maybe another 45 minutes or an hour, following the road farther into the dark. It grew increasingly desolate and forboding. We went further. There were no other cars, no more construction equipment. There had been no other signs, but we wondered if we had missed a turn. Just as we were discussing whether to turn around, it happened: The engine suddenly died!

"Oh shit!"

"Why'd you stop?" Dad asked.

"I didn't—the motor just stopped."

There was gas on the gauge. Turning the key did nothing. We tried, over and over. *"Don't flood it."* We sat, then tried again. Nothing. We got out and opened the hood. Nothing. We wiggled a few wires. Nothing.

"We're fucked!" I muttered.

"No. We're stuck."

"What do we do?"

"We wait" said Dad.

"For what?"

"Help."

"From who?"

"We'll have to see."

"What if no one comes?"

"We'll see."

A long time passed. Suddenly, a large truck, an 18-wheeler, came around the curve. We stood by our car, in his headlights waving as he approached…the truck slowed but just kept going.

"Shit!" I cursed. Dad shook his head, saying nothing.

More time went by, maybe another hour. I turned the key again—still nothing. It was very dark and getting colder. Suddenly, another set of headlights! This time a car. We waved, but it barreled by, going too fast, not even slowing. The driver honked his horn as he disappeared into the night.

Eleven o'clock came and went. We sat in the car, hood up. Not talking much.

Maybe an hour passed. Then another. It got even colder.

Then, headlights coming up the road toward us! We got out and waved. The pick-up truck slowed, then stopped. The driver rolled his window down.

"What's wrong?"

Dad spoke: *"We're stuck. The engine stopped and won't start. We've got plenty of gas."*

"Want me to take a look?"

"We'd sure appreciate it."

The man was white, wearing a jacket and a John Deere cap, looked to be in his mid or late 30s. His wife, bundled up, was sitting next to him. She was holding an infant or small child. Sleeping bundled up between them was a little girl, maybe 4 or 5, maybe a bit older.

He backed up his truck, faced his headlights under our hood, then got out and closed the cab door behind him. He leaned over the car and poked around, asking questions, wiggling this, checking that.

"What do you think?" Dad asked.
"I don't know—all your connections look OK."
"What do we do now?" I asked impatiently. Dad slipped me a look.
"It could be your gas line, but it sounds more electrical. Mind if I check a little more?"

The man went back to his pickup, behind the cab, and returned with a flashlight and a toolbox.
"Are you a mechanic?"
"Not really, but I like to fool around a little."
"Let me hold your light for you," said Dad.

Spark plugs were unscrewed and reversed. Nothing. Connections were loosened and retightened. Nothing. Hypotheses were formulated and tested. Nothing. Finally, he announced:

"Here it is! It's your rotator. It broke off. Too bad—I was hoping it was something we could rig up, at least to get you to town. There's nothing we can do—you'll need a new one. They should have one, but if not, they'll have to order it. You're going to need a tow into town."

"How far is it?" I asked.
"Not too bad—maybe an hour, little more."
I knew to be quiet. I let Dad speak.
"What should we do?"
"Well, your vehicle can't move, so I'll have to drive back and let them know you need help. It'll be better if I have them follow me to show them where you are."
"That's taking you way out of your way—I really appreciate all of your help."
"No problem."

The man went back to his truck, got in and talked with his wife for a few minutes. She listened, then nodded. He pulled up next to us.

"It'll take us maybe an hour to get there. There's an all-night service station. At this hour we should be able to get someone to come right away, so unless there's some problem, we'll be back in a couple of hours." He turned around and drove off.

A couple of hours later, two sets of headlights appeared. The pickup pulled up next to us, followed by the tow truck. The driver got out.

"That wasn't too bad. I've told Joe what the problem is, and he'll tow you right to the gas station. The parts store is right next to it, and it opens up at 8 a.m. They should be able to get you back on the road. There's an all-night coffee shop you can wait in until it opens at 8."

"Thank you."

"There's nothing more I can do. Like I said, you need a new rotor. You'll be OK with Joe. I think we're going to take off. We've got a way to go until we get home to Sacramento. But first, my wife's got some family in Los Angeles we're heading to see."

"You've really helped us out." Dad reached into his pocket. "I'd like to pay you for all of your time."

"Don't worry about it."

"That's very kind. But you really saved us, and it took you a long way out of your way in the middle of the night."

"I was glad to be able to help."

"I'd feel better if I could pay you—at least for your gas."

"Nahh."

"Well, then would you at least let me buy a little present for your girls?" Dad had a couple of $20s in his hand.

"It's not necessary."

"No, but you've really been great."

The man paused. "I don't want any money, but I'll tell you what you can do." We listened intently. "Sometime, if you ever see someone who's stuck or needs a hand, help them out, OK?"

Dad nodded. "I understand. You're a good man." I listened.

He shook our hands, wished us well, and drove off as we called out "Thanks, again!"

The tow driver hitched us up for the long ride into town.

"Wow! What luck! He wouldn't even take any money. That was far out!" I exclaimed.

"Nice guy, huh?" replied Dad.

"You know, we never even found out his name."

"Let's call him Sam, for short. Know what I mean?"

I did. I bought some battery cables. Paid for them myself. You never know when someone might need a jump.

13

How I Embody a Narrative Constructive Approach

I have noticed there are many human beings who do not twinkle.
—Vaslav Nijinsky, *Diary* (1918-1919/1973, p. 99)

My approach to psychological intervention can be subsumed under the general rubric of *constructive therapies*, which incorporates ideas from both *brief therapy* and *narrative constructivism*. The hallmarks of brief therapy are the development of a collaborative alliance and an emphasis on clients' strengths and competencies in the service of the efficient attainment of co-created goals. As I wrote in *Brief Therapy and Managed Care* (Hoyt, 1995a, pp. 326-327):

> The goal of brief psychotherapy, regardless of the specific theoretical approach or technical method, is to help the client resolve a problem, to get "unstuck" and to move on. Techniques are specific, integrated, and as eclectic as needed. Treatment is focused, the therapist appropriately active, and the patient responsible for making changes. Each session is valuable, and therapy ends as soon as possible. Good outcome, not good process, is most valued. More is not better; *better* is better. The patient carries on, and can return to treatment as needed.

The term *narrative constructivism*, as I use it, refers to the idea that we are actively building our worldview, that we are making meaning and constructing, not just uncovering, our psychological realities. This largely happens through language.

There are many constructivist traditions. Tracing my own particular path, I see signposts with names like *Aurelius* and *Vico* and *Adler* and *Kelly*, and others that say *Ericksonian, Solution-Focused,* and *Narrative Therapy*. Behind me and up ahead there are also many other intriguing possibilities (see Neimeyer & Mahoney, 1995; Neimeyer & Raskin, 2000; Neimeyer & Stewart, 2000; Rosen & Kuehlwein, 1996).

The literature is vast. I recently took *The Selected Writing of Ralph Waldo Emerson* on our annual family holiday at our cabin at Newfound Lake, New Hampshire. Opening to his famous essay, "The Transcendentalist," I read:

> The first thing we have to say respecting what are called *new views* here in New England, at the present time, is, that they are not new....What is popularly called Transcendentalism among us, is Idealism; Idealism as it appears in 1842. As thinkers, mankind has ever divided into two sects, Materialists and Idealists; the first class founding on experience, the second on consciousness; the first class beginning to think from the data of the senses, the second class perceive that the senses are not final, and say, The senses give us representations of things, but what are the things themselves, they cannot tell. The materialist insists on facts, on history, on the force of circumstances and the animal wants of man; the idealist on the power of Thought and of Will, on inspiration, on miracle, on individual culture. (Emerson, 1842/1950, p. 871, emphasis in original)

My favorite explanation of narrative constructivism is the famous joke about the three baseball umpires disputing their acumen:

> The first, the honest ethicist, says "I call 'em the way I see 'em." The second, the accurate objectivist, says "Well, that's good—but I call 'em the way they are." Finally, the third ump, the narrative constructivist, says: "They ain't nothin' until I call 'em!"

There are options to the ways we "call 'em," to how we put our stories together. *Some stories are better than others*, some ways of looking and thinking and acting are more invigorating and rewarding than others. How we look influences what we see, and what we see influences what we do, 'round and round.

Brief therapy and narrative construction and a competency focus are not merely a set of techniques. They are an overarching worldview, an orientation toward thinking and being. What I'm going to do here is discuss some ways I see myself embodying this orientation, some ways I see it informing my thinking and manifesting in my personal life. "Description begins in the writer's imagination, but should finish in the reader's," as Stephen King (2000, p. 174) says. Maybe by listening to us panelists trying to explain ourselves to ourselves, other people will get some ideas to help them see themselves.

I prefer, as Michael Schmidt (1999, p. 837) writes in *Lives of the Poets*:

> the language of embodiment, containing rather than describing meanings: 'With this ring I wed thee' rather than 'I give you this ring as a sign of our marriage.' Enactment in language—a function of rhythm, word order, diction—can impart a spiritual dimension to the work of secular writers; poems can mean more than a poet intends, as if touched by a grace the poet inadvertently accesses and cannot deny.

I'm going to describe a bit of how I see it. We each have the capacity to be successful versions of ourselves (I'm still working on mine), and I don't mean to suggest that my way is necessarily better for anyone but me. "Insist on yourself; never imitate" as Emerson (1841/1950, p. 166) said in his famous essay, "Self-Reliance." I also like the way Lucille Clifton (in Moyers, 1995, p. 85) put it:

> I don't know if you can put what is true into linear, rational terms. Faulkner gets at it this way—if the truth is one thing to you and another to me, how do we know which is true and not true? The answer is that the heart already knows.
>
> There is something in us that recognizes what is so; and even if it is not so for us, there is something in us that recognizes rightness. It may be that in our culture we've become accustomed not to listen to that voice, but just because we don't consciously listen to it with our ears doesn't mean we don't hear it.

So, looking through my lenses at myself[1], here are some ways I see me embodying my brief, narrative constructive orientation:

I'm very practical and pragmatic. I love to get things done and scratched off my endless 'to do' list. I tend to see quickly solutions to how things might work better and what might help people get 'unstuck.' This makes brief, outcome-oriented therapy consonant and attractive for me. At the same time, I'm more into curiosity than certainty. It's exciting not to know the ending at the beginning. This may go against the current call for treatment plans and our cultural and pro-

---

1. Again, Emerson (from his essay "Experience," 1844/1950, p. 345): "Life is a train of moods like a string of beads, and as we pass through them they prove to be many-colored lenses which paint the world their own hue, and each shows only what lies in its focus. From the mountain you see the mountain. We animate what we can, and we see only what we animate. Nature and books belong to the eyes that see them. It depends on the mood of the man whether he shall see the sunset or the fine poem."

fessional emphasis on prediction and control, but I'm learning to prefer 'Wow!' and 'How'd you do that?' to 'Uh-huh' and 'I told you so.'[2]

More and more, I find myself understanding the idea that what is, is. At the same time, once we get beyond the physical plane, we make our worlds. It's not all good or fair or the way I want it. I do think, however, that we make our psychological realities, together, by what we focus on, what we choose to highlight. One of the keys to happiness is knowing where to double-click! There is a *there* there, an external or objective reality, but we all have a wonderful *response-ability*, an ability to choose how we respond.

Knowing that I am constructing my version of this world has helped to open my vision. If we look, there is more to see. There is a lot to be learned, if we're willing to bend our ear toward the parable. As Dennis Olson has written in his beautiful book, *Shared Spirits* (1995, p. x): "We have, to this point, looked at multi-cultural education as learning 'about' other cultures. Because of our own world view, it hasn't occurred to us that we might learn 'from' other cultures."

I'm more interested in *local knowledge* than in overarching canons and models. I'm pretty smart and I can think critically and analytically but, as I heard Garrison Keillor say one morning on NPR's [National Public Radio] Prairie Home Companion, "Being intelligent doesn't make you happy. It just means you can get stuck in more remote places!"

Last year I went through a big decision about whether to move my practice to another clinic closer to home. It was a complicated decision. The commute was less and new opportunities would surely emerge, but it also entailed letting go of a lot—familiar colleagues and patients, a system I helped to build, a community I had come to know very well. As I talked with my various friends and confidants, asking their input and advice, I found it was very helpful to listen to the questions I asked as much as to their answers. Recognizing the ways in which I was co-constructing our dialogues, how I was framing my concerns, showed me the sticking points I needed to consider.

We are verbs more than nouns. *Life is*. In our family, we have an expression when we go for a walk: *"Let's see what we can see"* (not: "Let's see what there is to see"). The difference may seem subtle, but I hope that you'll see that the former puts the focus on the *activity of perception*. So, let's see what we can see...

---

2. For an extended discussion of the issue of *discovery and/or direction*, see *Interviews with Brief Therapy Experts* (Hoyt, 2001a), especially the conversations with Michael White, Donald Meichenbaum, and Steve de Shazer.

While not always, I have generally found that the harder I listen, the smarter people get. There is an internal logic to what they're thinking and doing. To me, it's not just "There's a pony in there somewhere." I usually assume people are telling their truth and that it's my job to help them figure out what that truth is about, what's right for them, and how they can use it better. Imposition tends to generate opposition, and life is better, I find, if you approach it with open eyes and open-heartedly.

I tend to take things as I find them, at face value. Sometimes I get enmeshed, or duped, but those risks are better than starting out by seeing the Other as a diagnostic specimen or a nut case or a medical-legal risk. We all need our polestars and lodestones lest we become awash in a sea of deconstruction, but one of the best ways to avoid burnout is to share the work and to embrace positives.

It is interesting to consider those times when we *don't* personally embody our theory or model. We may need to open up and revise our theory: "There are more things in heaven and earth, Horatio, Than are dreamt of in your philosophy" (*Hamlet*, Act I, Scene 5). Sometimes I do think that people are plain wrong, or crazy, or being jerks. I can be direct and confrontative, articulate, and persuasive, but when I start to cut off the other person's humanity I find it helpful to ask myself what is it in my story about myself that I am trying to protect and conserve? (See Gustafson, 1986; Rosenbaum, 1999.)

I think it's important to read widely[3] and, more important, to live widely.[4] Milton Erickson used to recommend sharpening one's observational skills and advised that "Anybody doing therapy ought to get to know the range of human behavior" (Erickson & Rossi, 1981, p. 86). To help me experience and value more than what my "proper education" and largely white upper-middle class professional lifestyle is likely to provide, I try to be with and learn from people (and other beings[5]) who grew up in other cultures, especially ones that aren't Eurocentric—and if I don't "get it," I try to be curious about what I may be missing, rather than quickly dismissing them as wrong or weird or, more politely and politically correct, as different or foreign.

While I can tell you that attending the heavy-metal Ozzfest concert and going to the Berkeley Repertory Theater to see *The Laramie Project* over the same weekend, as I did recently, can be a bit dizzying and "multiphrenic" (Gergen, 1991), I like both Emerson's (1841/1950, p. 152, "Self-Reliance") famous line about

---

3. I got a clue to this one day when I looked at Carl Whitaker's desk and saw the two open books were E.B. White's *Stuart Little* and Soren Kierkegaard's *Fear and Trembling*!

"foolish consistency is the hobgoblin of little minds" and Walt Whitman's (1892/1940, Stanza 51) proud stanza:

> Do I contradict myself?
> Very well then I contradict myself
> (I am large, I contain multitudes.)

Being a narrative constructivist has helped me recognize that a lot of our sense of rushing and pressure and frustration and boredom comes from how we set our expectations and attention. Anyone who has lugged firewood down a steep hillside or paddled a steady canoe across a lake or run a long distance knows that there is a pace, neither fast nor slow, that stays within your breath and heartbeat and gets you there.

When Yogi Berra was asked "What time is it?" he answered, "Do you mean Now?" In my briefcase I carry a fortune cookie slip that says, "If you're not here now, you're late!" (I also carry a chunk of iron pyrite, fools' gold, to remind me not to chase glittering illusions.) Now here's something interesting: Tomorrow never happens. There's a great *New Yorker* cartoon with two Zen monks sitting side by side, and one says to the other: "Next? There is no *next*. This is it!" There

---

4. In his study of the French poet and *enfant terrible* Arthur Rimbaud, Henry Miller (1956, p. 5) comments: "Rimbaud experienced his great crisis when he was eighteen, at which moment in his life he had reached the edge of madness; from this point on his life is an unending desert. I reached mine at the age of thirty-six to thirty-seven, which is the age at which Rimbaud dies. From this point on my life begins to blossom. Rimbaud turned from literature to life; I did the reverse. Rimbaud fled from the chimeras he had created; I embraced them....I halted and converted my energies to creation. I plunged into writing with the same fervor and zest that I had plunged into life....Rimbaud restored literature to life; I have endeavored to restore life to literature."

    In *To Begin Where I Am*, Czeslaw Milosz (2001, p. 2) also clarifies his priorities: "I have read many books, but to place all those volumes on top of one another and stand on them would not add a cubit to my stature. Their learned terms are of little use when I attempt to seize naked experience, which eludes all accepted ideas. To borrow their language can be helpful in many ways, but it also leads imperceptibly into a self-contained labyrinth, leaving us in alien corridors which allow no exit."

5. You can learn a lot about adaptation and coping in a botanical garden and a lot about endurance and patience from a mountain and, if you're lucky and pay attention, a lot about joy and curiosity from my two-year-old German shepherd puppy, Ranger.

is no time but the present. If you catch the flow and natural rhythm of things, you can be "in time" and "on time."[6]

We narrative constructivists pay a lot of attention to languaging. Appreciating how we "call 'em" as we construct our sense of reality is connected to my almost daily reading of poetry. As the Pulitzer-prize winning poet Ted Roethke (2001, p. 96) said, a good poem can "split the heart of reality." While language helps us find ourselves, however, it is important not to confuse *words* with *life*.[7]

Still, consider which description of *reframing* is richer, more inviting, more redolent with possibilities. This one which, with all due respect to my fine colleagues at the Mental Research Institute, is from their classic book *Change: Principles of Problem Formation and Problem Resolution* (Watzlawick, Weakland & Fisch, 1974, p. 95):

> To reframe, then, means to change the conceptual and/or emotional setting or viewpoint in relation to which a situation is experienced and to place it in another frame which fits the 'facts' of the same concrete situation equally well or even better, and thereby changes its entire meaning.

Or this, from Walt Whitman's *Leaves of Grass* (1891-92/1940, Stanza 21):

> I am the poet of the Body and I am the poet of the Soul,
> The pleasures of heaven are with me and the pains of hell are with me,
> The first I graft and increase upon myself,
> The latter I translate into a new tongue.

In my house there is a lot of storytelling and joking and word-play, as there was in my family of origin. Corny puns and double-entendres and curious etymologies and stories with funny twists that highlight semantic ambiguities and create surprise tickle our fancy. When he was a little guy, my son and I used to

---

6. Of course, one could also ask: If time is a human construct, why didn't we make more of it?
7. Emerson (1944/1950, p. 374), describing both the power and the limits of words, in a sweet line in his essay "Character" says, "we are painting the lightning with charcoal." And, in "The Poet" (1944/1950, p. 329) he writes: [I]n every word he speaks he rides on them as the horses of thought." Emerson explicates: "Every word was once a poem. Every new relation is a new word....For though the origin of most of our words is forgotten, each word was at first a stroke of genius, and obtained currency because for the moment it symbolized the world to the first speaker and to the hearer" (pp. 327-329).

play some games that sharpened our wits on the idea that there are multiple ways to look at a situation. Our master bedroom has a parade of masks, Mexican and African and Nepalese, ringing the four walls near the ceiling. We would lie in bed and each shine flashlights on different faces and improvise dialogues, switching roles and retelling the stories using different accents. In another game, which we called "Good or Bad?", we would make up and tell a story back and forth alternating (reframing) whether an event was positive or negative. For example:

> Someone is going on an airplane trip but the plane runs out of gas. Good or bad?
> *Bad.*
> No, good—the plane lands in a beautiful place. So, the plane lands in a beautiful place—good or bad?
> *Good.*
> No, bad—the place is on top of a volcano about to explode. So, landing on top of the volcano—good or bad?
> *Bad.*
> No, good—the person is a scientist and makes a great discovery. So, making the discovery—good or bad?
> *Good.*
> No, bad. Criminals steal the discovery and want to use it to conquer the world. So, criminals steal the discovery—good or bad?
> *Good.*
> *Good?*
> Yeah. The scientist is smart, so he reversed the discovery and it blew up the criminals when they tried to use it.

Once we realize that there is more than one way to look at a situation, that different visions yield different versions, we begin to "look around the corner" more and to recognize that we are making choices about which stories to pursue and embrace. More and more my interest in narrative construction has made me aware of the *politics of experience*—of power and control and who says what is *normal* and what is *valid* and *healthy*, and what is not. So much is culturally-bound taste or preference—much of which I agree with—but it is not Revealed Truth.

A narrative perspective has also helped me get more tuned into social justice issues. I've still got a way to go, but I don't countenance racist jokes anymore, and I wince (and usually overcome my shyness to speak up) when someone makes an anti-gay remark.[8] The stories we hear and repeat and tell ourselves do a lot to create the world we live in.

Social constructionism, which involves what we admit as evidence and understand as the truth, also can be used to consider how propaganda and misinformation can be used to manufacture consent (see Herman & Chomsky, 1988). I'm still appalled that the Supreme Court had the *chutzpah* to expropriate the last American Presidential election, and that 'we the people' (including me) did so little to protest. I don't believe that the old Jews in Florida voted for Buchanan or that a disproportionate number of Blacks couldn't mark ballots or find their way to the polling booths (see Moore, 2001). Now that we've gotten our tax rebate (read: hush money), what will they try to sell us next—certainly not something as unbelievable as that there's no global warming, or that it's not a good investment to clean up the environment, or that avaricious HMOs and managed-care companies shouldn't be liable to lawsuits (see Alter, 2001)? I almost resigned the APA [American Psychological Association] because it was taking political positions—now I'm thinking of resigning if it doesn't start taking stronger ones!

Let's go on to some things perhaps kinder and gentler. I live and practice in Marin County, just a long walk north from San Francisco across the beautiful Golden Gate Bridge. Our catchment area contains the highest percentage of seniors in Northern California. I'm now 52 years old—there are 52 weeks in a year, 52 cards in a deck—and getting older and working with an aging population, and having a Hospice nurse for a wife, has certainly amped my existential self to the wake-up-call words of Longfellow:

> *Though half-way up the hill, I see the Past*
> *Lying beneath me with its sounds and sights,—*
> *A city in the twilight dim and vast,*
> *With smoking roofs, soft bells, and gleaming lights.—*
> *And hear above me on the autumnal blast*
> *The cataract of Death far thundering from the heights.*
> —Henry Wadsworth Longfellow, "Mezzo Cammin."
> (1842/1943, p. 173)

Marin County is also a hotbed of spiritual seekers—in addition to Christians and Jews, some of my patients identify themselves as Buddhists, as Hindus, as Moslems and Sikhs, as pagans, and as Grateful Deadheads (Jerry Garcia was a local)! Almost every day I hear about *chi* and *Tao* and *yoga* and *karma*, about Ram Dass and Jack Kornfeld and Thich Nich Han, about catechism and kabbala and mindfulness and healing arts and sometimes about sweatlodges and prayer

---

8. "The more I feel an American, the more this situation pains me. I can escape the feeling of complicity with it only by speaking out."—Albert Einstein (1946/1950, p. 9)

arrows. Over and over, I am confronted with the question of whether spiritual experience is ultimately just a juicy neuropsychological epiphenomenon, a "buzz" we get off a certain set of brainwave symphonies; or is there truly something outside of us—call it Great Spirit or Allah or Yaweh or whatever? In his eloquent Foreword in *The Handbook of Constructive Therapies*, Kenneth Gergen (1998, p. xiv) spoke of "the teeming number of therapists whose practices are nourished by the discourse of spirit, love, and God, and yet who are unable to gain legitimacy in speaking of these matters." We are creatures and well as creators. How can (or should?) this be integrated into what we do as clinical psychologists? Some of it seems too New Age and flaky for me, but I also recall the story Martin Buber (1947, p. 53) recounts about the fiddler who

> played so sweetly that all who heard him began to dance and whoever came near enough to hear, joined in the dance. Then a deaf man, who knew nothing of music, happened along, and to him all he saw seemed the action of madmen—senseless and in bad taste.

To conclude (for now): We need more rationality, for sure, and we also need more curiosity and flexibility. Sometimes we need to appreciate "the nobility of the imagination," to "let things shimmer" (Roethke, 2001, p. 120). *We need an expanded sense of spaciousness.* As Robert Frost (reported in Roethke, 2001, p. 108) said, "Let's be accurate, but not too accurate." And it was Albert Einstein (1930/1954, p. 11) in his essay "The World As I See It" who said: "The most beautiful experience we can have is the mysterious. It is the fundamental emotion which stands at the cradle of true art and true science."

Narrative constructivism, which highlights the language-based meaning-making aspects of awareness, has made me more appreciative of both what is really real and what is often assumed and taken-for-granted but can be examined and questioned and sometimes changed.

I hope that considering what I have been describing will help you notice your noticing, help you pay attention to the way that you choose where to place your attention, and that you will allow room for the growth of more stories that bring you more of what you want. We all get to decide: *Will our life be prose, or poetry?*

14

I've Always Been This Way—Thanks to Them!

i thank You God for most this amazing
day: for the leaping greenly spirits of trees
and a blue true dream of sky; and for everything
which is natural which is infinite which is yes
  —e.e. cummings (1958/1991, p. 663)

Specialists in these areas will easily recognize the names of each of my consultants—I honor myself by recording them here. They have been generous beyond my expectation.
  —Sherwin B. Nuland (1995, p. xiii)

We all have potentials that can be blessed and brought forward, some combination of nature and nurture and autonomous choice. For many of us, as psychologists and students of mental health we have an urge toward understanding, toward language and logic and communication and, dare I say, toward healing and love. We have energy and a desire to make the world a better place. I've certainly needed some shaping and encouragement—and still do—but I've always been this way.

I resonate with the "acorn theory" that James Hillman (1996), borrowing from Plato at the end of *The Republic*, describes in his book, *The Soul's Code*:

> In a nutshell, then, this....is about calling, about fate, about character, about innate image. Together they make up the "acorn theory," which holds that

each person bears a uniqueness that asks to be lived and that is already present before it can be lived. [p. 6]

He suggests the value of thinking about how we "grow down" into the world, not just how we "grow up."[1] A similar view is expressed by Roger Housden (2001) in his book, *Ten Poems to Change Your Life*:

> We spend much of our lives trying to make ourselves—to create the life we want, to forge some reality from our dreams. We live in a culture wedded to the fantasy of self-determination and self-made men. Yet there is another school of thought that looks at a human life from the other direction. Instead of making ourselves, this more ancient tradition would say we ourselves are there in embryo from the start, and we unfurl as we go along, colored by circumstances and climate. Just as the oak tree is there already in the acorn, the babe carries on its brow and in its eyes the mark and signature of its later life. Not the details, perhaps, but the particular energetic response to life, the quality of engagement that is unique to him [or her]. It is as if our joys and trials are there in seed from the beginning. [pp. 97-98][2]

---

1. I also resonate with Hillman when he writes, "Repression, the key to personality structure in all therapy schools, is not of the past but of the acorn and the past mistakes we have made in our relation to it" (p. 5). He derides models that would reduce us to explanations based on developmental theories of compensation rather than embracing those that would champion romance, adventure, passion, mystery, imagination, myth, spirit, and beauty. "A theory so degrading to inspiration deserves the derision I am giving it" (Hillman, 1996, p. 25).
2. In this connection, Meryl Streep (Burns, 2002, p. 7) made an interesting comment about acting: "There are certain things in the script that will evoke a past part, or some corner of a remembered building or someone's gesture. It's like while I'm reading and feel some kind of improvisational response that comes from I don't know where. People write books about acting, but I don't think they've ever pierced this mystery. Because it is something, and I think the secret of it does have something to do with our shared DNA—that everyone in Europe went through Charlemagne. [Interviewer:....the kinship of the soul that we have. You're saying your performances are not based on your personal experience, but something you evoke from within to bring the 'moment' to that role?] Yes. Because I believe in imagination. I did *Kramer vs. Kramer* before I had children. But the mother I would be was already inside me. People say, 'When you have children, everything changes.' But maybe things are awakened that were already there. I think actors can awaken things that are in all of us: our evil, our cruelty, our grace. Actors can call these things up more easily than other people."

Let me make clear: While I recognize the importance of not imposing our personal issues upon our clients/patients, I reject invitations to overly psychologize (read: pathologize) my therapeutic motivations and commitments.[3][4] I appreciate and honor the influence of my father's intellect and honesty and storytelling; my mother's concern and passion and energy; my brother's demands for quality and accountability, as well as his sharp wit, on which I honed mine; my grandfather's immigrant drive and *joie d'vive* and my grandmother's shrewdness; as well as my wife's love and sincerity and kindness and my teenage son's pressure to be the father he thinks I am and to be contemporary and to keep it real.[5] My dogs, Rocky and Snowball and now Ranger, have also influenced me, repeatedly reminding me about having fun and living life in the present.

So who, then, beyond family and friends, are some of my influences?[6] Looking from this point in time and space, here are a few who have influenced me, and how. There are others who confirmed and encouraged me, blessed me, helped me to become more of myself, but let me at least mention these:

I have always been more interested in literature and art and philosophy and how and why people do what they do than in things like cars and electricity. My parents would tell family stories about me asking, when I was in grade school or junior high, questions like 'Why does Mr. Goldberg always go out to have a cigarette whenever Mrs. Goldberg starts to talk about their daughter?' I was also very interested in going up to my junior high school teacher's desk (Mrs. Jordan was her name) to check her out more closely—so interested, in fact, that she gently referred me to the school counselor. We had a couple of talks, and then he lent me a book that he thought I'd be interested in. It was called *The Interpretation of Dreams* by Sigmund Freud!

A couple of my UCLA psychology professors, in their different ways, took the time to nurture the interest of a bright undergraduate. Dr. John Liebeskind let me visit him in his physiological lab; and Dr. Carl Faber, a psychotherapist with a Jungian bent toward myth and ritual, let me serve as a teaching assistant, reading and grading student projects in consultation with him. Professor Richard Centers let me work as his social psychology research assistant and initiated me into the publication club by encouraging and co-authoring a couple of my first papers. Another of my UCLA professors, the anthropologist Joseph Birdsell, inspired me with his knowledge and expository abilities and got me to think about adapta-

---

3. I am grateful to Dr. George Zimmar at Brunner-Routledge Publishers for pointing out to me that in 167 A.D. Marcus Aurelius (1964) spent the first several pages of his *Meditations* thanking his grandfather, teachers, parents, and the gods for their specific lessons and influences.

tion, how environment influences development; and the sociologist, Melvin Seeman, got me to really think about the *social* in social psychology and also got me to shift my political thinking when he cut through all the Vietnam War rhetoric by simply saying something that I already knew: "It's wrong to kill people."

I'm grateful to Dr. Jerome Singer at Yale, who let me switch from the social to the clinical graduate program.

During my predoctoral internship at the University of Wisconsin-Madison, in 1974-75, I was most fortunate to study with the well-known family therapist, Carl Whitaker, who I count as one of my mentors. (*The Family Crucible* and *Midnight Musings of a Family Therapist* are two of my favorite books.) As some of you may know, Carl was extraordinarily adept at saying things that would stir people up and put them in better touch with themselves.[7] He was a master of both authenticity and absurdity; he had a way of embracing the genuine person while separating them from their pretense and games. I remember once talking

---

4. Back a few years, in the book *The First Session in Brief Therapy*, I somewhat tongue-in-cheek wrote: "I was born to be a brief therapist. My mother, a loving and wonderful woman bless her soul, was a major-league worrier. I often consoled her, and soon learned to do it quickly. When the story got old, I told her not to be such a worrier (my first second-order intervention) and began to find ways to enhance her self-understanding as well as to anticipate, outflank, and redirect her. This involved my whole family, including myself. My academic pedigree includes a Yale Ph.D., extended training with Whitaker, Horowitz, and the Gouldings, numerous long-term and short-term therapy courses and workshops, plus lots of side trips through various psychospiritual schools of enlightenment (est, Zen, the Sufis, Hasidic Masters, etc.), bodywork, and personal therapy. By temperament and attention span, I prefer the 'action' and excitement of brief therapy. As staff psychologist and [then] Director of Adult Services at a large HMO (Kaiser), my delight in new problems, stimulating contact, and human experience is constantly aroused. Now, if I could only get my mother to stop worrying!" (in Hoyt, Rosenbaum & Talmon, 1992, p. 81). This notwithstanding, I agree with my Australian colleague, Michael White: "I always believe that this privileging of psychological accounts of motive to be a profoundly conservative endeavor, one that is counterinspiration, one that could only contribute significantly to therapist experiences of fatigue and burnout. For various reasons, I could never be persuaded into the pathologizing of my motives for my interest in joining this profession, and mostly managed to hold on to what were my favored notions of conscious purpose and commitment. I have no doubt that over the years that expressions of these notions have been a source of invigoration to me, and in recent years I have been encouraging therapists to join together in identifying, articulating, and elevating notions of conscious purpose and commitment" (in Hoyt & Combs, 1996, p. 54).

with him about a personal decision I was trying to make. He listened for a while as I ambivalated, then remarked: "Don't worry—whatever you do, you'll regret it!" Pop! That was Carl! Another time, I confessed to him during a supervision session that I had been also presenting the same case to another supervisor, and getting different advice. He laughed, then said: "I guess you'll have to think for yourself." I also recall sitting in their kitchen eating delicious Brunswick stew with him and his wife, Muriel, after working in the woodshop he had in his garage. I had spent the day making a large bookcase/entertainment center; when Carl came out, he could see that it was kind of artsy and creative, but that it lacked strength and durability, so he added a few structural supports and some large nails—both a reality and a metaphor.

He inspired me, or maybe I should say he influenced me, to bring more of myself into my work. Let me tell you, though, that while there are lots of 'Whitaker-as-Zen-Master' stories, many of which highlight his saying seemingly wacky or off-the-wall things, it was not 'anything goes.' He was 'crazy like a fox.' For six months, he sat in the room once a week and watched me do intakes and then spent time debriefing with me, often being very linear as he coached me about the interviewing, asked me about differential diagnoses, possibly overlooked issues, and so on.

One day, when Carl wasn't there, I was doing an intake with a married couple and the man indicated that he and his wife had made the appointment because they wanted to be in family therapy with Dr. Whitaker. When I went to Carl and told him of their request, he said I should call the couple and tell them that he would see them, under one condition: that *I* would be his co-therapist! (I was an intimidated and somewhat overwhelmed pre-doc—but as I found out, doing co-therapy was one of Whitaker's, and now one of my, favorite training methods.)

---

5. In October 2001, Alex and I took the opportunity of spending 18 days together in Japan in conjunction with my speaking at a brief therapy conference in Osaka (see Chapter 1, this volume). We had a great time and did a lot. One day in Kyoto, however, we were a bit worn out when we got to the famous Sansjusangendo Temple. I had been there before, six years prior, and wanted to share the experience of the fabulous 700-year-old Buddhist temple, with its hundreds of life-like statues surrounding a large gilded Kannon, the goddess of mercy. Alex was less than enthralled, and I quickly got irritated, then pissed off: "Pay attention! We came all this way, why don't you appreciate this? Why don't you stop whining? Damnit, why don't you just go outside and play." Alex responded in kind (where did he ever learn that?), then sort of slinked away toward the outside courtyard. I stood there, exasperated, then looked up at Kannon, who looked back at me and seemed to say, "You're not getting the point here, are you?" I went outside and apologized—and then Alex did, too.

While Carl did most of the heavy lifting, from my junior position I learned a great deal about creativity, the use of self, the magic of the moment, and intergenerational family dynamics.[8]

In a session near the end of our many meetings with the family, the grandmother had not shown up. It was one of the kids' birthdays and they had brought a cake, and I was ready to dig in at the end of the session. Carl knew better. He said we could sing 'Happy Birthday,' but not cut the cake. "Take it home and share it with grandmother—she needs to know that she means more to you than we do."

At the end of my pre-doc year, as I was saying goodbye to Carl, I stopped in the doorway and looked around his office, then asked: "Would you please give me a momento, something I can take with me?" He smiled that smile, then went to his shelves and pulled off a book, took it to his desk and signed it, and handed it to me. We embraced, wished each other well, and I walked away. Going down the hall, I looked at what was in my hand: it was a first edition of Joseph Campbell's (1949) *The Hero with a Thousand Faces*! I saw Carl a number of times after that. Although he died a few years ago, I'd like to think that Carl Whitaker and I have stayed in touch.

---

6. As I noted in my chairman's introduction at the APA symposium where this paper was first presented, the term *influence* came from the Latin *influent*, in-flowing, and referred originally to the astrological idea of an ethereal fluid thought to flow from the stars and to affect the actions of humans—an emanation or transmission. When speaking of "an influence" we usually mean something more than just new information: an infusion, a major shift or turning point, a quantum leap, power arising from station or character, and so forth. Influences can come from family and friends, of course, as well as professional teachers and books, but also from a variety of sources—art and literature; philosophy and religion; history and popular culture; songs, sports, and films; Nature and Mother Earth; and so on. Sometimes, as the old saying has it, "When the student is ready, the teacher appears."

7. As Salvador Minuchin wrote in his Foreword to Whitaker's collected papers, *From Psyche to System: The Evolving Therapy of Carl Whitaker* (1982, p. ix): "Any statement presented as complete is turned into a fragment; like James Joyce, Whitaker creates a revolution in the grammar of life….Though seemingly random, his interventions are all directed to challenge the meaning that people give to events. Whitaker's assumption seems to be that out of his challenge to form, creative processes in individual members as well as the family as a whole can arise. Out of this experiential soup, a better arrangement among family members can result….By the end of therapy, every family member has been touched by Whitaker's distorting magic. Each member feels challenged, misunderstood, accepted, rejected, or insulted. But he has been put in contact with a less familiar part of himself."

I would also like to tip my hat to Lady Luck, Fortuna, Trickster, Chance, Opportunity, Serendipity, Happy Coincidences, Good Timing, Fate, The Breaks, and their kindred spirits. Back at Yale after my year in Wisconsin, working on my doctoral dissertation, I was wandering around Dr. Singer's office one evening, planning to borrow a book, when he walked in and told me that he had just had a phone conversation with a colleague in San Francisco who had just gotten a grant—and asked if I would be interested in doing my post-doc there. That 'accidental' meeting led to my being in several 'right places' at the right time—to my getting back to California, to my getting my first job, to my making certain lifelong friends, to my meeting my wife…to a path that has brought me here today. "We live life forwards but understand it backwards," as Kierkegaard (1843/1959) said.

We also often encounter significant patients and colleagues—and teachers—by accident or coincidence. While chance or luck may play a role, of course, it's what we do with the opportunities that really makes a difference. As Epictetus said two millennia ago, "It's not so much events, but our reactions to those events, that determine our destinies." True, but I keep a set of dice on the corner of my office bookcase, arranged with a 7 up and a 7 showing toward the client, but with snake eyes also staring out sideways at me, to remind me that everything is not under our control.[9]

---

8. I do think I may have scored some points with Carl when, in an early session, the father, trying to split us, challengingly asked me: "What's your role here?" I paused, then replied: "Me? I'm the ventriloquist!"

    In another session I watched as Carl worked beautifully with the husband about his unresolved grief concerning the long-ago death of his father; in a subsequent session, when the father came back and was describing his experience having visited the father's grave, the kids grew restless and fidgety. This was a sensitive moment, and they were being goofy and pretty annoying. Finally, I leaned over and whispered in one kid's ear, who then leaned to the next and whispered something, down the line. They stopped being disruptive and paid attention. Afterwords, when Carl asked me what I had said to get the kids to settle down, I told him: "I whispered, 'Tell the kid next to you that this may seem kind of boring now, but it'll be really interesting after your Dad dies.'"

9. James Hillman (1996, p. 55) elaborates: "Heidegger or Camus, for instance, places the human being into the situation of 'thrownness.' We are merely thrown into being here (*Dasein*). The German word for 'thrown' (*Wurf*) combines senses of the throw of the dice, a projection, and a litter of pups or piglets cast by a bitch or a sow." To mix gambling metaphors, it's how you play the cards you're dealt.

Dr. Albert Ellis, who was sitting next to me at the APA symposium where this paper was first presented, has also been an influence. When I was a graduate student at Yale, in the mid-1970s, Dr. Ellis came and gave a talk. I had heard of him, but this was the first time I actually heard him. Yale's psychiatric establishment was deep into psychoanalysis then, and I recall that Al's talk about R.E.T.—despite his brilliance, wit, and clear thinking—was not entirely, shall we say, 'well received.' I was fascinated. Here was this guy who was famous and clearly knew his stuff, yet was not part of the academic establishment. It helped me open my lenses wider. What most impressed me then, and still does—even beyond the cognitive-behavioral therapy and constructivist theory—was the way Al listened to but really wasn't intimidated by what the pooh-bahs and muckymucks thought! He was himself. For me, an upstart crow, this was an important lesson about paying attention but following your own drummer.

After I finished my dissertation, I then did a two-year postdoctoral fellowship at the Langley Porter Institute of the University of California, San Francisco, with the psychiatrist-psychoanalyst Mardi Horowitz. While I learned some ideas about brief psychodynamic therapy and process-outcome research, what stayed with me the most—what really influenced me—was Mardi's example of hard work and productivity. This was also reinforced, years later, by watching my colleague Don Meichenbaum at the 1995 and 2000 Evolution of Psychotherapy conferences. If you have ever seen Don present, you know he is a brilliant walking encyclopedia, but what I also noticed is that even in the short panel discussions, when some of the other presenters would just sort of fluff their way through, Don had carefully planned what would be most useful to say in his allotted few minutes. I've tried to take that as an exemplar for my own presentations.

Another influence for me has been the *est* training. I know that many people barely know about *est* or think it was some 1970s cult in which you were locked in a room, insulted, and not allowed to go to the bathroom. I also know that *est* had fallen out of favor and that the personal life of the founder, Werner Erhard, seems to have turned out to be a mess, but for many of us who were there, the actual training was a wonderful, life-affirming experience. Over two long weekends and a mid-week evening, we were led through a series of processes, drawn from Gestalt, psychodrama, psychoanalysis, psychosynthesis, hypnosis, Eastern religions, group therapy, and so on, in which we came to recognize undeniably how much of how we experience life is of our own making. We talked a lot about *It*, the realization that we make our reality in the sense that we are responsible for our perceptions. This understanding is pivotal. We were confronted and empowered with our abilities to choose and the consequences of keeping our agreements and having integrity. By the end, when the trainer went around the room and asked, "Did you get it?" I had become a confirmed constructivist and responded: "Did I get *it*? I brought *it* with me!"[10]

My style of thinking and ways of knowing tend to be divergent and synthesizing, cross-cutting schools, disciplines, and departments in search of sources, connections, and solutions. These tendencies were strongly reinforced when I was fortunate to spend some time with Joseph Campbell, the great mythologist whose book Carl Whitaker had handed to me. I heard his famous call to "Follow your bliss and doors will open where there were no doors before" (quoted in Hart, 1990, p. 45). Even beyond the richness and rapture of his mind, Campbell's lasting influence on me is helping to open the space for me to follow my interests and to think outside the box.

Another influence has been a psychiatrist-colleague, Norman Weinstein, who hired me for my first job at Kaiser Permanente back in 1979. Norm was a 'can-do' kind of guy. One day when Norm came to work the wooden arm on the staff parking lot gate wouldn't go up—there was a long line of cars. Norm got out, tried to get it to function and, when it wouldn't, he simply broke it off and tossed it aside, allowing us all to get parked and to get to work. I saw him do it. When he was subsequently asked, later that day, by the head of the medical center about this unusual action, he readily acknowledged he had done it: "Of course. I figured with what we're paying staff, we were losing hundreds of dollars an hour, plus lots of patients were waiting and were going to be inconvenienced." We psychologists sometimes get more caught up in the *why?* and *what's wrong?* than the *how?* and *what works?*, and over the years Norm taught me a lot about getting involved and intervening, about taking responsibility for doing something to make things right.[11]

Another mentor[12] was Robert Goulding, M.D. We met in 1985. When I approached Bob after a lecture at the first Evolution of Psychotherapy conference and asked him what I would learn if I attended his Redecision Therapy training

---

10. Talk about luck: It must have been around 1980. I took a one-day workshop with Salvador Minuchin at the Family Therapy Institute of Berkeley. I wasn't sure I would stay the whole day, so I sat in the back of the room, in one of the few unfilled seats. As the workshop started, someone else slipped in and sat down next to me. Minuchin was brilliant, of course, and when we got to a point in the morning when he had us turn to the person next to us to discuss some aspect of the family session we had been observing, I turned to discover that my fellow discussant was Werner Erhard! I stayed for the day, and learned a lot.

program, he replied: "Well, that will depend a lot on what you choose to do!" From Bob (along with his wife, Mary Goulding, M.S.W.), I learned the concepts and techniques of their creative amalgam of TA and Gestalt work, and also got some much-needed personal therapy (see Hoyt, 1992, 2001b; Hoyt & Goulding, 1989). I'm not a redecision therapist, but over several years of training programs I learned a lot about motivation and imagination and how much *The Power Is in the Patient*—the title of one of the Gouldings' books. Their influence on me, like that of *est*, was really existential: about the power of choice and experience and about focus and personal autonomy and accountability. Following the Gouldings, I still ask "What's the patient's contract?" and I learned quickly from them how to hear whether people would just say they were "Going to try" or whether they really would take responsibility for their thoughts, feelings, and actions—therapeutic and otherwise.

How you look influences what you see, and what you see influences what you do. A lot of what I see, I see because I've been able to look through the eyes of so many different teachers. More recent influences include Insoo Kim Berg and Steve de Shazer, the co-originators of Solution-Focused Therapy; and Michael White, the co-originator (with David Epston) of Narrative Therapy. Michael and I and a colleague, Gene Combs, were having a conversation (see Hoyt & Combs, 1996/2001) when Michael made a comment that affected me deeply: "We do not just walk a path but, rather, we create our path as we walk it."[13] Again, I've been clued to the significance of languaging and belief systems, as well as to the

---

11. Many years later, when Norm was retiring, we gave him a party. One of my colleagues, Stewart Proctor, gave a nice little speech and then (to our surprise) presented Norm with a token of our appreciation…a broken-off parking gate mounted on a lovely piece of mahogany with an inscribed brass plaque! Well done, Stewart, well done!
12. Mentors instruct and teach, but they do more. Bill Russell, the captain of the Boston Celtics basketball team, had this to say: "Mentoring is about creating an awakening. It is breathing life into abilities, capabilities, and potential that are living under the surface but need to see the sunlight. Mentoring is as old as the human race and is about redefining teamwork in a new context. It's a collaboration. Mentoring is the gift of a relationship" (Russell, 2001, p. 232).
13. Michael told us that he had heard these lines from Humberto Maturana while walking along the quay in Lisbon; subsequently, my co-panelist Lillian Comas-Diaz, in her paper (2002) presented at the symposium where this paper was first delivered, called my attention to the composition by the great Spanish poet Antonio Machado (1983) entitled *"Caminante No Hay Camino, Se Hace Camino al Andar"* ("There Is No Way, the Way Is Made by Walking").

importance of power and politics in therapy—including the significance of choosing what meanings you privilege and elevate. The influences of solution-focused therapy and narrative therapy are abundantly apparent in my recent books, especially in *Some Stories Are Better than Others* and *Interviews with Brief Therapy Experts*.

I never really set out to be a *brief* therapist.[14] I'm just attracted to things that are efficient at reducing suffering and that are lively and creative and respectful of people's existing talents and abilities. I'm interested in being an *expander*, not a *shrink* (Hoyt, 1985/1995a). I think most of my clients will tell you that I am practical and very personal, that I talk from the heart and to the heart. We're in the room together. My overarching theory is narrative constructivism and I think I'm what Stanley Messer (1992) would call an "assimilative integrationist": *I'm interested in what works*. My approach is pragmatic and technically eclectic. I like to help people put their stories together in ways that gets them more of what they want. I'm drawn to the romantic, the heroic, and the comedic. Some days I'm my solution-focused/narrative/client-centered self (with an existential-experiential strategic twist); other days (or even hours) I'm doing something more akin to a form of problem-solving cognitive therapy. I'm interested in thoughts, feelings, and behavior; I try to attend to intrapsychic as well as interpersonal aspects. Sometimes I teach skills, like communication and relaxation; occasionally I'm confrontative and even downright directive. Nothing works all the time.

I remember when I first read Jay Haley's brilliant 1973 book, *Uncommon Therapy: The Psychiatric Techniques of Milton H. Erickson, M.D.* I never had the privilege of meeting Dr. Erickson. Haley, who had studied with him for a couple of decades, had organized Erickson's work around a family lifecycle concept and beautifully depicted case after case of the master's innovative methods. A world of *utilization* and *reframing* and *metaphor* and *strategy* and *therapeutic artistry* opened before me. What struck me most, and still does, is how creative and respectful and sometimes even fun were many of Erickson's interventions.[15]

Patients, of course, are also a great influence, one would hope the *sine qua non*, especially if you pay attention to what works and what doesn't work—something one needs to do constantly when working in a large HMO, as I have done since 1979. I've come to understand that much—but not all—of what we call *patient*

---

14. The term *brief* has come to mean two (sometimes) interrelated things: (1) efficient or time sensitive; and (2) a set of theories and practices, loosely based on certain epistemological principles described as having to do with constructivism and social constructionism.

resistance is really *therapist heavy-handedness*, our failing to connect and inspire with sufficient art and craft.

Early on Bill O'Hanlon was very encouraging and helpful in my career as a workshop presenter. I'm also grateful to the many workshop attendees and sponsors who continue to provide encouragement and an in-flow of new ideas.

I'd also like to mention my colleague, Scott Miller. While I was getting interested in narrative constructive approaches to therapy, in the early 1990s, I took a workshop with Scott, and then sent him some papers I had published back then. After some time, Scott wrote back. He said, in essence: "Michael, I have to tell you that while reading your papers, after awhile I began to find myself arguing with you. You're clearly smart, but I found that the way they were written, I kept feeling like you were saying that you were right and that if I didn't agree with you I had to be wrong." When I first read this, I quickly thought "You're wrong!" but then I took some time and reflected on what Scott had written. I re-read some things I had sent him and, damn, he was right! For someone like myself, who believes that resistance is mostly co-created by the therapist, this was certainly an eye-opener. Scott's feedback influenced the way I write and teach, as well as the way I practice therapy—and the way I relate to others. This has been strongly reinforced by my time abroad, especially in my visits to Japan, where I have seen how courtesy is used to allow each person their space.

When you attempt to acknowledge your gratitude, you can sometimes recognize how complicated and non-linear influence can be. Did they tell me, did I tell them, or did it come out of our conversation together? Pay in forward, backward, and sideways. Let me illustrate—here's a cool story: My political sympathies have always tended to lean left, but I'm usually passive and inactive. A few years ago I was inspired by a public interview I did with two Canadian colleagues, Karl Tomm and Stephen Madigan (Tomm, Hoyt & Madigan, 1998/2001), in which

---

15. I am also a great admirer of Haley (see Hoyt, 2002a, 2002b). Sometime in 1992 I contacted him, by letter and telephone, asking him to participate in an interview for a book I was working on at the time. He indicated his preference not to do a formal interview, but then graciously added, "How about if we just get together for a drink?" And so we did, at the Fifth International Ericksonian Congress, held in Phoenix in December 1992. Sitting atop the Hyatt-Regency, we got a bit acquainted. I had no specific agenda, other than to enjoy the pleasure of his company. Finally, however, an important issue came to my mind. "Jay, may I ask you a question?" "Sure," he replied. I paused, then asked: "What do you feed your twinkle?" He smiled: "Well, you have one, too, don't you?" "Well, yeah...but yours is older—I want to make sure I'm feeding mine the right stuff!" We both laughed.

we talked about, amongst other topics, some of Karl's efforts toward political protest. A couple of years later, it happened that I had a patient in my office who worked as an attorney in the area of civil rights. When I asked him, in an early session, how he had gotten into that area, he explained to me that as a child he had lived in Birmingham, Alabama. When the neighborhood church had been bombed, in 1963, a minister came from Georgia to help the community. The minister stayed at my patient's house. "I was only a boy then," he said, "but every night for a week I sat at the dinner table with The Rev. Martin Luther King, and I listened." Wow!

As it happened, many months later I observed an incident at my local postoffice in which I thought the patrons had treated the workers quite rudely, and I could see the institutions of race and social class in their actions. While not thinking consciously of my interview with Karl and Stephen, or the story of my patient and Dr. King, I took what for me was the unusual step of writing a letter, under the title of "Decency," to the local newspaper, calling attention to what had happened. The letter got printed (Hoyt, 2001c). I sent a copy of the letter to Karl Tomm, with a note thanking him for the encouragement. A couple of weeks later, when my patient next came to see me, he started the session by asking, "Are you the Michael Hoyt who wrote the letter in the paper?" I was surprised, and acknowledged that I was. "Very interesting," he said, and I could feel our therapeutic alliance strengthen. So, his influence on me influenced my influence on him; Dr. King's efforts resonated through the system; and my conversation with Drs. Tomm and Madigan continued. I don't know if a butterfly in the Amazon really changes the weather in New York, as some chaos theorists (see Briggs & Peat, 1989; Burke, 1996) would suggest, but I do know that we are in this world together, that "As in the universe, every atom has an effect, however miniscule, on every other atom, so that to pinch the fabric of Time and Space at any point is to shake the whole length and breadth of it" (Gardner, 1991, p. 46). "One Love," as Bob Marley said.

The humanities and popular culture and Nature open my eyes and ears and mind. Art has delighted my spirit and has helped me, as the Scottish sculptor Andy Goldsworthy (in Riedelsheimer, 2001) says, "to see something you never saw before, that was always there but you were blind to it." This is what the great architect Frank Lloyd Wright (1957/1992, p. 396) said:

> I guess I use the word *nature*, as I always have, in rather a confusing way because I always put a capital "N" on the word, and why? Because we write the word God with a capital "G" don't we? Now *Nature* is all the body of God

we are ever going to see! As you study it, instead of looking *at* it, look *into* Nature. The reason is the *why* of this or that and by way of such interior *Nature* study, increase your knowledge of what constitutes *truth*. Do this concerning anything and you will soon find that its Nature is the *beauty* of it.

Literature and poetry have influenced me to put my roots deeper into the world and become more, as James Broughton (1990) says, "the I am that I am."[16] As Jim Harrison (2002, p. 39) wrote, "I'm sure that there's a scientific explanation for this though for a poet the science is doomed to be less interesting than the experience." A really good poem can shake you, start a fire, change your life (Housden, 2001). A really good poem can enrich your perception and get under your skin and stay with you. Sometimes when we're "verging" (Hoffman, 2002) on something in our life—perhaps a beginning or ending, an interest that keeps calling, a shift or change in our thinking or work or relationships, maybe a way out of one of the "swamplands of the soul" (Hollis, 1996)—a really good poem speaks to us when we're ready to hear it, helping to encourage and tip us toward our authentic self. T'was Shakespeare who said "This above all: to thine own self be true" (*Hamlet*, Act I, Scene 3, line 78); and it was Emerson, in his essay "Self-Reliance," who echoed, "Insist on yourself; never imitate" (1841/1950, p. 166). Readers who already know Mary Oliver's (1986/1992) wonderful poem, "The Journey," will understand what I am trying to say.

I hope these words will encourage and influence you in your own journeys. I've gone so far in mine, so many twists and turns, so many inputs and inspira-

---

16. My palate is amateur and barely educated, more autodidactic than apodictic (whew!), and somewhat biased toward Americans and the English-speaking world. Many of my favorites are obvious, like Walt Whitman and e.e. cummings and Langston Hughes, and (in translation) Rumi and Rilke and Basho. I love James Broughton and Charles Bukowski, and enjoy the various anthologies put together by Robery Bly and by Bill Moyers, and lately I've been listening to great poets reading their works in the *Poetry Speaks* (Paschen & Mosby, 2001) oral history collection. Another recent favorite is Ric Masten, the poet laureate of Carmel, California, who wrote: "The words minister and minstrel come from the same Latin root word meaning servant. I believe a poet is a servant who helps us see things more clearly, who helps us recognize what we already know, who serves the human hive as a spokesman...." (DiGirolamo, n.d., p. 14). Robert Coles (1989, p. 101), in a lovely chapter about bringing poems to medical school teaching, writes: "Poets try to sharpen the sight, to nurture language carefully in the hope of calling upon it for an understanding of what is happening." As Stanley Kunitz (1995, p. 11), the Pulitzer-prize winner, has also said: "Poetry....is ultimately mythology, the telling of the stories of the soul—moving through time."

tions, that I could never find my way back to where I started—not that I'd ever really want to. I think I'll just keep my ears open, look around, await my next influence, and carry on.

In closing, I say: Be open to wisdom, wherever you find it—especially within yourself.

References

Adams, J.F., Piercy, F.P., & Jurich, J.A. (1991) Effects of solution-focused therapy's "formula first session task" on compliance and outcome in family therapy. *Journal of Marital and Family Therapy*, 17, 277-290.

Adler, A. (1968) *What Life Should Mean to You*. New York: Capricorn Books. [original work published 1931]

Alter, M. (2001, Aug. 6) Fighting the HMO meanies. *Newsweek*, 138(6), 33.

American Psychological Association Task Force on Psychological Intervention Guidelines. (1994) Washington, DC: Author.

Anderson, H. (1997) *Conversation, Language, and Possibilities: A Postmodern Approach to Therapy*. New York: Basic Books.

Anderson, H. (2000) Reflections on and the appeals and challenges of postmodern psychologies, societal practice, and political life. In L. Holtzman & J. Morss (Eds.), *Postmodern Psychologies, Societal Practice, and Political Life* (pp. 202-208). New York: Routledge.

Anderson, H., & Goolishian, H.A. (1992) The client is the expert: A not-knowing approach to therapy. In S. McNamee & K.J. Gergen (Eds.), *Therapy as Social Construction* (pp. 25-39). Newbury Park, CA: Sage.

Anderson, W.T. (1990) *Reality Isn't What It Used to Be: Theatrical Politics, Ready-to-Wear Religion, Global Myths, Primitive Chic, and Other Wonders of the Postmodern World*. San Francisco: HarperCollins.

Appignanesi, R. (Ed.) (2002) *Postmodernism and Big Science: Einstein Dawkins Kuhn Hawking Darwin*. Cambridge, England: Totem Books.

Appignanesi, R., & Garratt, C. (1995) *Postmodernism for Beginners*. New York: Writers and Readers Publishing.

Atwood, J.D. (1993) Social constructionist couple therapy. *The Family Journal: Counseling and Therapy for Couples and Families*, 1, 116-130.

Atwood, J.D. (1997) Social construction theory and therapy. In J.D. Atwood (Ed.), *Challenging Family Therapy Situations: Perspectives in Social Construction* (pp. 1-40). New York: Springer.

Auden, W.H. (1966) Robert Frost. In *The Dyer's Hand and Other Essays* (pp. 337-353). New York: Random House.

Aurelius, M. (1964) *Meditations*. (M. Staniforth, Trans.) London: Penguin Books. (original work written in A.D. 167)

Bachelard, G. (1964). *The Poetics of Space*. (M. Jolas, Trans.). Boston: Beacon Press.

Bakhtin, M.M. (1981) *The Dialogic Imagination: Four Essays by M.M. Bakhtin* (M. Holquist, T.C. Emerson & M. Holquist, Eds.). Austin, TX: University of Texas Press.

Barber, J. (1990) Miracle cures? Therapeutic consequences of clinical demonstrations. In J.K. Zeig & S. Gilligan (Eds.), *Brief Therapy: Myths, Methods, and Metaphors* (pp. 437-442). New York: Brunner/Mazel.

Bateson, G. (1972) *Steps to an Ecology of Mind*. New York: Ballantine.

Bateson, G. (1979) *Mind and Nature: A Necessary Unity*. New York: Dutton.

Baudrillard, J. (1990) *Seductions*. (trans. by B. Singer) New York: St. Martin's Press. [original French work published 1979]

Baudrillard, J. (1994) *Simulacra and Simulation*. (Trans. by S.F. Glaser) Ann Arbor. MI: University of Michigan Press. (original French work published in 1981]

Beaulieu, D. (2004) Lessons well learned: How to help your clients hold on to their gains. *Psychotherapy Networker*, 28(1), 27-28.

Berendt, J. (1994) *Midnight in the Garden of Good and Evil*. New York: Random House.

Berg, I.K. (1989) Of visitors, complainants, and customers. *Family Therapy Networker*, 13(1), 27.

Berg, I.K. (1994a) *Family-Based Services: A Solution-Focused Approach*. New York: Norton.

Berg, I.K. (1994b) *Irreconcilable Differences: A Solution-Focused Approach to Marital Yherapy*. [videotape] New York: Norton.

Berg, I.K. (1994c) *So What Else is Better? Solutions for Substance Abuse*. [videotape] Milwaukee, WI: Brief Family Therapy Center.

Berg, I.K., & de Shazer, S. (1993) Making numbers talk: Language in therapy. In S. Friedman (Ed.), *The New Language of Change: Constructive Collaboration in Psychotherapy* (pp. 5-24). New York: Guilford Press.

Berg, I.K., & Dolan, Y.D. (2000) *Tales of Solutions: A Collection of Hope-Inspiring Stories*. New York: Norton.

Berg, I.K., & Kelly, S. (2000) *Building Solutions in Child Protective Services*. New York: Norton.

Berg, I.K., & Miller, S.D. (1992) *Working with the Problem Drinker: A Solution-Focused Approach*. New York: Norton.

Berg, I.K., & Reuss, N.H. (1997) *Solutions Step by Step: A Substance Abuse Treatment Manual*. New York: Norton.

Beutler, L.E., & Harwood, T.M. (2001) Antiscientific attitudes: What happens when scientists are unscientific? *Journal of Clinical Psychology*, 57(1), 43-52.

Beyebach, M., & Morejon, A.R. (1999) Some thoughts on integration in solution-focused therapy. *Journal of Systemic Therapies*, 18(1), 24-42.

Bogard, M. (1992, November-December). The duel over dual relationships. *Family Therapy Networker*, 16(6), 32-37.

Bohart, A.C., & Tallman, K. (1999) *How Clients Make Therapy Work: The Process of Active Self-Healing*. Washington, DC: American Psychological Association.

Bonjean, M.J. (1997) Solution-focused brief therapy with aging families. In T.D. Hargrave & S.M. Hanna (Eds.), *The Aging Family: New Visions in Theory, Practice, and Reality* (pp. 81-100). New York: Brunner/Mazel.

Bonjean, M.J. (2003) Solution-focused therapy: Elders enhancing exceptions. In J.L. Ronch & J. Goldfield (Eds.), *Mental Wellness in Aging: Strengths-Based Approaches* (pp. 201-234). Baltimore, MD: Health Professions Press.

Borges, J.L. (1964) A new refutation of time. In *Labyrinths: Selected Stories and Other Writings* (pp. 217-234). New York: New Directions.

Boscolo, L., & Bertrando, P. (1993) *The Times of Time*. New York: Norton.

Blum, J.D. (1978) On changes in psychiatric diagnosis over time. *American Psychologist*, 33, 1017-1031.

Briggs, J., & Peat, F.D. (1989) *Turbulent Mirror: An Illustrated Guide to Chaos Theory and the Science of Wholeness*. New York: Harper & Row.

Brockelman, T.P. (2001) *The Frame and the Mirror: On Collage and the Postmodern*. Evanston, IL: Northwestern University Press.

Brodribb, S. (1992) *Nothing Mat(t)ers: A Feminist Critique of Postmodernism*. North Melbourne, Australia: Spinifex Press.

Broughton, J. (1990) "I am the I am that I am." In *Special Deliveries: New and Selected Poems* (p. xvii). Seattle, WA: Broken Moon Press.

Bruner, J. (1986) *Actual Minds, Possible Worlds*. Cambridge, MA: Harvard University Press.

Bruner, J. (1987) Life as narrative. *Social Research*, 54, 11-32.

Buber, M. (1947) *Tales of the Hasidim: Early Masters*. New York: Schocken.

Budman, S.H., Hoyt, M.F., & Friedman, S. (Eds.) (1992) *The First Session in Brief Therapy*. New York: Guilford Press.

Burke, J. (1996) *The Pinball Effect: How Renaissance Water Gardens Made the Carburetor Possible and Other Journeys through Knowledge*. Boston: Little, Brown.

Burns, K. (2002) Interview: Meryl Streep. *Marin Independent Journal/USA Weekend*, November 29-December 1, pp. 6-7.

Butler, C. (2002) *Postmodernism: A Very Short Introduction.* Oxford, England: Oxford University Press.

Cade, B. (1986) The reality of "reality" (or the "reality") of reality. *American Journal of Family Therapy*, 14, 49-56.

Cade, B., & O'Hanlon, W.H. (1993) *A Brief Guide to Brief Therapy.* New York: Norton.

Campbell, J. (1949) *The Hero with a Thousand Faces.* Princeton, NJ: Bollingen/Princeton University Press.

Carlson, J. (2000) How to prevent relapse: Treatment strategies for long-term change. *Family Therapy Networker*, 24(5), 23, 84.

Carroll, L. (1946) *Alice in Wonderland and Through the Looking Glass.* New York: Grosset & Dunlap. [work originally published 1887]

Chessick, R.D. (1990) Hermeneutics for psychotherapists. *American Journal of Psychotherapy*, 44(2), 256-273.

Clavell, J. (1975) *Shogun.* New York: Random House.

Coe, D.M., & Zimpfer, D.D. (1996) Infusing solution-oriented theory and techniques into group work. *Journal for Specialists in Group Work*, 21(1), 49-57.

Coles, R. (1989) *The Call of Stories: Teaching and the Moral Imagination.* Boston: Houghton Mifflin.

Comas-Diaz, L. (2002, August) Traveling companions: The teachings of culture, ethnicity, and gender. Paper presented at symposium on *Honoring Our Teachers—Eminent Psychotherapists Describe Who Influenced Them, and How* (M.F. Hoyt, Chair), held at the annual convention of the American Psychological Association, Chicago.

Combs, G., & Freedman, J. (1994) Milton Erickson: Early postmodernist. In J.K. Zeig (Ed.), *Ericksonian Methods: The Essence of the Story* (pp. 267-281). New York: Brunner/Mazel.

Coyne, J.C. (1982) A brief introduction to epistobabble. *Family Therapy Networker*, 6(4), 27-28.

cummings, e.e. (1991) "i thank You God for most this amazing day." In *E.E. Cummings: Complete Poems 1904-1962* (G.J. Firmage, Ed.), p. 663. New York: Liveright Publishing Company. (work originally published 1950)

Cummings, N.A., & Cummings, J.L. (2000) *The Essence of Psychotherapy: Reinventing the Art in the New Era of Data*. San Diego, CA: Academic Press.

Cummings, N.A., Cummings, J.L., & Johnson, J.N. (Eds.) (1997) *Behavioral Health in Primary Care: A Guide for Clinical Integration*. Madison, CT: Psychosocial Press.

Cummings, N.A., & Follette, W.T. (1976) Brief psychotherapy and medical utilization. In H. Dorken et al. (Eds.), *The Professional Psychologist Today*. San Francisco: Jossey-Bass.

Cummings, N.A., & Sayama, M. (1995) *Focused Psychotherapy: A Casebook of Brief, Intermittent Psychotherapy Throughout the Life Cycle*. Philadelphia: Brunner/Mazel.

Cushman, P. (1990) Why the self is empty: Toward a historically situated psychology. *American Psychologist*, 45(5), 599-611.

Cushman, P. (1995) *Constructing the Self, Constructing America: A Cultural History of Psychotherapy*. New York: Addison-Wesley.

DeJong, P., & Berg, I.K. (1997) *Interviewing for Solutions*. Pacific Grove, CA: Brooks/Cole.

DeJong, P., & Hopwood, L.E. (1996) Outcome research on treatment conducted at the Brief Family Therapy Center, 1992-1993. In S.D. Miller, M.A. Hubble, & B.L. Duncan (Eds.), *Handbook of Solution-Focused Brief Therapy* (pp. 272-298). San Francisco: Jossey-Bass.

Derrida, J. (1972) *Limited, Inc.* Evanston, IL: Northwestern University Press.

Derrida, J. (1976) *On Grammatology*. Baltimore, MD: Johns Hopkins University Press. [original French work published 1967]

Derrida, J. (1978) *Writing and Difference* (A. Bass, Trans.). Chicago: University of Chicago Press.

Derrida, J. (1981) *Positions* (A. Bass, Trans.). Chicago: University of Chicago Press.

de Shazer, S. (1982) *Patterns of Brief Family Therapy*. New York: Guilford Press.

de Shazer, S. (1984) The death of resistance. *Family Process*, 23, 79-93.

de Shazer, S. (1985) *Keys to Solution in Brief Therapy*. New York: Norton.

de Shazer, S. (1988) *Clues: Investigating Solutions in Brief Therapy*. New York: Norton.

de Shazer, S. (1991a) *Putting Difference to Work*. New York: Norton.

de Shazer, S. (1991b) Foreword. In Y.M. Dolan, *Resolving Sexual Abuse: Solution-FocusedTherapy and Ericksonian Hypnosis for Adult Survivors* (pp. ix-x). New York: Norton.

de Shazer, S. (1993a) Creative misunderstanding: There is no escape from language. In S.G. Gilligan & R. Price (Eds.), *Therapeutic Conversations* (pp. 81-90). New York: Norton.

de Shazer, S. (1993b) Commentary: de Shazer & White: Vive la differance. In S. Gilligan & R. Price (Eds.), *Therapeutic Conversations* (pp. 112-120). New York: Norton.

de Shazer, S. (1994a) *Words Were Originally Magic*. New York: Norton.

de Shazer, S. (1994b) Essential, non-essential: Vive la difference. In J.K. Zeig (Ed.), *Ericksonian Methods: The Essence of the Story* (pp. 240-253). New York: Brunner-Mazel.

de Shazer, S. (2001) Internet.http//maelstrom.stjohns.edu./archives/sf-l.html. 27.1.2001.

de Shazer, S. (2002) Getting to the surface of the problem: The bricks and mortar of our constructions. In J.K. Zeig (Ed.), *Brief Therapy: Lasting Impres-*

sions (pp. 243-258). Phoenix, AZ: The Milton H. Erickson Foundation Press.

de Shazer, S., & Berg, I.K. (1985) A part is not apart: Working with only one of the partners present. In A.S. Gurman (Ed.), *Casebook of Marital Therapy* (pp. 97-110). New York: Guilford Press.

de Shazer, S., & Berg, I.K. (1992) Doing therapy: A post-structural re-vision. *Journal of Marital and Family Therapy*, 18, 71-81.

de Shazer, S., & Berg, I.K. (1997) "What works?" Remarks on research aspects of Solution-Focused Brief Therapy. *Journal of Family Therapy*, 19, 121-124.

de Shazer, S., Berg, I.K., Lipchik, E., Nunnally, E., Molnar, A., Gingerich, W., & Weiner-Davis, M. (1986) Brief therapy: Focused solution development. *Family Process*, 25, 207-227.

de Shazer, S., & Molnar, A. (1984) Four useful interventions in brief family therapy. *Journal of Marital and Family Therapy*, 10(3), 297-304.

DiClemente, C.C. (1991) Motivational interviewing and the stages of change. In W.R. Miller & S. Rollnick, *Motivational Interviewing: Preparing People to Change Addictive Behaviors* (pp. 191-202). New York: Guilford Press.

DiGirolamo, V. (n.d.) Full circle: The life and work of Ric Masten. In R. Masten, *Let It Be a Dance: Words and One-Liners* (pp. 8-17). Carmel, CA: Carmel Publishing Company.

Dilthey, W. (1988) *Introduction to the Human Sciences*. Detroit, MI: Wayne State University Press.

Doan, R.E. (1997) Narrative therapy, postmodernism, social constructionism, and constructivism: Discussion and distinctions. *Transactional Analysis Journal*, 27(2), 128-133.

Doan, R.E. (1998) The king is dead; long live the king: Narrative therapy and practicing what we preach. *Family Process*, 37(3), 379-385.

Doherty, W.J. (1991) Family therapy goes postmodern. *Family Therapy Networker*, 15(5), 36-42.

Dolan, Y.M. (1985) *A Path with a Heart: Ericksonian Utilization with Resistant and Chronic Clients.* New York: Brunner/Mazel.

Dolan, Y.M. (1991) *Resolving Sexual Abuse: Solution-Focused Therapy and Ericksonian Hypnosis for Adult Survivors.* New York: Norton.

Driver-Linn, E. (2003) Where is psychology going? Structural fault lines revealed by psychologists' use of Kuhn. *American Psychologist*, 58, 269-278.

Duncan, B.L., Hubble, M.A., & Miller, S.D. (1997) *Psychotherapy with "Impossible" Cases: The Efficient Treatment of Therapy Veterans.* New York: Norton.

Duncan, B.L., & Miller, S.D. (2000) *The Heroic Client: Doing Client-Directed, Outcome-Oriented Therapy.* San Francisco: Jossey-Bass.

Ecker, B., & Hulley, L. (1996) *Depth Oriented Brief Therapy.* San Francisco: Jossey-Bass.

Efran, J.S., & Fauber, R.L. (1995) Radical constructivism: Questions and answers. In R.A. Neimeyer & M.J. Mahoney (Eds.), *Constructivism in Psychotherapy* (pp. 275-304). Washington, DC: American Psychological Association.

Efran, J.S., Lukens, M.D., & Lukens, R.J. (1990) *Language, Structure, and Change: Frameworks of Meaning in Psychotherapy.* New York: Norton.

Efran, J.S., & Schenker, M.D. (1993) A potpourri of solutions: How new and different is solution-focused therapy? *Family Therapy Networker*, 17, 71-74.

Einstein, A. (1950) The Negro question. In *Essays in Humanism* (pp. 8-11). New York: Philosophical Library. (work originally published 1946)

Einstein, A. (1954) The world as I see it. In *Ideas and Opinions* (pp. 8-11). New York: Crown. (work originally published 1930)

Elliott, T.R., Shewchuk, R., Hagglund, K., Rybarczyk, B., & Harkins, S. (1996) Occupational burnout, tolerance for stress, and coping among nurses in rehabilitation units. *Rehabilitation Psychology*, 41, 267-284.

Ellis, A. (1994) *Reason and Emotion in Psychotherapy* (rev. ed.). New York: Birch Lane Press.

Ellis, A. (1998) How rational emotive behavior therapy belongs in the constructivist camp. In M.F. Hoyt (Ed.), *The Handbook of Constructive Therapies* (pp. 83-99). San Francisco: Jossey-Bass.

Emerson, R.W. (1950) *The Selected Writings of Ralph Waldo Emerson* (B. Atkinson, Ed.). New York: Modern Library/Random House. (works originally published 1841-1844)

Emerson, R.W. (1950) Self-reliance. In *The Selected Writings of Ralph Waldo Emerson* (B. Atkinson, Ed.; pp. 145-169). New York: Modern Library/Random House. (works originally published 1841-1844).

Epston, D., & White, M. (1992) *Experience, Contradiction, Narrative and Imagination: Selected Papers of David Epston and Michael White, 1989-1991*. Adelaide, Australia: Dulwich Centre Publications.

Erickson, B.A. (2002) Ericksonian, cognitive, behavioral, strategic, or all four? In J.K. Zeig (Ed.), *Brief Therapy: Lasting Impressions* (pp. 277-291). Phoenix, AZ: The Milton H. Erickson Foundation Press.

Erickson, B.M., & Simon, J.S. (1996) Scandinavian families: Plain and simple. In M. McGoldrick, J. Giordano, & J.K. Pearce (Eds.), *Ethnicity and Family Therapy* (2nd ed., pp. 595-608). New York: Guilford.

Erickson, M.H. (1980) *Collected Papers* (Vol. 1). New York: Irvington.

Erickson, M.H., & Rossi, E.L. (1981) *Experiencing Hypnosis*. New York: Irvington.

Erickson, M.H., Rossi, E.L., & Rossi, S.I. (1976) *Hypnotic Realities: The Induction of Clinical Hypnosis and Forms of Indirect Suggestion*. New York: Irvington.

Eron, J.B., & Lund, T.W. (1996) *Narrative Solutions in Brief Therapy*. New York: Guilford Press.

Erwin, E. (2001) The rejection of natural science approaches to psychotherapy: Language and the world. *Journal of Clinical Psychology*, 57(1), 7-18.

Feiler, B.S. (1991) *Learning to Bow: Inside the Heart of Japan*. New York: Ticknor & Fields.

Fillingham, L.A. (1993) *Foucault for Beginners.* New York: Writers and Readers Publishing.

Fisch, R., Weakland, J.H., & Segal, L. (1982) *The Tactics of Change: Doing Therapy Briefly.* San Francisco: Jossey-Bass.

Fish, J.M. (1997) Paradox for complainants: Strategic thoughts about solution-focused therapy. *Journal of Systemic Therapies,* 16(5), 266-273.

Fish, V. (1993) Poststructuralism in family therapy: Interrogating the narrative/conversational mode. *Journal of Marital and Family Therapy,* 19(3), 221-232.

Foerster, H. von (1984) On constructing a reality. In P. Watzlawick (Ed.), *The Invented Reality* (pp. 41-61). New York: Norton.

Foerster, H. von (1985) Apropos epistemologies. *Family Process,* 24, 517-524.

Foucault, M. (1980) *Power/Knowledge: Selected Interviews and Other Writings, 1972-1977.* New York: Pantheon.

Frank, R.G., & Elliott, T.R. (Eds.) (2000) *Handbook of Rehabilitation Psychology.* Washington, DC: American Psychological Association.

Fraser, J.S. (1998) Solution-focused therapy—as a problem. In W. Ray & S. de Shazer (Eds.), *Evolving Brief Therapies: Essays in Honor of John Weakland* (pp. 178-194). Iowa City, IA: Geist & Russell.

Freedman, J., & Combs, G. (1996) *Narrative Therapy: The Social Construction of Preferred Realities.* New York: Norton.

Freixas, G. (1995) Personal constructs in systemic practice. In R.A. Neimeyer & M.J. Mahoney (Eds.), *Constructivism in Psychotherapy* (pp. 305-337). Washington, DC: American Psychological Association.

Freud, S. (1961) Introductory lectures on psycho-analysis. In J. Strachey (Ed. and Trans.), *The Standard Edition of the Complete Psychological Works of Sigmund Freud* (Vols. 15-16, pp. 3-463). London: Hogarth Press. [original German language work published in 1915]

Friedman, S. (1992) Constructing solutions (stories) in brief family therapy. In S.H. Budman, M.F. Hoyt, & S. Friedman (Eds.), *The First Session in Brief Therapy* (pp. 282-305). New York: Guilford Press.

Friedman, S. (1993a) Does the miracle question always create miracles? *Journal of Systemic Therapies*, 12(1), 71-74.

Friedman, S. (1993b) Possibility therapy with couples: Constructing time-effective solutions. *Journal of Family Psychotherapy*, 4(4), 35-52.

Friedman, S. (1996) Couples therapy: Changing conversations. In H. Rosen & K.T. Kuehlwein (Eds.), *Constructing Realities: Meaning-Making Perspectives for Psychotherapists* (pp. 413-453). San Francisco: Jossey-Bass.

Friedman, S. (1997) *Time-Effective Psychotherapy: Maximizing Outcomes in an Era of Minimized Resources*. Boston: Allyn & Bacon.

Friedman, S., & Lipchik, E. (1999) A time-effective, solution-focused approach to couple therapy. In J.M. Donovan (Ed.), *Short-Term Couple Therapy* (pp. 325-359). New York: Guilford Press.

Frykman, J. (2001) *Nicole: An Erickson Case, Followed for 22 Years*. Workshop presented at the Eighth International Congress on Ericksonian Approaches to Hypnosis and Psychotherapy, Phoenix, AZ, December 8.

Fuchs, S., & Ward, S. (1994) What is deconstruction, and where and when does it take place? Making facts in science, building cases in law. *American Sociological Review*, 59, 481-500.

Furman, B., & Ahola, T. (1992) *Solution Talk: Hosting Therapeutic Conversations*. New York: Norton.

Gadamer, H.G. (1999) *Truth and Method*. (2nd ed.) New York: Continuum Publishing Co.

Gale, J., & Newfield, N. (1992) A conversation analysis of a solution-focused marital therapy session. *Journal of Marital and Family Therapy*, 18(2), 153-165.

Gardner, J. (1991) *The Art of Fiction: Notes on Craft for Young Writers*. New York: Vintage.

George, E., Iveson, C., & Ratner, H. (1999) *Problem to Solution: Brief Therapy with Individuals and Families.* (rev. ed.) London: Brief Therapy Press.

Gergen, K.J. (1985). The social constructionist movement in modern psychology. *American Psychologist,* 40, 266-275.

Gergen, K.J. (1991) *The Saturated Self: Dilemmas of Identity in Contemporary Life.* New York: Basic Books.

Gergen, K.J. (1993) Foreword. In S. Friedman (Ed.), *The New Language of Change: Constructive Collaboration in Psychotherapy* (pp. ix-xi). New York: Guilford Press.

Gergen, K.J. (1994) Therapeutic professions and the diffusion of deficit. In *Realities and Relationships: Soundings in Social Construction.* Cambridge, MA: Harvard University Press.

Gergen, K.J. (1994a) Exploring the postmodern: Perils or potentials? *American Psychologist,* 49, 412-416.

Gergen, K.J. (1994b) *Realities and Relationships: Soundings in Social Construction.* Cambridge, MA: Harvard University Press.

Gergen, K.J. (1995) Postmodern psychology: Resonance and reflection. *American Psychologist,* 50(5), 394.

Gergen, K.J. (1998) Foreword. In M.F. Hoyt (Ed.), *The Handbook of Constructive Therapies* (pp. xi-xv). San Francisco: Jossey-Bass.

Gergen, K.J. (1999) *An Invitation to Social Constructionism.* Thousand Oaks, CA: Sage.

Gergen, K.J. (2000) From identity to relational politics. In L. Holzman & J. Morss (Eds.), *Postmodern Psychologies, Societal Practice, and Political Life* (pp. 130-150). New York: Routledge.

Gergen, K.J. (2000a) *Social Construction in Context.* Thousand Oaks, CA: Sage.

Gergen, K.J. (2001b) Psychological science in a postmodern context. *American Psychologist,* 56(10), 803-813.

Gergen, K.J., & Kaye, J. (1992) Beyond narrative in the negotiation of therapeutic meaning. In S. Kvale (Ed.), *Psychology and Postmodernism*. Newbury Park, CA: Sage.

Gergen, K.J., & McNamee, S. (1997) Foreword. In E. Riikonen & G.M. Smith, *Re-Imagining Therapy: Living Conversations and Relational Knowing* (pp. xii-ix). Thousand Oaks, CA: Sage.

Giddens, T. (1991) *Modernity and Identity: Self and Society in the Late Modern Age*. Stanford, CA: Stanford University Press.

Gilligan, S.P. (1996) The relational self: The expanding of love beyond desire. In M.F. Hoyt (Ed.), *Constructive Therapies, Volume 2* (pp. 211-237). New York: Guilford Press.

Gladfelter, J. (2001) Videotape review: Interview by Michael Hoyt, Ph.D. *Newsletter of the Milton H. Erickson Foundation*, 23, 3.

Glaserfeld, E. von (1984) An introduction to radical constructivism. In P. Watzlawick (Ed.), *The Invented Reality*. (pp. 17-40). New York: Norton.

Glass, J.M. (1993) *Shattered Selves: Multiple Personality in a Postmodern World*. Ithaca, NY: Cornell University Press.

Glasser, W., & Glasser, C. (2000) *Getting Together and Staying Together: Solving the Mystery of Marriage*. New York: HarperCollins.

Goffman, E. (1963) *Stigma: Notes on the Management of Spoiled Identity*. Englewood Cliffs, NJ: Prentice-Hall.

Gottman, J.M. (1994) *Why Marriages Succeed or Fail: What You can Learn from the Breakthrough Research to Make Your Marriage Last*. New York: Fireside/Simon & Schuster.

Gottman, J.M., & Silver, N. (1999) *The Seven Principles for Making Marriage Work*. New York: Three Rivers Press/Random House.

Goulding, M.M., & Goulding, R.L. (1979) *Changing Lives through Redecision Therapy*. New York: Grove Press.

Goulding, M.M., & Hillman, J. (1995, December) *Growth and Development of the Therapist.* Dialogue held at the Evolution of Psychotherapy Conference, Las Vegas, NV.

Goulding, R.L., & Goulding, M.M. (1978) *The Power Is in the Patient: A Gestalt/TA Approach to Psychotherapy.* San Francisco: Transactional Analysis Press.

Green, S., & Flemons, D. (Eds.) (2004) *Quickies: The Handbook of Brief Sex Therapy.* New York: Norton.

Greenberg, D., & O'Malley, S. (1983) *How to Avoid Love and Marriage.* New York: Freundlich Books/Schribner.

Gross, P.R., & Levitt, N. (1994) *Higher Superstition: The Academic Left and Its Quarrels with Science.* Baltimore, MD: Johns Hopkins University Press.

Gustafson, J.P. (1986) *The Complex Secret of Brief Psychotherapy.* New York: Norton.

Habermas, J. (1985) *The Philosophical Discourse of Modernity: Twelve Lectures* (Trans. by F.G. Lawrence) Cambridge, England: Polity Press.

Haley, J. (1969) *The Power Tactics of Jesus Christ, and Other Essays.* New York: Avon.

Haley, J. (1969) The art of psychoanalysis. In *The Power Tactics of Jesus Christ and Other Essays* (pp. 9-26). New York: Avon.

Haley, J. (1973) *Uncommon Therapy: The Psychiatric Techniques of Milton H. Erickson, M.D.* New York: Norton.

Haley, J. (1976) *Problem Solving Therapy.* San Francisco: Jossey-Bass.

Haley, J. & Richeport, M. (1993) *Milton H. Erickson, M.D.: Explorer in Hypnosis and Therapy.* [videotape] New York: Brunner/Mazel.

Hanna, F.J. (2002) *Therapy with Difficult Clients: Using the Precursors Model to Awaken Change.* Washington, DC: American Psychological Association.

Hansen, N.B., Lambert, M.J., & Forman, E.M. (2002) The psychotherapy dose-response effect and its implications for treatment delivery services. *Clinical Psychology: Science and Practice*, 9(3), 329-343).

Harrison, J. (2002) *Off to the Side: A Memoir*. New York: Grove Press.

Hart, B. (1995) Re-authoring the stories we work by: Situating the narrative approach in the presence of the family of therapists. *Australian and New Zealand Journal of Family Therapy*, 16(4), 181-189.

Hart, M. (1990) *Drumming at the Edge of Magic: A Journey into the Spirit of Percussion*. (with J. Stevens & F. Lieberman) New York: HarperCollins.

Hearn, L. (1984) *Writings from Japan: An Anthology* (ed. by F. King). New York: Penguin. [work originally published 1898]

Heidegger, M. (1971) *On the Way to Language*. San Francisco: Harper & Row.

Held, B.S. (1990) What's in a name? Some confusions and concerns about constructivism. *Journal of Marital and Family Therapy*. 16(2), 179-186.

Held, B.S. (1995) *Back to Reality: A Critique of Postmodern Theory in Psychotherapy*. New York: Norton.

Held, B.S. (1999) How brief therapy got postmodern, or where's the brief? In W.J. Matthews & J.H. Edgette (Eds.), *Current Thinking and Research in Brief Therapy: Solutions, Strategies, Narratives* (Vol. 3, pp. 135-164 and 174-178). Philadelphia: Brunner/Mazel.

Held, B.S. (2001a) Introduction: Antiscientific attitudes within psychotherapy: Philosophical, scientific, and political/psychological considerations. *Journal of Clinical Psychology*, 57(1), 3-6.

Held, B.S. (2001b) Antiscientific attitudes within psychology: Concluding comments. *Journal of Clinical Psychology*, 57(1), 53-62. Herman, E.S., & Chomsky, N. (1988) *Manufacturing Consent: The Political Economy of the Mass Media*. New York: Pantheon Books.

Herman, E.S., & Chomsky, N. (1988) *Manufacuring Consent: The Political Economy of the Mass Media*. New York: Pantheon Books.

Hillman, J. (1983) The fiction of case history. In *Healing Fiction* (pp. 3-49). Woodstock, CT: Spring Publications.

Hillman, J. (1996) *The Soul's Code: In Search of Character and Calling.* New York: Random House.

Hirsch, E. (1999) *How to Read a Poem: And Fall in Love with Poetry.* San Diego, CA: Harcourt.

Hirshfield, J. (1997) *Nine Gates: Entering the Mind of Poetry.* New York: Harper-Collins.

Hjerth, M. (1995, February) *New Developments in Solution-Focused Therapy.* Workshop presented in Salamanca, Spain.

Hoeg, P. (1993) *Smilla's Sense of Snow.* New York: Delta.

Hoffman, L. (1990) Constructing realities: An art of lenses. *Family Process,* 29(1), 1-12.

Hoffman, L. (2002) *Family Therapy: An Intimate History.* New York: Norton.

Hollis, J. (1996) *Swamplands of the Soul: New Life in Dismal Places.* Toronto: Inner City Books.

Holzman, L., & Morss, J. (Eds.) (2000) *Postmodern Psychologies, Societal Practice, and Political Life.* New York: Routledge.

Hopwood, L., & de Shazer, S. (1994) From here to there and who knows where: The continuing evolution of solution-focused brief therapy. In M. Elkaim (Ed.), *Therapies Familiales: Les Approches Principaux* (pp. 555-576). Paris, France: Editions de Seuil.

Horgan, J. (1996) *The End of Science: Facing the Limits of Knowledge in the Twilight of the Scientific Age.* Reading, MA: Addison-Wesley.

Horn, S. (1996) *Shalom, Japan.* New York: Kensington Books.

Hoskisson, P. (2003) Solution-focused groupwork. In B. O'Connell & S. Palmer (Eds.), *Handbook of Solution-Focused Therapy* (pp. 25-37). London: Sage.

Housden, R. (2001) *Ten Poems to Change Your Life.* New York: Harmony Books.

Hoyt, M.F. (1985) "Shrink" or "expander": An issue in forming a therapeutic alliance. *Psychotherapy*, 22, 814-814. Reprinted in M.F. Hoyt, *Brief Therapy and Managed Care* (pp. 209-211). San Francisco: Jossey-Bass, 1995.

Hoyt, M.F. (1992) Personal and powerful. In C.L. Pelton & L. Myers-Pelton (Eds.), *Reflections of Robert L. Goulding* (pp. 179-182). Aberdeen, SD: Family Health Media.

Hoyt, M.F. (Ed.) (1994a) *Constructive therapies*. New York: Guilford Press.

Hoyt, M.F. (1994b) On the importance of keeping it simple and taking the patient seriously: A conversation with Steve de Shazer and John Weakland. In M.F. Hoyt (Ed.), *Constructive therapies* (pp. 11-40). New York: Guilford Press. Reprinted in M.F. Hoyt, *Interviews with brief therapy experts* (pp. 1-33). New York: Brunner-Routledge, 2001.

Hoyt, M.F. (1994c) Single session solutions. In M.F. Hoyt (Ed.), *Constructive therapies* (pp. 140-159). New York: Guilford Press. Reprinted in M.F. Hoyt, *Brief Therapy and Managed Care: Readings for Contemporary Practice* (pp. 141-162). San Francisco: Jossey-Bass, 1995.

Hoyt, M.F. (1995a) *Brief Therapy and Managed Care: Readings for Contemporary Practice*. San Francisco: Jossey-Bass.

Hoyt, M.F. (1995b) On time in brief therapy. In *Brief Therapy and Managed Care: Readings for Contemporary Practice* (pp. 69-104). San Francisco: Jossey-Bass.

Hoyt, M.F. (Ed.) (1996a) *Constructive Therapies* (Volume 2). New York: Guilford Press.

Hoyt, M.F. (1996b) Solution building and language games: A conversation with Steve de Shazer (and some after words with Insoo Kim Berg. In M.F. Hoyt (Ed.), *Constructive Therapies* (Volume 2, pp. 60-86). New York: Guilford Press. Reprinted in M.F. Hoyt, *Interviews with Brief Therapy Experts* (pp. 158-183). New York: Brunner-Routledge, 2001.

Hoyt, M.F. (1996c) Cognitive-behavioral treatment of posttraumatic stress disorder from a narrative constructivist perspective: A conversation with Donald Meichenbaum. In M.F. Hoyt (Ed.), *Constructive Therapies*, Volume 2 (pp. 124-147). New York: Guilford Press. Reprinted in M.F. Hoyt, *Interviews with Brief Therapy Experts* (pp. 97-120). New York: Brunner-Routledge, 2001.

Hoyt, M.F. (1996d) Welcome to Possibilityland: A conversation with Bill O'Hanlon. In M.F. Hoyt (Ed.), *Constructive Therapies,* Volume 2 (pp. 87-123), New York: Guilford Press. Reprinted in M.F. Hoyt, *Interviews with Brief Therapy Experts* (pp. 34-70). New York: Brunner-Routledge, 001.

Hoyt, M.F. (1996e) Postmodernism, the relational self, constructive therapies, and beyond: A conversation with Kenneth Gergen. In M.F. Hoyt (Ed.), *Constructive Therapies,* Volume 2 (pp. 347-368). New York: Guilford Press. Reprinted in M.F. Hoyt, *Interviews with Brief Therapy Experts* (pp. 184-205). New York: Brunner-Routledge, 2001.

Hoyt, M.F. (1996f) A golfer's guide to brief therapy (with footnotes for baseball fans). In M.F. Hoyt (Ed.), *Constructive Therapies* (Volume 2, pp. 306-318). New York: Guilford. Reprinted in M.F. Hoyt, *Some Stories Are Better than Others* (pp. 5-15). Philadelphia: Brunner/Mazel, 2000.

Hoyt, M.F. (Ed.) (1998) *The Handbook of Constructive Therapies.* San Francisco: Jossey-Bass.

Hoyt, M.F. (2000a) *Some Stories Are Better than Others: Doing What Works in Brief Therapy and Managed Care.* Philadelphia: Brunner/Mazel.

Hoyt, M.F. (2000b) Likely future trends and attendant ethical concerns regarding managed mental health care. M.F. Hoyt, *Some Stories Are Better than Others* (pp. 77-108). Philadelphia: Brunner-Mazel.

Hoyt, M.F. (2001a) *Interviews with Brief Therapy Experts.* New York: Brunner-Routledge.

Hoyt, M.F. (2001b) Contact, contract, change, encore: A conversation about redecision therapy with Bob Goulding. In M.F. Hoyt, *Interviews with Brief Therapy Experts* (pp. 121-143). Philadelphia: Brunner-Routledge.

Hoyt, M.F. (2001c) Decency. *Marin Independent Journal,* February 16, p. A4. (Letter to the Editor)

Hoyt, M.F. (2002a) Review of *Learning and Teaching Therapy with Jay Haley: A Videotape Series*. *American Journal of Family Therapy*, 30(1), 105-112.

Hoyt, M.F. (2002b) Book review of J.K. Zeig's *Changing Directives: The Strategic Therapy of Jay Haley*. *The Milton H. Erickson Foundation Newsletter*, 22(2), 17.

Hoyt, M.F. (2002c) Solution-focused couple therapy. In A.S. Gurman & N.S. Jacobson (Eds.), *Clinical Handbook of Couple Therapy* (3rd ed., pp. 335-369). New York: Guilford Press.

Hoyt, M.F. (2003) Brief psychotherapies. In A.S. Gurman & S.B. Messer (Eds.), *Essential Psychotherapies* (2nd ed., pp. 350-399). New York: Guilford Press.

Hoyt, M.F., & Berg, I.K. (1998) Solution-focused couple therapy: Helping clients construct self-fulfilling realities. In M.F. Hoyt (Ed.), *The Handbook of Constructive Therapies* (pp. 314-340). San Francisco: Jossey-Bass. Reprinted in M.F. Hoyt, *Some Stories Are Better than Others* (pp. 143-166). Philadelphia: Brunner/Mazel, 2000.

Hoyt, M.F., & Combs, G. (1996) On ethics and the spiritualities of the surface: A conversation with Michael White. In M.F. Hoyt (Ed.), *Constructive Therapies* (Volume 2, pp. 33-59). New York: Guilford Press. Reprinted in M.F. Hoyt, *Interviews with Brief Therapy Experts* (pp. 71-96). Philadelphia: Brunner-Routledge, 2001.

Hoyt, M.F., & Friedman, S. (2000) Dilemmas of postmodern practice under managed care and some pragmatics for increasing the likelihood of treatment authorization. In M.F. Hoyt, *Some Stories Are Better than Others* (pp. 109-117). Philadelphia: Brunner-Mazel, 2000. (A version originally appeared in *Journal of Systemic Therapies*, 1998, 17(3), 23-33.)

Hoyt, M.F., & Goulding, R.L. (1989) Resolution of a transference-countertransference impasse using Gestalt techniques in supervision. *Transactional Analysis Journal*, 19, 201-211. Reprinted in M.F. Hoyt, *Brief Therapy and Managed Care* (pp. 237-256). San Francisco: Jossey-Bass, 1995.

Hoyt, M.F., & Miller, S.D. (2000) Stage-appropriate change-oriented brief therapy strategies. In M.F. Hoyt, *Some Stories Are Better than Others* (pp. 207-235). Philadelphia: Brunner/Mazel.

Hoyt, M.F., Miller, S.D., Held, B.S., & Matthews, W.J. (2000) About constructivism (or, if four colleagues talked in New York, would anyone hear it?). *Journal of Systemic Therapies*, 19(4), 76-92. Reprinted in M.F. Hoyt, *Interviews with Brief Therapy Experts* (pp. 206-225). New York: Brunner-Routledge, 2001.

Hoyt, M.F., & Nylund, D. (2000) The joy of narrative: An exercise for learning from our internalized clients. In M.F. Hoyt, *Some Stories Are Better than Others* (pp. 201-206). Philadelphia: Brunner-Mazel.

Hoyt, M.F., Rosenbaum, R., & Talmon, M. (1992) Planned single-session psychotherapy. In S.H. Budman, M.F. Hoyt, & S. Friedman (Eds.), *The First Session in Brief Therapy* (pp. 59-86). New York: Guilford Press.

Hubble, M.A., Duncan, B.L., & Miller, S.D. (Eds.) (1999) *The Heart and Soul of Change: What Works in Therapy*. Washington, DC: American Psychological Association.

Hubble, M.A., & O'Hanlon, W.H. (1992). Theory countertransference. *Dulwich Centre Newsletter*, 1, 25-30.

Hudson, P., & O'Hanlon, W.H. (1991) *Rewriting Love Stories: Brief marital Therapy*. New York: Norton.

Hyde, L. (1983) A draft of Whitman. In *The Gift: Imagination and the Erotic Life of Property* (pp. 160-215). New York: Vintage.

Iveson, C. (2003) Solution-focused couples therapy. In B. O'Connell & S. Palmer (Eds.), *Handbook of Solution-Focused Therapy* (pp. 61-73). London: Sage.

Iyer, P. (1992) *The Lady and the Monk: Four Seasons in Kyoto*. New York: Vintage.

Jameson, F. (1998) *The Cultural Turn: Selected Writings on the Postmodern 1983-1998*. London: Verso.

Jeffers, R. (1960) "Fire on the Hills." In *The Complete Works of Robinson Jeffers*. New York: Random House. [work originally published 1932]

Johnson, C.E., & Goldman, J. (1996) Taking safety home: A solution-focused approach with domestic violence. In M.F. Hoyt (Ed.), *Constructive Therapies* (Volume 2, pp. 184-196). New York: Guilford Press.

Johnson, S. (1998) *Who Moved My Cheese?: An A-Mazing Way to Deal with Change in Your Work and in Your Life.* New York: G.P. Putnam's Sons.

Jopling, D.A. (2001) Placebo insight: The rationality of insight-oriented psychotherapy. *Journal of Clinical Psychology*, 57(1), 19-36.

Jordan, K., & Quinn, W.H. (1994) Session two outcome of the formula first session task in problem-and solution-focused approaches. *Journal of Family Therapy*, 22, 3-16.

Jung, C.G. (1966) Problems of modern psychotherapy. In *The Collected Works of C.G. Jung* (2nd ed., Vol. 16, pp. 53-75). Princeton, NJ: Bollingen/Princeton University Press. (original work published 1929)

Kaslow, F.W. (Ed.) (1984) *Psychotherapy with Psychotherapists.* New York: Haworth.

Katie, B. (2002) *Loving What Is: Four Questions that Can Change Your Life.* New York: Harmony Books.

Kazantzakis, N. (1965) *Report to Greco.* New York: Bantam Books. (original Greek language work published 1961)

Keats, J. (1974) *Selected Letters of John Keats.* (R. Pack, Ed.) New York: Signet. (original letter written 1817)

Keats, J. (1988) Ode on a Grecian urn. In *The Complete Poems* (3rd ed., pp. 344-346; J. Barnard, Ed.) New York: Penguin Books.

Keeney, B.P. (1983) *The Aesthetics of Change.* New York: Guilford.

Kegan, R. (1994) *In Over Our Heads: The Mental Demands of Modern Life.* Cambridge, MA: Harvard University Press.

Kellner, D. (Ed.) (1994) *Baudrillard: A Critical Reader.* Cambridge, MA: Blackwell.

Kelly, G.A. (1955) *The Psychology of Personal Constructs*. New York: Norton.

Kendrick, S. (2000, January-February) Zen in the art of Sherlock Holmes. *Utne Reader*, No. 97, 65-69.

Kernberg, O., Marmor, J., Masterson, J., & Polster, E. (2000, May). *Transference/Countertransference*. Panel discussion held at the Evolution of Psychotherapy Conference, Anaheim, CA.

Kerr, A. (1996) *Lost Japan*. Melbourne, Australia: Lonely Planet Publications.

Kierkegaard, S. (1959) *Journals*. (A. Dru, Ed.) New York: Harper. (work originally published 1843)

King, E. (1998) Role of affect and emotional context in solution-focused therapy. *Journal of Systemic Therapies*, 17(2), 51-64.

King, S. (2000) *On Writing: A Memoir of the Craft*. New York: Simon & Schuster.

Korngold, M. (2004) *First Draft: A Life to Talk About*. Paris: Valmy Press.

Kottler, J.A., & Carlson, J. (2003) Michael F. Hoyt: "I was blind at the time." In *Bad Therapy: Master Therapists Share Their Worst Failures* (pp. 157-164). New York: Brunner-Routledge.

Kreider, J.W. (1998) Solution-focused ideas for briefer therapy with longer-term clients. In M.F. Hoyt (Ed.), *The Handbook of Constructive Therapies* (pp. 341-357). San Francisco: Jossey-Bass.

Kroker, A. (1988) *Excremental Culture and Hyper-Aesthetics*. Montreal, Canada: New World Perspectives.

Kroker, A., Kroker, M., & Cooks, D. (Eds.) (1989) *Panic Encyclopedia*. Montreal, Canada: New World Perspectives.

Kuhn, T. (1970) *The Structure of Scientific Revolutions*. Chicago: University of Chicago Press.

Kunitz, S. (1995) Instead of a foreword: Speaking of poetry. In *Passing Through: The Later Poems New and Selected* (pp. 11-12). New York: Norton.

Kvale, S. (Ed.) (1992) *Psychology and Postmodernism*. Thousand Oaks, CA: Sage.

Lankton, S., & Lankton, C. (1998) Ericksonian emergent epistemologies. In M.F. Hoyt (Ed.), *The Handbook of Constructive Therapies* (pp. 116-136). San Francisco: Jossey-Bass.

Larner, G. (1995) The real as illusion: Deconstructing power in family therapy. *Journal of Family Therapy*, 17, 191-217.

Lau, M.Y. (2002) Postmodernism and the values of science. *American Psychologist*, 55(12), 1126-1127.

Lax, W.D. (1992) Postmodern thinking in a clinical practice. In S. McNamee & K.J. Gergen (Eds.), *Therapy as Social Construction* (pp. 69-85). Newbury Park, CA: Sage.

Lazarus, A.A. (1995) Different types of eclecticism and integration: Let's be aware of the dangers. *Journal of Psychotherapy Integration*, 5, 27-39.

Lazarus, A.A. (1997). *Brief but Comprehensive Psychotherapy: The Multimodal Way*. New York: Springer.

Lesser, W. (2002) *Nothing Remains the Same: Rereading and Remembering*. Boston: Houghton Mifflin.

Lethem, J. (1994) *Moved to Tears, Moved to Action: Solution Focused Brief Therapy with Women and Children*. London: Brief Therapy Press.

Levine, P. (1999) "Keats in California." In M. Collier & S. Plumly (Eds.), *The New Bread Loaf Anthology of Contemporary American Poetry* (pp. 160-161). Hanover, NH: University Press of New England.

Lipchik, E. (Ed.) (1987) *Interviewing*. Rockville, MD: Aspen.

Lipchik, E. (1993) "Both/and" solutions. In S. Friedman (Ed.), *The New Language of Change: Constructive Collaboration in Psychotherapy* (pp. 25-49). New York: Guilford Press.

Lipchik, E. (1994) The rush to be brief. *Family Therapy Networker*, 18(2), 34-39.

Lipchik, E. (1997) My story about solution-focused brief therapist/client relationships. *Journal of Systemic Therapies*, 16(2), 159-172.

Lipchik, E. (2002) *Beyond Technique in Solution-Focused Therapy: Working with Emotions and the Therapeutic Relationship*. New York: Guilford Press.

Lipchik, E., & de Shazer, S. (1986) The purposeful interview. *Journal of Strategic and Systemic Therapies*, 5, 88-89.

Lipchik, E., & Kubicki, A.D. (1996) Solution-focused domestic violence views: Bridges toward a new reality in couples therapy. In S.D. Miller, M.A. Hubble, & B.L. Duncan (Eds.), *Handbook of Solution-Focused Brief Therapy* (pp. 65-98). San Francisco: Jossey-Bass.

Lodge, D. (2002) *Consciousness and the Novel*. London: Penguin Books.

Longfellow, H.W. (1943) "Morituri Salutamus." In *The Poems of Henry Wadsworth Longfellow* (pp. 427-439; L. Untermeyer, Ed.) New York: Heritage Press. (original work published 1875)

Longfellow, H.W. (1943) "Mezzo Cammin." In *The Poems of Henry Wadsworth Longfellow* (p. 173; L. Untermeyer, Ed.). New York: Heritage Press. (work originally published 1842)

Lonnrot, E. (Compiler) (1963) *The Kalevala, or Poems of the Kaleva District*. (Trans. by F.P. Magoun, Jr.) Cambridge, MA: Harvard University Press. (original Finnish language work published 1849)

Lopez, J., & Potter, G. (Eds.) (2001) *After Postmodernism: An Introduction to Critical Realism*. New York: Athlone Press.

Luhrmann, T.M. (2000) *Of Two Minds: The Growing Disorder in American Psychiatry*. New York: Knopf.

Lyon, D. (1994) *Postmodernity*. Minneapolis: University of Minnesota Press.

Lyotard, J.-F. (1984) *The Postmodern Condition: A Report on Knowledge*. Minneapolis: University of Minnesota Press. (original French publication, 1979)

Macdonald, A.J. (2003) Research in solution-focused brief therapy. In B. O'Connell & S. Palmer (Eds.), *Handbook of Solution-Focused Therapy* (pp. 12-24). London: Sage.

Macey, D. (2000) *The Penguin Dictionary of Critical Theory*. London: Penguin Books.

Machado, A. (1983) "Caminante No Hay Camino, Se Hace Camino al Andar"/ "There is No Way, the Way is Made by Walking." In *Times Alone: Selected Poems of Antonio Macado* (R. Bly, Trans). Middletown, CT: Wesleyan University Press.

Madigan, S.P., & Epston, D. (1995) From "spy-chiatric gaze" to communities of concern: From professional monologue to dialogue. In S. Friedman (Ed.), *The Reflecting Team in Action: Collaborative Practice in Family Therapy* (pp. 257-276). New York: Guilford.

Mahoney, M.J. (1991) *Human Change Processes: The Scientific Foundations of Psychotherapy*. New York: Basic Books.

Mahoney, M.J. (1995) The psychological demands of being a constructive psychotherapist. In R.A. Neimeyer & M.J. Mahoney (Eds.), *Constructivism in Psychotherapy* (pp. 385-399). Washington, DC: American Psychological Association.

Malinen, T. (2001) On using appreciative language in constructing promising/ illusionistic realities. *Australian and New Zealand Journal of Family Therapy*, 25(4), 214-216.

Martel, Y. (2001) *Life of Pi: A Novel*. Orlando, FL: Harcourt.

Martin, J., & Sugarman, J. (2000) Between the modern and the postmodern: The possibility of self and progressive understanding in psychology. *American Psychologist*, 55(4), 397-406.

Matthews, W.J. (1985). A cybernetic model of Ericksonian hypnotherapy: One hand draws the other. *Ericksonian Monographs*, 1, 42-60.

Matthews, W.J. (1998) Let's get real: The fallacy of postmodernism. *Journal of Theoretical and Philosophical Psychology*, 18, 16-33.

Matthews, W.J. (2002) Reality exists: A critique of antirealism in brief therapy. In J.K. Zeig (Ed.), *Brief Therapy: Lasting Impressions* (pp. 147-168). Phoenix, AZ: The Milton H. Erickson Foundation Press.

Maturana, H.R., & Varela, F.J. (1980) *Autopoiesis and Cognition: The Realization of the Living*. Boston: Reidel Publishing Company. [original Chilean publication, in Spanish, in 1972]

McBroom, A. (1979) "The Rose." Song on Bette Midler album, *The Rose*. New York: Atlantic Records/Warner Communications Group.

McKee, R. (1997) *Story: Substance, Structure, Style, and the Principles of Screenwriting*. New York: HarperCollins.

McKeel, A.J. (1996) A clinician's guide to research on solution-focused brief therapy. In S.D. Miller, M.A. Hubble, and B.L. Duncan (Eds.), *Handbook of Solution-Focused Brief Therapy* (pp. 251-271). San Francisco: Jossey-Bass.

McNamee, S., & Gergen, K.J. (Eds.) (1992) *Therapy as Social Construction*. Newbury Park, CA: Sage.

McNamee, S., & Gergen, K.J. (1999) *Relational Responsibility*. Thousand Oaks, CA: Sage.

Mente, D. (1995) Whose truth? Whose goodness? Whose beauty? *American Psychologist*, 50(5), 391.

Merleau-Ponty, M. (1968) *The Visible and the Invisible*. Evanston, IL: Northwestern University Press.

Messer, S.B. (1992) A critical examination of belief structures in integrative and eclectic psychotherapy. In J. Norcross & M. Goldfried (Eds.), *Handbook of Psychotherapy Integration* (pp. 130-164). New York: Basic Books.

Messer, S.B., Sass, L.A., & Woolfolk, R.L. (Eds.) (1988) *Hermeneutics and Psychological Theory*. New Brunswick, NJ: Rutgers University Press.

Messer, S.B., & Warren, C.S. (1995) *Models of Brief Psychodynamic Therapy: A Comparative Approach*. New York: Guilford Press.

Metcalf, L. (1998) *Solution-Focused Group Work*. New York: The Free Press.

Miller, G. (1997) *Becoming Miracle Workers: Language and Meaning in Brief Therapy*. Hawthorne, NY: Aldine de Gruyter.

Miller, G., & de Shazer, S. (1998) Have you heard the latest about...? Solution-focused therapy as a rumor. *Family Process*, 37, 363-378.

Miller, G., & de Shazer, S. (2000) Emotions in solution-focused therapy: A re-examination. *Family Process*, 39(1), 5-23.

Miller, H. (1956) *The Time of the Assassins: A Study of Rimbaud*. New York: New Directions.

Miller, S.D. (1992) The symptoms of solution. *Journal of Strategic and Systemic Therapies*, 11, 1-11.

Miller, S.D. (1994) Some questions (not answers) for the brief treatment of people with drug and alcohol problems. In M.F. Hoyt (Ed.), *Constructive Therapies* (pp. 92-110). New York: Guilford Press.

Miller, S.D., & Berg, I.K. (1995) *The Miracle Method*. New York: Norton.

Miller, S.D., & Duncan, B.L. (2000) Paradigm lost: From model-driven to client-directed, outcome-informed clinical work. *Journal of Systemic Therapies*, 19(1), 20-34.

Miller, S.D., Duncan, B.L., & Hubble, M.A. (1997) *Escape from Babel: Toward a Unifying Language for Psychotherapy Practice*. New York: Norton.

Miller, S.D., Hubble, M.A., & Duncan, B.L. (Eds.) (1996) *Handbook of Solution-Focused Brief Therapy*. San Francisco: Jossey-Bass.

Miller, W.R., & C'de Baca, J. (2001) *Quantum Change: When Epiphanies and Sudden Insights Transform Ordinary Lives*. New York: Guilford.

Miller, W.R., & Rollnick, S. (1991) *Motivational Interviewing: Preparing People to Change Addictive Behavior*. New York: Guilford.

Milosz, C. (2001) *To Begin Where I Am: Selected Essays*. New York: Farrar, Straus and Giroux.

Minuchin, S. (1982) Foreword. In J.R. Neill & D.P. Kniskern (Eds.), *From Psyche to System: The Evolving Therapy of Carl Whitaker* (pp. vii-ix). New York: Guilford Press.

Minuchin, S. (1991) The seductions of constructivism. *Family Therapy Networker*, 15(5), 47-50.

Minuchin, S. (1992) The restoried history of family therapy. In J.K. Zeig (Ed.), *The Evolution of Psychotherapy: The Second Conference* (pp. 3-12). New York: Brunner/Mazel.

Minuchin, S. (1998) Where is the family in narrative family therapy? *Journal of Marital and Family Therapy*, 24(4), 397-403.

Mirowsky, J., & Ross, C.E. (1987) *Social Causes of Psychological Distress*. Hawthorne, NY: Aldine de Gruyter.

Monk, G., Winslade, J., Crocket, K., & Epston, D. (Eds.) (1997) *Narrative Therapy in Practice: The Archaeology of Hope*. San Francisco: Jossey-Bass.

Moore, M. (2001) *Stupid White Men*. New York: HarperCollins.

Moyers, B. (1995) *The Language of Life: A Festival of Poets*. New York: Broadway Books/Doubleday.

Muggeridge, M. (1971) *Something Beautiful for God*. New York: Ballantine Books.

Mumford, E., Schlesinger, H.J., Glass, G., Parick, C., & Cuerdon, T. (1984) A new look at evidence about reduced cost of medical utilization following mental-health treatment. *American Journal of Psychiatry*, 141, 1145-1158.

Mura, D. (1991) *Turning Japanese: Memoirs of a Sansei*. New York: Anchor Books.

Murphy, M. (1972) *Golf in the Kingdom*. New York: Delta.

Murphy, M. (1992) *The Future of the Body*. New York: Tarcher.

Murphy, M., & White, R. (1978) *The Psychic Side of Sports*. Reading, MA: Addison-Wesley.

Napier, A.Y., & Whitaker, C.A. (1978) *The Family Crucible*. New York: HarperCollins.

Nau, D.S., & Shilts, L. (2000) When to use the miracle question: Clues from a qualitative study of four SFBT practitioners. *Journal of Systemic Therapies*, 19(1), 129-135.

Neimeyer, R.A. (1995) Constructivist psychotherapies: Features, foundations, and future directions. In R.A. Neimeyer & M.J. Mahoney (Eds.), *Constructivism in Psychotherapy* (pp. 11-38). Washington, DC: American Psychological Association.

Neimeyer, R.A. (1998) Cognitive therapy and the narrative trend: A bridge too far? *Journal of Cognitive Psychotherapy*, 12, 57-65.

Neimeyer, R.A. (2000a) Research and practice as essential tensions: A constructivist confession. In L.M. Valliant & S. Soldz (Eds.), *Empirical Knowledge and Clinical Experience* (pp. 123-150). Washington, DC: American Psychological Association.

Neimeyer, R.A. (2000b) Performing psychotherapy: Reflections on postmodern practice. In L. Holzman & J. Morss (Eds.), *Postmodern Psychologies, Societal Practice, and Political Life* (pp. 190-201). New York: Routledge.

Neimeyer, R.A. (2002) The relational co-construction of selves: A postmodern perspective. *Journal of Contemporary Psychotherapy*, 32, 51-59.

Neimeyer, R.A., & Bridges, S.K. (2003) Postmodern approaches to psychotherapy. In A.S. Gurman & S.B. Messer (Eds.), *Essential Psychotherapies* (rev. ed.). New York: Guilford Press.

Neimeyer, R.A., & Mahoney, M.J. (1995) Glossary. In R.A. Neimeyer & M.J. Mahoney (Eds.), *Constructivism in Psychotherapy* (pp. 401-409). Washington, DC: American Psychological Association.

Neimeyer, R.A., & Mahoney, M.J. (1995) (Eds.) *Constructivim in Psychotherapy*. Washington, DC: American Psychological Association.

Neimeyer, R.A., & Raskin, J.D. (Eds.) (2000) *Constructions of Disorder: Meaning-Making Frameworks for Psychotherapy*. Washington, DC: American Psychological Association.

Neimeyer, R.A., & Stewart, A.R. (2000) Constructivist and narrative psychotherapies. In C.R. Snyder & R.E. Ingram (Eds.), *Handbook of Psychological Change* (pp. 337-357). New York: Wiley.

Nelson, T.S., & Kelly, L. (2001) Solution-focused couples group. *Journal of Systemic Therapies*, 20(4), 47-66.

Nichols, M.P., & Schwartz, R.C. (1997) *Family Therapy: Concepts and Methods*. Needham Heights, MA: Allyn & Bacon.

Nicholson, L.J. (Ed.) (1990) *Feminism/Postmodernism*. New York: Routledge.

Nijinsky, V. (1918-1919) *The Diary of Vaslav Nijinsky*. (R. Nijinsky, Ed.) Berkeley: University of California Press. (work originally published 1936)

Norris, C. (1992) *Uncritical Theory: Post-Modernism, Intellectuals, and the Gulf War*. Amherst, MA: University of Massachusetts Press.

Norris, C. (1993) *The Truth about Postmodernism*. Cambridge, MA: Blackwell.

Norum, D. (2000) The family has the solution. *Journal of Systemic Therapies*, 19(1), 3-15.

Nuland, S.B. (1995) Acknowledgments. In *How We Die: Reflections on Life's Final Chapter* (pp. xi-xiv). New York: Vintage Books.

Nunnally, E. (1993) Solution-focused therapy. In R.A. Wells & V.J. Giannetti (Eds.), *Casebook of the Brief Psychotherapies* (pp. 271-286). New York: Plenum Press.

Nylund, D., & Corsiglia, V. (1994) Becoming solution-forced/focused in brief therapy: Remembering something important we already knew. *Journal of Systemic Therapies*, 13(5), 5-12.

O'Connell, B., & Palmer, S. (Eds.) (2003) *Handbook of Solution-Focused Therapy*. London: Sage.

O'Hanlon, W.H. (1998) Possibility therapy: An inclusive, collaborative, solution-based model of psychotherapy. In M.F. Hoyt (Ed.), *The Handbook of Constructive Therapies* (pp. 137-158). San Francisco: Jossey-Bass.

O'Hanlon, W.H. (1999) *Do One Thing Different: And Other Uncommonly Sensible Solutions to Life's Persistent Problems.* New York: William Morrow.

O'Hanlon, W.H., & Hudson, P. (1994) Coauthoring a love story: Solution-oriented marital therapy. In M.F. Hoyt (Ed.), *Constructive Therapies* (pp. 160-188). New York: Guilford Press.

O'Hanlon, W.H., & Weiner-Davis, M. (1989) *In Search of Solutions: A New Direction in Psychotherapy.* New York: Norton.

O'Hanlon, W.H., & Wilk, J. (1987) *Shifting Contexts: The Generation of Effective Psychotherapy.* New York: Guilford Press.

O'Hara, M., Anderson, W.T. (1991) Welcome to the postmodern world. *Family Therapy Networker*, 15(5), 18-25.

Oliver, M. (1992) "The Journey." In *New and Selected Poems* (pp. 114-115). Boston: Beacon Press. (work originally published 1986)

Olkin, R. (1999) *What Psychotherapists Should Know about Disability.* New York: Guilford Press.

Olson, D.L. (1995) *Shared Spirits: Wildlife and Native Americans.* Minnetonka, MN: Northword Press.

Omer, H. (1993) Quasi-literary elements in psychotherapy. *Psychotherapy*, 30, 59-66.

Palmer, D.D. (1999) *Structuralism and Poststructuralism for Beginners.* New York: Writers and Readers Publishing.

Parker, I. (2000) Four story-theories about and against postmodernism in psychology. In L. Holzman & J. Morss (Eds.), *Postmodern Psychologies, Societal Practice, and Political Life* (pp. 29-48). New York: Routledge.

Parry, A. (1997) Why we tell stories: The narrative construction of reality. *Transactional Analysis Journal*, 27(2), 118-127.

Parry, A., & Doan, R.E. (1994) *Story Re-Visions: Narrative Therapy in the Postmodern World.* New York: Guilford Press.

Paschen, E., & Mosby, R.P. (Eds.) (2001) *Poetry Speaks* (C. Osgood, Narrator) Naperville, IL: Sourcebooks.

Penn, P. (1985) Feed-forward: Future questions, future maps. *Family Process*, 24, 289-310.

Pinkson, T.S. (1995) *Flowers of Wiricuta: A Gringo's Journey to Shamanic Power.* Mill Valley, CA: Wakan Press.

Pirsig, R. (1974) *Zen and the Art of Motorcycle Maintenance: An Inquiry into Values.* New York: Vintage.

Polkinghorne, D. (1999) Foreword. In J. Martin & J. Sugarman, *The Psychology of Human Possibility and Human Constraint* (pp. vii-xiv). Albany, NY: SUNY Press.

Powell, J. (1997) *Derrida for Beginners.* New York: Writers and Readers Publishing.

Prilleltensky, I. (1997) Values, assumptions, and practices: Assessing the moral implications of psychological discourse and action. *American Psychologist*, 52(5), 517-535.

Prochaska, J.O. (1999) How do people change and how can we change to help many more people? In M.A. Hubble, B.L. Duncan, & S.D. Miller (Eds.), *The Heart and Soul of Change: What Works in Therapy.* Washington, DC: American Psychological Association.

Quick, E.K. (1996) *Doing What Works in Brief Therapy: A Strategic Solution-Focused Approach.* San Diego, CA: Academic Press.

Ram Dass. (2000) *Still Here: Embracing Aging, Changing, and Dying.* New York: Riverhead Books/Penguin Putnam.

Ram Dass & Gorman, P. (1993) *How Can I Help? Stories and Reflections on Service*, New York: Knopf.

Raskin, J.D. (2001) The modern, the postmodern, and George Kelly's personal construct psychology. *American Psychologist*, 56(4), 368-369.

Riedelsheimer, T. (Director) (2001) *Rivers and Tides: Andy Goldsworthy Working with Time*. Film.

Riikonen, E., & Smith, G.M. (1997) *Re-Imagining Therapy: Living Conversations and Relational Knowing*. London: Sage Publications.

Rilke, R.M. (1981) "My Life Is Not This Steeply Sloping Hour." In *Selected Poems of Rainer Maria Rilke* (p. 31; R. Bly, Trans.). New York: Harper & Row.

Robertiello, R.C., & Schoenewolf, G. (1987). *101 Common Therapeutic Blunders: Countertransference and Counterresistance in Psychotherapy*. Northvale, NJ: Jason Aronson.

Roethke, T. (2001) *On Poetry and Craft: Selected Prose*. Port Townsend, WA: Copper Canyon Press.

Rogers, C. (1989) Do we need "a" reality? In *The Carl Rogers Reader* (pp. 420-429; H. Kirschenbaum & V.L. Henderson, Eds.). Boston: Houghton Mifflin. [work originally published 1978]

Rosen, H., & Kuehlwein, K.T. (1996) (Eds.) *Constructing Realities: Meaning-Making Perspectives for Psychotherapists*. San Francisco: Jossey-Bass.

Rosenau, P.M. (1992) *Post-Modernism and the Social Sciences: Insights, Inroads, and Intrusions*. Princeton, NJ: Princeton University Press.

Rosenbaum, R. (1999) *Zen and the Heart of Psychotherapy*. Philadelphia: Brunner/Mazel.

Rosenbaum, R., & Dyckman, J. (1996) No self? No problem! Actualizing empty self in psychotherapy. In M.F. Hoyt (Ed.), *Constructive Therapies, Volume 2* (pp. 238-274). New York: Guilford Press.

Rosenbaum, R., Hoyt, M.F., & Talmon, M. (1990) The challenge of single-session therapies: Creating pivotal moments. In R.A. Wells & V.J. Giannetti (Eds.), *Handbook of the Brief Psychotherapies* (pp. 165-189). New York: Plenum Press. Reprinted in M.F. Hoyt, *Brief Therapy and Managed Care: Readings for Contemporary Practice* (pp. 105-139). San Francisco: Jossey-Bass, 1995.

Rosenberg, B. (2000) Mandated clients and solution focused therapy: "It's not my miracle." *Journal of Systemic Therapies*, 19(1), 90-99.

Roth, P. (2001) *The Dying Animal*. Boston: Houghton Mifflin.

Roth, S., & Chasin, R. (1994) Entering one another's worlds of meaning and imagination: Dramatic enactment and narrative couple therapy. In M.F. Hoyt (Ed.), *Constructive Therapies* (pp. 189-216). New York: Guilford Press.

Roth, S., & Epston, D. (1996) Consulting the problem about the problematic relationship: An exercise for experiencing a relationship with an externalized problem. In M.F. Hoyt (Ed.), *Constructive Therapies* (Volume 2, pp. 148-162). New York: Guilford Press.

Rowen, T., & O'Hanlon, W.H. (1999) *Solution-Oriented Therapy for Chronic and Severe Mental Illness*. New York: Wiley.

Rukeyser, M. (1996) *The Life of Poetry*. (New foreword by J. Cooper) Ashfield, MA: Paris Press. (original work published 1949)

Russell, R.L., & Gaubatz, M.D. (1995) Contested affinities: Reactions to Gergen's (1994) and Smith's (1994) postmodernisms. *American Psychologist*, 50(5), 389-390.

Russell, W.F. (2001) *Russell Rules: 11 Lessons on Leadership from the Twentieth Century's Greatest Winner*. (with A. Hilburg & D. Falkner) New York: New American Library.

Saarelainen, R. (1999) Narratives that Finnish families tell themselves about themselves. In U.P. Gielen & A.L. Communian (Eds.), *International Approaches to the Family and Family Therapy* (pp. 235-247). Padova, Italy: Unipress.

Saggese, M.L., & Foley, F.W. (2000) From problems or solutions to problems and solutions: Integrating the MRI and solution-focused models of brief therapy. *Journal of Systemic Therapies*, 19(1), 59-73.

Sarlo, B. (2001) *Scenes from Postmodern Life*. Minneapolis: University of Minnesota Press.

Sartwell, C. (2002) The "New Realism" takes over: Eminem goes beyond Clinton and Madonna. *San Francisco Chronicle*, November 24, Section D, p. 4.

Schmidt, M. (1999) *Lives of the Poets*. New York: Knopf.

Schon, D.A. (1982) *The Reflective Practitioner: How Professionals Think in Action*. New York: Basic Books.

Schorr, M. (1997) Finding solutions in a roomful of angry people. *Journal of Systemic Therapies*, 16(3), 201-210.

Schultheis, G.M., O'Hanlon, W.H., & O'Hanlon, S. (1998) *Brief Couples Therapy Homework Planner*. New York: Wiley.

Schweitzer, A. (1948) *The Psychiatric Study of Jesus: Exposition and Criticism*. Boston: Beacon Press. (originally published 1913)

Searles, J.R. (1995) *The Construction of Social Reality*. New York: Free Press.

Sharry, J. (2003) *Solution-Focused Groupwork*. London: Sage.

Sharry, J., Madden, B., & Darmody, M. (2001) *Becoming a Solution Detective: A Strengths-Based Guide to Brief Therapy*. London: BT Press.

Slawson, D.A. (1999) *Secret Teachings in the Art of Japanese Gardens*. Tokyo: Kodansha International.

Shawver, L. (1996) What postmodernism can do for psychoanalysis: A guide to the postmodern vision. *American Journal of Psychoanalysis*, 56, 371-394.

Shewchuck, R., & Elliott, T.R. (2000) Family caregiving in chronic disease and disability. In R.G. Frank & T.R. Elliott (Eds.), *Handbook of Rehabilitation Psychology* (pp. 553-563). Washington, DC: American Psychological Association.

Shields, D. (2001) (Comp.) *"Baseball is Just Baseball"—The Understated Ichiro*. Seattle, WA: TNI Books.

Shoham, V., & Rohrbaugh, M.J. (2002) Brief strategic couple therapy. In A.S. Gurman & N.S. Jacobson (Eds.), *Clinical Handbook of Couple Therapy* (3rd ed., pp. 5-25). New York: Guilford Press.

Shoham, V., Rohrbaugh, M., & Patterson, J. (1995) Problem- and solution-focused couple therapies: The MRI and Milwaukee models. In N.S. Jacobson & A.S. Gurman (Eds.), *Clinical Handbook of Couple Therapy* (2nd ed., pp. 142-163). New York: Guilford Press.

Short, D. (1997) Interview: Steve de Shazer and Insoo Kim Berg. *The Milton H. Erickson Foundation Newsletter*, 17, 1, 18-20.

Short, D. (2002, Fall) Interview: Nicholas Cummings, Ph.D., Sc.D. *The Milton H. Erickson Foundation Newsletter*, 22(3), 1, 21-24.

Simon, R. (2001, July/August) Psychotherapy soothsayer: Nick Cummings foretells your future. *Psychotherapy Networker*, 25(4), 34-39, 62.

Sluzki, C.E. (1992) Transformations: A blueprint for narrative changes in therapy. *Family Process*, 31, 217-230.

Sluzki, C.E. (1998) Strange attractors and the transformation of narratives in family therapy. In M.F. Hoyt (Ed.), *The Handbook of Constructive Therapies* (pp. 159-179). San Francisco: Jossey-Bass.

Smith, C. (1997) Introduction. In C. Smith & D. Nylund (Eds.), *Narrative Therapies with Children and Adolescents*. New York: Guilford Press.

Smith, M.B. (1994) Selfhood at risk: Postmodern perils and the perils of postmodernism. *American Psychologist*, 49, 405-411.

Smith, M.B. (1995) About postmodernism: Reply to Gergen and others. *American Psychologist*, 50(5), 393.

Smith, M.B. (2001) Sigmund Koch as critical humanist. *American Psychologist*, 56(5), 441-444.

Snyder, M. (1996) Our "other history": Poetry as a meta-metaphor for narrative therapy. *Journal of Family Therapy*, 18, 337-359.

Sokal, A., & Bricmont, J. (1998) *Fashionable Nonsense: Postmodern Intellectuals' Abuse of Science*. New York: Picador/St. Martin's Press.

Spence, D.P. (1982) *Narrative Truth and Historical Truth: Meaning and Interpretation in Psychoanalysis*. New York: Norton.

Spence, D.P. (2001) Dangers of anecdotal reports. *Journal of Clinical Psychology*, 57(1), 37-42.

Sodergren, E. (1993) Chambers of consciousness. In W.R. Mead (Ed.), *An Experience of Finland* (pp. 54-66). London: Hurst.

Stern, D.N. (2004) *The Present Moment in Psychotherapy and Everyday Life*. New York: Norton.

Sternberg, R.J. (1998) *Love is a Story: A New Theory of Relationships*. New York: Oxford University Press.

Taffel, R. (1993, January/February). In praise of countertransference. *Family Therapy Networker*, 17(1), 52-57.

Talmon, M. (1990) *Single Session Therapy: Maximizing the Effect of the First (and Often Only) Therapeutic Encounter*. San Francisco: Jossey-Bass.

Taylor, C. (1989) *Sources of the Self*. Cambridge, MA: Harvard Univrsity Press.

Taylor, M.C. (Ed.) (1986) *Deconstruction in Context: Literature and Philosophy*. Chicago: University of Chicago Press.

Tohn, S.L., & Oshlag, J.A. (1996) *Crossing the Bridge: Integrating Solution-Focused Therapy into Clinical Practice*. Natick, MA: Solutions Press.

Tohn, S.L., & Oshlag, J.A. (1996) Cooperating with the uncooperative. In S.D. Miller, M.A. Hubble, & B.L. Duncan (Eds.), *Handbook of Solution-Focused Brief Therapy* (pp. 152-183). San Francisco: Jossey-Bass.

Tolle, E. (1999) *The Power of Now: A Guide to Spiritual Enlightenment*. Novato, CA: New World Library.

Tomm, K. (1987) Interventive interviewing: I. Strategizing as a fourth guideline for the therapist. *Family Process*, 26, 3-13.

Tomm, K. (1990) A critique of the *DSM*. *Dulwich Centre Newsletter*, 3, 5-8.

Tomm, K. (1991) Beginnings of a "HIPs and PIPs" approach to psychiatric assessment. *Calgary Participator*, 1(Spring), 25-28.

Tomm, K., Hoyt, M.F., Anderson, H., & Gilligan, S.P. (1996, June 28). Discussion panel. Held at Therapeutic Conversations 3 conference, Denver, CO.

Tomm, K., Hoyt, M.F., & Madigan, S.P. (1998) Honoring our internalized others and the ethics of caring: A conversation with Karl Tomm. In M.F. Hoyt (Ed.), *The Handbook of Constructive Therapies* (pp. 198-218). San Francisco: Jossey-Bass.

Trautman, P. (2000) The key to the pharmacy: Integrating solution-focused brief therapy and psychopharmacological treatment. *Journal of Systemic Therapies*, 19(1), 100-110.

Tucker, N.L., Stith, S.M., Howell, L.W., McCollum, E.E., & Rosen, K.H. (2000) Meta-dialogues in domestic violence-focused couples treatment. *Journal of Systemic Therapies*, 19(4), 56-72.

Turnell, A., & Lipchik, E. (1999) The role of empthy in brief therapy: The overlooked but vital context. *Australian and New Zealand Journal of Family Therapy*, 20(4), 177-182.

Uken, A., & Sebold, J. (1996) The Plumas Project: A solution-focused goal-directed domestic violence diversion program. *Journal of Collaborative Therapies*, 4, 10-17.

Walter, J.L., & Peller, J.E. (1988) Going beyond the attempted solution: A couple's meta-solution. *Family Therapy Case Studies*, 3(1), 41-45.

Walter, J.L., & Peller, J.E. (1992) *Becoming Solution-Focused in Brief Therapy*. New York: Brunner/Mazel.

Walter, J.L., & Peller, J.E. (1994) "On track" in solution-focused brief therapy. In M.F. Hoyt (Ed.), *Constructive Therapies* (pp. 111-125). New York: Guilford Press.

Walter, J.L., & Peller, J.E. (2000) *Recreating Brief Therapy: Preferences and Possibilities*. New York: Norton.

Watzlawick, P. (Ed.) (1984) *The Invented Reality: How Do We Know What We Believe We Know? (Contributions to Constructivism)*. New York: Norton.

Watzlawick, P. (1990) *Munchhausen's Pigtail, or Psychotherapy and "Reality": Essays and Lectures.* New York: Norton.

Watzlawick, P., & Hoyt, M.F. (1998) Constructing therapeutic realities. In M.F. Hoyt (Ed.), *The Handbook of Constructive Therapies* (pp. 183-197). San Francisco: Jossey-Bass. Reprinted in M.F. Hoyt, *Interviews with Brief Therapy Experts* (pp. 144-157). New York: Brunner-Routledge, 2001.

Watzlawick, P., Weakland, J.H., & Fisch, R. (1974) *Change: Principles of Problem Formation and Problem Resolution.* New York: Norton.

Weakland, J.H. (1993) Conversation—but what kind? In S.G. Gilligan & R. Price (Eds.), *Therapeutic Conversations* (pp. 136-145). New York: Norton.

Weakland, J.H., & Fisch, R. (1992) Brief therapy—MRI style. In S.H. Budman, M.F. Hoyt & S. Friedman (Eds.), *The First Session in Brief Therapy* (pp. 306-323). New York: Guilford Press.

Weiner-Davis, M. (1992) *Divorce-Busting: A Revolutionary and Rapid Program for Staying Together.* New York: Simon & Schuster/Fireside.

Weiner-Davis, M. (1993) Pro-constructed realities. In S.G. Gilligan & R. Price (Eds.), *Therapeutic Conversations* (pp. 149-157). New York: Norton.

Weiner-Davis, M. (1995) *Change Your Life and Everyone in It.* New York: Fireside/Simon & Schuster.

Weiner-Davis, M. (1998) *A Woman's Guide to Changing Her Man.* New York: Golden Books.

Weiner-Davis, M. (2000, October 12-13). *Putting "Marriage" Back into Marriage Therapy: An Advanced Workshop in Solution-Based, Marriage-Saving Methods.* Workshop sponsored by the Institute for the Advancement of Human Behavior, San Francisco, CA.

Weiner-Davis, M., de Shazer, S., & Gingerich, W.J. (1987) Using pretreatment change to construct a therapeutic solution: An exploratory study. *Journal of Marital and Family Therapy,* 13, 359-363.

Whitaker, C.A. (1989). *Midnight Musings of a Family Therapist.* New York: Norton.

Whitaker, C.A., & Napier, A.Y. (1978) *The Family Crucible*. New York: Harper & Row.

White, D.R., & Wang, A.Y. (1995) Universalism, humanism, and postmodernism. *American Psychologist*, 50(5), 392-393.

White, M. (1989) The externalizing of the problem and the re-authoring of lives and relationships. In *Selected Papers* (pp. 5-28). Adelaide, Australia: Dulwich Centre Publications.

White, M. (1993) Deconstruction and therapy. In S. Gilligan & R. Price (Eds.), *Therapeutic Conversations* (pp. 22-61). New York: Norton.

White, M. (1995) *Re-Authoring Lives: Interviews and Essays*. Adelaide, Australia: Dulwich Centre Publications.

White, M., & Epston, D. (1990) *Narrative Means to Therapeutic Ends*. New York: Norton.

White, M., Hoyt, M.F., & Zimmerman, J. (2000) Direction and discovery: A conversation about power and politics in narrative therapy. In M. White, *Reflections on Narrative Practice: Essays and Interviews* (pp. 97-116). Adelaide, Australia: Dulwich Centre Publications. Reprinted in M.F. Hoyt, *Interviews with Brief Therapy Experts* (pp. 265-293). New York: Brunner-Routledge, 2001.

Whitman, W. (1940) "Song of Myself." In *Leaves of Grass* (rev. ed., pp. 29-74). New York: Modern Library/Random House. (original work published 1891-1892)

Wilbur, K. (1998) *The Marriage of Sense and Soul*. New York: Random House.

Williams, M. (1972). "Drift Away." Song on Dobie Gray record album, *Drift Away*. Universal City, CA: MCA Records, 1973. (Almo Music Corp./ASCAP)

Williams, W.C. (1969a). "Asphodel, That Greeny Flower." In *Selected Poems of William Carlos Williams* (pp. 142-155) (Intro. by R. Jarrell). New York: New Directions.

Williams, W.C. (1969b). "The Descent." In *Selected Poems of William Carlos Williams* (pp. 132-133). (Intro. by R. Jarrell). New York: New Directions.

Winnicott, D.W. (1949). Hate in the countertransference. *International Journal of Psychoanalysis, 30*, 69-74.

Winslade, J., & Monk, G. (1999) *Narrative Counseling in Schools: Powerful and Brief.* Thousand Oaks, CA: Corwin Press.

Wittgenstein, L. (1968) *Philosophical Investigations* (3rd ed.; G.E.M. Anscombe, Trans.). New York: Macmillan.

Wittgenstein, L. (1980) *Culture and Value.* (P. Winch, Trans.) Chicago: University of Chicago Press.

Wright, B.A. (1991) Labeling: The need for greater person-environment individuation. In C.R. Snyder & D.R. Forsyth (Eds.), *Handbook of Social and Clinical Psychology: The Health Perspective* (pp. 469-487). New York: Permagon.

Wright, F.L. (1992) Building for local government: The Marin County Civic Center. In *Truth Against the World: Frank Lloyd Wright Speaks for an Organic Architecture* (pp. 381-411; P.J. Meehan, Ed.). Washington, DC: The Preservation Press/National Trust for Historic Preservation. (speech originally given 31 July 1957).

Yeats, W.B. (1989). "Among School Children." In R.J. Finneran (Ed.), *The Collected Poems of W.B. Yeats* (pp. 215-217). New York: Collier. (original work published 1928)

Yeats, W.B. (1989) "The Second Coming." In *The Collected Poems of W.B. Yeats* (R.J. Finneran, Ed.; p. 187). New York: CollierBooks/Macmillan Publishing Company. [work originally published 1921]

Yeats, W.B. (1999) *Autobiographies.* (W.H. O'Donnell & D.N. Archibald, Eds.) New York: Scribner/Simon & Schuster. (work originally published 1935)

Zeig, J.K. (2002) Clinical heuristics. In J.K. Zeig (Ed.), *Brief Therapy: Lasting Impressions* (pp. 41-62). Phoenix, AZ: The Milton H. Erickson Foundation Press.

Zeig, J., & Gilligan, S. (Eds.) (1990) *Brief Therapy: Myths, Methods, and Metaphors*. New York: Brunner/Mazel.

Ziegler, P.B. (1998) Solution-focused therapy for the not-so-brief clinician. *Journal of Collaborative Therapies*, 6(1), 22-25.

Ziegler, P.B. (2000, April 8) *Recreating Partnership: A Solution-Focused, Competency-Based Approach to Couples Therapy*. Workshop sponsored by John F. Kennedy University, Orinda, CA.

Ziegler, P.B., & Hiller, T. (2001) *Recreating Partnership: A Solution-Oriented, Collaborative Approach to Couples Therapy*. New York: Norton.

Ziegler, P.B., & Hiller, T. (2002) Good story/bad story: Collaborating with violent couples. *Psychotherapy Networker*, 26(2), 63-68.

Zimbardo, P.G. (2002) President's column: Rediscovering disability. *APA Monitor on Psychology*, 33(9), 5.

Zimmerman, J.L., & Dickerson, V.C. (1993) Separating couples from restraining patterns and the relationship discourses that support them. *Journal of Marital and Family Therapy*, 19(4), 403-413.

Zinn, H. (2002) *You Can't Be Neutral on a Moving Train: A Personal History of Our Time*. Boston: Beacon Press.

About the Author

MICHAEL F. HOYT, PH.D. (Yale '76), is a senior staff psychologist at the Kaiser Permanente Medical Center in San Rafael, California, and is a member of the clinical faculty of the University of California School of Medicine in San Francisco. An expert clinician and an internationally respected teacher and lecturer, Hoyt is the author of *Brief Therapy and Managed Care* (1995), *Some Stories Are Better than Others* (2000), and *Interviews with Brief Therapy Experts* (2001); the editor of *Constructive Therapies, Volumes 1 & 2* (1994, 1996) and *The Handbook of Constructive Therapies* (1998); and the co-editor of *The First Session in Brief Therapy* (1992).

Dr. Hoyt has been honored as a Woodrow Wilson Fellow, as a Continuing Education Distinguished Speaker by the American Psychological Association, as a Distinguished Presenter by the International Association of Marriage and Family Counselors, and as a Contributor of Note by the Milton H. Erickson Foundation.

He resides in Mill Valley, California, with his wife and son.

Credits

Chapter 1. Keynote address presented 2 November 2001 in Osaka, Japan, at The 2nd Pan-Pacific Brief Psychotherapy Conference. Special thanks to Tatsumi Kojima, Satoru Yoshikawa, and the Japanese Association for Brief Psychotherapy; as well as to my co-presenters, from both sides of the Pacific; and to the fine audience that attended the conference. A version of this paper appeared [in Japanese] in the *Japanese Brief Therapy Journal*, 2003. Used by agreement.

Chapter 2. A version, with changes, originally appeared in *Journal of Clinical Psychology/In Session: Psychotherapy in Practice*, 2001, 57(8), 1-8. A version of the extended case report that concludes the chapter also appeared under the title "Love, Dr. Lagerfeld" in *Psychotherapy Networker*, 2002, 26(2), 44-45, 77. Used by agreement.

Chapter 3. Originally presented on 9 March 2001 at the Finnish Rehabilitation Foundation conference held in Helsinki. Special thanks to Karin Olssen and Ritva Saarelainen; as well as to Jeff Ordover and Tapio Malinen. An abbreviated version of this paper appeared (in Finnish) in the rehabilitation journal *Kuntoutus*, 2001, May/June. Used by agreement.

Chapter 4. A version, with changes, originally appeared in N.A. Cummings & J.L. Cummings (2000), *The Essence of Psychotherapy: Reinventing the Art in the New Era of Data* (pp. 193-208). San Diego, CA: Academic Press. Used by agreement.

Chapter 5. A version of this interview, with changes, was originally posted on the Internet at www.psychotherapist.net in November 2002. Randall Wyatt served as editor. Used by agreement.

Chapter 6. A version, with changes, originally appeared in A.S. Gurman & N.S. Jacobson (Eds.), 2002, *Clinical Handbook of Couple Therapy* (3rd ed., pp. 335-369). New York: Guilford Press. Used by agreement.

Chapter 7. A version, with changes, originally appeared in *Family Therapy Networker*, 25(1), 19-20. Used by agreement.

Chapter 8. A version, with changes, originally appeared in *Context: The Magazine for Family Therapy and Systemic Practice*, 2001, No. 58, p. 23. Used by agreement.

Chapter 9. No prior publication.

Chapter 10. A version, with changes, originally appeared (in Finnish) in *Ratkes*, 2001, 3, 4-11. Used by agreement. The Finnish word *Ratkes* can be loosely translated as "Right on!" or "Got it!"

Chapter 11. A version, with changes, was originally posted (in Finnish) on the Internet at www.paihdelinkki.fi. Used by agreement.

Chapter 12. A version, with changes, originally appeared in J.H. Frykman and T.S. Nelson (Eds.), 2003, *Making the Impossible Difficult: Tools for Getting Unstuck* (pp. 62-65). New York: iUniverse. Used by agreement.

Chapter 13. Originally presented 25 August 2001 at a symposium (chaired by Alvin H. Mahrer) entitled *How Do Eminent Psychotherapists Personally Embody Their Own Theories?* held at the American Psychological Association annual convention in San Francisco, California. The other panelists were Laura S. Brown, Albert Ellis, John C. Norcross, and Ernesto Spinelli. A version, with changes, was published in *Journal of Constructivist Psychology*, 2002, 15(4)279-289. Used by agreement.

Chapter 14. An abbreviated version of this paper was first presented at a symposium entitled *Honoring Our Teachers: Eminent Psychotherapists Describe Who Influenced Them, and How* (M.F. Hoyt, chair) held at Chicago on 23 August 2002 at the annual convention of the American Psychological Association. The other panelists were Laura S. Brown, Lillian Comas-Diaz, Albert Ellis, and Alvin H. Mahrer. In his *Autobiographies*, William Butler Yeats (1935/1999) wrote: "Education is not about filling buckets. It is about starting fires." Not mere encomium or panegyric, the symposium was intended to inspire reflection on how attendees and readers—like each of the panelists—has been influenced, is still being influenced, and may be influencing others.

0-595-31105-9